EPICURUS: AN INTRODUCTION

EPICURUS

AN INTRODUCTION

J. M. RIST

Professor of Greek, University of Toronto

CAMBRIDGE UNIVERSITY PRESS

CAMBRIDGE

LONDON · NEW YORK · MELBOURNE

Published by the Syndics of the Cambridge University Press
The Pitt Building, Trumpington Street, Cambridge CB2 IRP
Bentley House, 200 Euston Road, London NW1 2DB
32 East 57th Street, New York, NY 10022, USA
296 Beaconsfield Parade, Middle Park, Melbourne 3206, Australia

© Cambridge University Press 1972

Library of Congress catalogue card number: 70-177939

ISBN 0 521 08426 1 hard covers
ISBN 021 29200 X paperback

First published 1972
First paperback edition 1977

Printed in Great Britain at the
University Press, Cambridge

CONTENTS

CONTENTS

TO MY FRIEND
HENRY BLUMENTHAL

PREFACE

According to Diogenes Laertius, Epicurus wrote more than any philosopher before him, but of these writings there remain only three letters – of which one (to Pythocles) is sometimes said to be spurious, the so-called 'Basic Doctrines' (Κύριαι Δόξαι), and a quantity of fragments. Fragments are all that is left of the writings of many other Epicureans: Metrodorus, Polyaenus, Demetrius Laco, Philodemus and Diogenes of Oenoanda. Lucretius' poem survives almost intact. And from this varied evidence, eked out by the expositions of hostile critics like Cicero and Plutarch, we must reconstruct Epicureanism.

Progress has been impressive since the pioneering labours of Gassendi, Giussani and Usener. Perhaps the greatest credit is due to Bignone, who first realized how much we must emphasize Epicurus' reaction to the thought of Plato and Aristotle. But Bignone misled us for a while because he thought that it was only the early Aristotle, the Aristotle of the dialogues, that Epicurus knew. Later work, particularly by Diano and recently by Furley, has disposed of that unnecessary hypothesis. For while Bignone was limited by disputable interpretations of what the 'early' Aristotle taught, we have since learned that precise parallels can be found in ethics, physics and psychology between Plato and the Aristotle of the treatises on the one hand and Epicurus on the other. We even have a fragment of Epicurus which speaks of Aristotle's physical treatises – though not necessarily of our *Physics* – and of his *Analytics* (fr. 118 Arr.).

Epicurus has proved himself a hard man to help. From ancient times his philosophy has aroused both vehement opposition and enthusiastic approval. Judgments about it have often been emotional, and for this Epicurus himself must bear much of the responsibility. He himself set a depth of polemic hitherto unplumbed among ancient philosophers, and reserved some of his bitterest contempt for those from whom he learned the most. He is an ideologist, with an ideologist's loves and hatreds, and among his modern admirers many of the most devoted are those who see his importance primarily as that of a man who condemned the subordination of ethics to politics, of the happiness of the individual to the good of society, and, as Lucretius held, who liberated us both from the tyranny of the gods and from the opiates of false religious belief.

The scope of the present book is unambitious: it is to present an elementary account of what we know about the philosophy of Epicurus. Much of what is here has been said before somewhere. Yet several chapters will present a different Epicurus from that which emerges from other books in English. If we pass over the work of Farrington, especially his *Faith of Epicurus*, not because it is unhelpful – indeed to a considerable degree the reverse is true – but because his Marxist interpretations can only be properly evaluated by those already possessed of a firm grasp of the basic principles of Epicureanism, we are still to all intents and purposes left with the books of Bailey and De Witt. Bailey's *Greek Atomists and Epicurus* has been very useful and its appearance marked a substantial advance in Epicurean studies, but much of it has now been superseded. In particular the work of Diano on Epicurean ethics and psychology, still unnoticed by Bailey in his edition of Lucretius, cannot be passed over, and Bailey's discussion of Epicurean religion must be supplemented by a number of later studies, especially those of Kleve and Merlan. As for De Witt's *Epicurus and his Philosophy*, it is essentially a work of special pleading, and his theses about Epicurus' canonic and the general nature of the ethical writings have not won wide acceptance.

The present contribution to Epicurean studies is an attempt to redescribe the basic tenets of Epicurus himself. It is not a history of Epicureanism. I have only discussed other Epicureans, such as Philodemus and Lucretius, in so far as they enable us to understand the thought of Epicurus. In general too I have avoided more specialized problems of interpretation, though a few are touched on in appendices.

The most convenient collection of the writings and fragments of Epicurus is that of G. Arrighetti, entitled *Epicuro: Opere* (Turin 1960). Usener's *Epicurea* (Leipzig 1887, reprinted Rome 1963) is an invaluable source-book of passages relating to Epicureanism.

ACKNOWLEDGMENTS

I should like to thank Professor T. M. Robinson, Professor F. H. Sandbach and the advisers of the Cambridge University Press for reading and commenting on *Epicurus* in manuscript. It is a better book for their criticisms.

J.M.R.

Toronto, May 1971

ABBREVIATIONS

AAHG	*Anzeiger für die Altertumswissenschaft, hrsg. von der Österreichischen Humanistischen Gesellschaft*
ACGB	*Actes du VIIIe Congrès, Association Guillaume Budé* (Paris 1969)
AJA	*American Journal of Archaeology*
AJP	*American Journal of Philology*
Arr.	G. Arrighetti, *Epicuro: Opere* (Turin 1960)
ASNP	*Annali della Scuola Normale di Pisa, Classe di Lett., Storia e Filosofia*
BD	Epicurus, *Basic Doctrines*
BICS	*Bulletin of the Institute of Classical Studies of the University of London*
CN	Plutarch, *De communibus notitiis*
CP	*Classical Philology*
CQ	*Classical Quarterly*
CR	*Classical Review*
DK	*Die Fragmente der Vorsokratiker*, ed. H. Diels and W. Kranz
E. Pap.	*Études de Papyrologie*
GCFI	*Giornale critico di filosofia italiana*
GIF	*Giornale italiano di filologia*
JHI	*Journal of the History of Ideas*
JP	*Journal of Philology*
Mus. Helv.	*Museum Helveticum*
ND	Cicero, *De Natura Deorum*
PP	*La Parola del Passato*
PR	*Philosophical Review*
RAC	*Reallexikon für Antike und Christentum*
RAL	*Rendiconti dell'Accademia dei Lincei*
RE	*Paulys Real-Encyclopädie der classischen Altertumswissenschaft*
REA	*Revue des études anciennes*
REG	*Revue des études grecques*
RFIC	*Rivista di filologia e di istruzione classica*
Rh. Mus.	*Rheinisches Museum*

ABBREVIATIONS

SBB	*Sitzungsberichte der Kön. Akademie zu Berlin*
SIFC	*Studi italiani di filologia classica*
SO	*Symbolae osloenses*
SR	Plutarch, *De Stoicorum Repugnantiis*
TAPA	*Transactions and Proceedings of the American Philological Association*
VS	Epicurus, *Vatican Sayings*
WS	*Wiener Studien*

1

EPICURUS AND HIS FRIENDS

Every philosopher has a personal history, and it is often helpful
to understand his history if we want to understand his philosophy.[1] In the case of Epicurus an account of his life before the
foundation of his school in Athens in 306 is particularly informative, and although there is no need to consider all the details
of the biographical problem, a brief survey is essential. Epicurus
was an Athenian citizen born in Samos in 341 B.C.[2] His father
Neocles was a cleruch, an Athenian colonist, who, after the
expulsion of the Athenians from the island, earned his living as
a schoolmaster – a profession which accorded little status.[3]
His mother is said at some time to have been a priestess who
performed purificatory rites.[4] He had three brothers, all of
whom were later devoted to him.[5]

We know little about Epicurus' childhood except that he
seems to have become interested in philosophy at an early age –
twelve or fourteen.[6] Sextus Empiricus tells us that he had been
puzzled by references in Hesiod to chaos as the first thing
formed in the cosmos and had asked his schoolteacher from
what it had been formed. The teacher said that was a matter
for the philosophers; and Epicurus said that he must therefore
listen to what the philosophers had to say.[7] Whether he read
the works of Democritus at this early stage is uncertain but
unlikely. Who in Samos would have put him on to Democritus?
The only philosopher we know he heard was of a quite different
kind, the Platonist Pamphilus.[8] If we may judge by Epicurus'
later attitude, he may have learned a great deal from Pamphilus
and recognized the importance of Plato's work.[9] At any rate

---

[1] For more detailed biographical material see the article *Epikur* in *RE* Supp.
11, col. 579ff.   [2] D.L. 10.1.

[3] D.L. 10.4; cf. 10.8.   [4] D.L. 10.4.

[5] D.L. 10.3; *Suda*, s.v. Epicurus.   [6] D.L. 10.2; 10.14.

[7] Sext. Emp., *Adv. Math.* 10.18–19; cf. D.L. 10.2.   [8] Cic., *ND* 1.72.

[9] Book 14 of the Περὶ φύσεως is largely an attack on Plato's theory of the
elements; cf. Schmid, *Epikurs Kritik*.

he came to think that Platonism demanded vehement rebuttal. Not only are the followers of the 'golden' Plato to be dismissed as ham-actors in politics,[1] but their basic educational theories are to be categorically denied. Abandon all *paideia*, Epicurus urges Pythocles,[2] and those who see this as above all an attack on the Platonic mathematical and dialectical training are probably in the right.[3]

Epicurus arrived in Athens to do his national service as an *ephebos* in 323. Despite his military duties he now had some opportunity to hear the major philosophers of the day. The most powerful, albeit unpopular, thinker in the city was Aristotle, back in Athens since 335/4 and, we can hardly doubt, making a considerable impression on the intellectual élite. But Epicurus would have had little chance to hear him in person, since Aristotle found it necessary to retire to Chalcis lest he be condemned as pro-Macedonian. There seems to have been a charge of impiety,[4] but the underlying political reasons for hostility are obvious. Theophrastus, however, presumably remained behind in Athens, and the influence of Aristotle could not have immediately disappeared. His close associates must have continued to discuss his views whether or not they were generally available in published form. As for the Academy, it was still important and flourishing under Xenocrates, the second successor of Plato and a fairly conservative Platonist.[5] In this situation it is natural that Epicurus' attention would have been directed to the current views in the Academy and among the friends of Aristotle, and to the various controversies surrounding them. As we proceed to a more detailed examination of Epicureanism, we shall see the fruits of Epicurus' inspection of Platonic and Aristotelian philosophy. We may begin, however, by observing at once that Epicurus' later hostility to Theophrastus was unconcealed; and he accorded Aristotle little more respect.[6] Plutarch remarks that, although Epicurus was fond

---

[1] D.L. 10.8; Sext. Emp., *Adv. Math.* 1.3.   [2] D.L. 10.6.

[3] E.g. De Witt, *Epicurus* 44–5.   [4] D.L. 5.5.

[5] According to Demetrius of Magnesia Epicurus attended the lectures of Xenocrates (D.L. 10.13).

[6] Cf. De Witt, *Epicurus* 50–1. For Epicurus' hostile attitude to Aristotle, see Usener, 171.

of listening to music, he claimed to feel only loathing at the prospect of reading Theophrastus on musical theory.[1]

Besides observing the philosophical scene at this formative period of Epicurus' life, we cannot entirely neglect what was happening politically. Epicurus must have reflected on the death of Alexander and the incipient quarrels of his successors. At any rate he had the chance to notice a new and ominous feature of Greek politics, the power of a monarch. And the power of a monarch meant the weakness and destruction of his enemies. Hypereides was executed and Demosthenes committed suicide in the wake of the failure of Athens to resist Macedonian power. The dangers of politics were obvious, as well as the attractions (or the necessity, if one wished for security) of life as a private individual. Without accepting in its entirety Zeller's thesis that the career of Alexander and the subsequent near-destruction of the political importance of Greek city-states was perhaps the principal cause of a change in emphasis in Greek philosophy after Aristotle, we have to admit that in a society where the traditional forms of political life had had such an influence on philosophy, the importance of the eclipse of those forms must not be underestimated. Yet there is no clear break with the past on Aristotle's death. Many of the problems with which Epicurus became familiar during his early stay in Athens were the problems we find in Aristotle's writings; the new social and political scene did not generate the problems so much as affect the kind of answers given them.

While Epicurus was away in Athens, his family, together with the remainder of the Athenian colonists, had been evicted from Samos by order of the Macedonians.[2] The family ended up at Colophon in Asia Minor, and Epicurus joined them there in 321. The next ten years provided Epicurus' formal philosophical training. It has been suggested that he studied first with the Peripatetic Praxiphanes in Rhodes, but chronologically that is impossible. Praxiphanes and Epicurus were near contemporaries.[3] At some stage during this period, however, he became

---

[1] Plut., *Non posse* 1095c.
[2] D.L. 10.1.
[3] Cf. Brink, 'Callimachus and Aristotle', 23.

3

the pupil of Nausiphanes of Teos, and though Epicurus later vilified his teacher, his debt to him was great. We know comparatively little of Nausiphanes, but a few significant facts emerge.[1] In the first place he was a professed follower of Democritean atomism. In the second place he had associated with the sceptic Pyrrho,[2] who argued against the possibility of knowledge (though probably without claiming that it was absolutely impossible to attain). Even in Democritus, of course, there had been a sceptical strain, for he had argued that what we see and describe is the world of convention; the real world consists of atoms and the void. But Nausiphanes was not only an atomist with sceptical inclinations; he also held novel views on the end of life, which he defined as 'undisturbedness' (ἀκαταπληξία),[3] a position which resembles that of Epicurus in its negative formulation – Epicurus talked of 'untroubledness' (ἀταραξία) – though we have no evidence that Nausiphanes worked out a theory of the emotions in any way resembling the sophisticated treatment accorded the subject by Epicurus.

It is known that Nausiphanes wrote a book called *The Tripod*,[4] which was held to have been a formative influence on Epicurus and to have affected his *Canon* or treatise on the bases of knowledge. It is probable that in *The Tripod* Nausiphanes argued that knowledge depends on observation, the evidence of history and inference based on analogy.[5] It appears from Philodemus' *Rhetoric* that he also argued that the methodology of rhetoric is similar to that of the physical sciences and is therefore an acceptable pursuit for the student of nature[6] – a view to which Epicurus later came to take violent exception.

Epicurus must have learned from Nausiphanes the basic principles of atomism – of which he may have already acquired something in Athens – but of an atomism which led to the rule of 'necessity' in physics and the denial of 'free will' in psychology. He would have learned an atomism in which ethics is

[1] For Nausiphanes see DK 75A and 75B.
[2] D.L. 9.64. For Epicurus' interest in and reaction against Pyrrho, see Barigazzi, 'Épicure et le scepticisme', 290–1.
[3] Clem., *Strom.* 2.130 (=DK 75B3).
[4] D.L. 10.14.
[5] Cf. De Lacy, *Philodemus* 128.   [6] Cf. DK 75B2.

4

comparatively unimportant – though perhaps more closely integrated with physics than in Democritus – and which is concerned not so much to change human life and to promote happiness as to describe the world in which we live and the psychological realities which govern our behaviour. In later life his hostility to all his teachers, and indeed to virtually all previous philosophers, was very great, but it has always seemed particularly strange that Nausiphanes should be so fiercely attacked. But, as we shall have occasion to mention again, Epicurus' hostility is ideological. Nausiphanes said many of the right things for the wrong reasons; and though he taught much that is true, he did not understand the importance for the individual of what he taught. Worse than an opponent, he was in ideological terms a deviationist. And as for Nausiphanes, so also for the earlier masters of atomism, Democritus and Leucippus. Epicurus even went so far as to say that Leucippus did not exist,[1] a fabrication which has sometimes deceived modern scholars. Democritus is condemned as a natural philosopher (φυσικός) – a physical philosopher – whose views are warped; Epicurus never thought of himself as primarily a natural philosopher.

Epicurus seems to have had personal as well as philosophical grounds for his dislike of Nausiphanes. Among other insults he flung at his teacher he referred to Nausiphanes as a 'lung-fish', an 'illiterate', a 'deceiver', and, oddly enough, a 'prostitute'.[2] Obviously Nausiphanes was not strictly speaking illiterate, and Epicurus perhaps meant to suggest that he was incapable of seeing the true implications of his own learning. De Witt translates ἀγράμματος as 'dumb-animal', thus tying the accusation in with that of being a lung-fish.[3] Sextus Empiricus observes that lung-fishes are insensitive;[4] presumably Epicurus meant that Nausiphanes was insensitive to the truth, that is, unable to see it! As for the charges that he was a deceiver and a prostitute, they may be mere statements of fact – neither would be unknown among Greek philosophers – though Epicurus may have been following the established ancient practice of hurling

[1] D.L. 10.13.   [2] D.L. 10.8; cf. Sext. Emp., *Adv. Math.* 1.4.
[3] De Witt, *Epicurus* 62.   [4] Sext. Emp., *Adv. Math.* 1.4.

sexual insults without any serious justification. A further remark of Sextus may shed light on the matter.[1] Epicurus speaks of people thinking that he studied with Nausiphanes in company with a group of youths with permanent hangovers. For, continues Epicurus, Nausiphanes was an evil man whose practices were not such as to be conducive to wisdom. This has been taken as a further reference to homosexuality, but Sextus tells us that the practices were merely those of mathematics, which we know Epicurus condemned. Generally speaking, it is unusual for the ancients to miss an allegation of homosexuality if it is made.

Whatever the reason, whether personal, philosophical or ideological, for Epicurus' hostility to the master from whom he probably derived most, there is no doubt that Epicurus claimed to be self-taught. The only thing this could mean if we try and look at it in a friendly light, is that what he most valued in his own philosophy, his ethical attitudes, his views on freedom and necessity and on the gods, was the product of his own thought. Only the raw material of that thought was provided by his actual teachers, such as Nausiphanes, and his spiritual ancestors such as Democritus and Leucippus.

After a period of ten years spent in learning and thinking Epicurus presented himself in 311 as a teacher at Mytilene. His stay there was brief and seems to have been ended by forcible expulsion or at least by his being forbidden to teach. We know no details of the quarrels in which he became involved, though an allusion in a fragmentary life of Epicurus to the power of a mob, of a monarch and of a gymnasiarch, may suggest that the authorities in some way connived at popular violence against Epicurus and his friends.[2] Beyond that we cannot safely go; all we know is that Epicurus left Mytilene, which was at this time under the control of Antigonus Monophthalmus, and took refuge in Lampsacus, a town now probably controlled by Polemeus, a rebel against Antigonus' authority.[3] Epicurus' hostility to his fellow-teachers at Mytilene is shown by the fact that he wrote a tract *Against the Philosophers in Mytilene*.

[1] Sext. Emp., *Adv. Math.* 1.3; cf. De Witt, *Epicurus* 63.
[2] Cf. fr. 6, col. 2, 9–12 (Vogliano, *Epicuri et Epicureorum Scripta* 59).
[3] Cf. Momigliano, 'Su alcuni dati', 304.

It was probably in the winter of 310 that Epicurus hastily left Mytilene for Lampsacus, where he remained until the summer of 306. We know that at least for the first part of this period Lampsacus was not controlled by Lysimachus. Probably, therefore, it was not at this time that Epicurus began his association with Mithres, Lysimachus' minister.[1] The debt to Mithres which he sometime incurred, and which provided much material for his later detractors, who taunted him as a flatterer of barbarians, may have been incurred at a later stage in his career. We cannot date it at all, nor do we even know when Epicurus and Mithres were first acquainted. But, Mithres apart, Epicurus seems to have been welcomed in Lampsacus and to have won the support of various prominent citizens, including Idomeneus, who proved of great importance financially, Leonteus and his wife Themista, and above all Metrodorus, who was to become his deputy in the headship of the school. Batis, Metrodorus' sister, later married Idomeneus.

Two other prominent associates of Epicurus must be mentioned. Polyaenus of Cyzicus seems to have been at some time a member of the Cyzicene school of mathematicians which had been founded by Eudoxus. The mistress of Polyaenus, perhaps Hedeia, was also a follower of Epicurus and also originated from Cyzicus.[2] This city seems to have witnessed a struggle between Epicureanism and older forms of philosophy. Something of the polemic has come down to us in Epicurean attacks on the philosophers of Cyzicus as enemies of Greece.[3] The reason for the charge is presumably that, following Eudoxus, they were worshippers of astral gods whose origin was in Babylonia. Epicurus held that only Greeks could be serious philosophers.[4]

Finally we come to Hermarchus, Epicurus' eventual successor as head of the school in Athens. Hermarchus came from Mytilene, though we do not know when he joined Epicurus. The natural assumption is that it was during Epicurus' brief stay in Mytilene; but there is no certainty that this is the case. We

---

[1] Momigliano, ibid. 304. Diodorus 20.107.2 tells us that Lysimachus 'freed' Lampsacus in 302.   [2] Cf. Usener, pp. 407, 416.
[3] D.L. 10.8. There is no need to read 'Cynics' instead of 'Cyzicenes' here.
[4] Clem. Alex., Strom. 1.15 (Us. 226).

know that Hermarchus had once been a student of rhetoric, an activity which Epicurus disliked. Epicurus had probably studied it himself, at least with Nausiphanes, but it is unlikely that he ever taught it.[1] A passage of Philodemus, in which the author argues that it is legitimate for a philosopher skilled in rhetoric to teach it for a short period if it will ease his financial difficulties has sometimes been thought to refer to Epicurus himself.[2] Perhaps Hermarchus, the second head of the school, is the short-term rhetorician in question.

A few more adherents who joined Epicurus at this time should be noticed: Colotes, the student whose destructive attack on rival schools of philosophy, dedicated to Ptolemy I of Egypt, was able to attract the ire of Plutarch, who wrote a rebuttal four hundred years later; Pythocles, the youth to whom a letter on meteorological phenomena, reputedly by Epicurus himself, was addressed – a letter which is preserved by Diogenes Laertius; Timocrates, the brother of Metrodorus, who later left the school and, in company with Herodotus, began publishing scurrilous attacks on Epicurus and impugning his status as an Athenian citizen.[3]

It would be interesting to know in detail what Epicurus taught during the early part of his philosophical career. It would be interesting to know whether his views in Lampsacus differed significantly from those he later taught in Athens. Unfortunately we have no evidence; we must rely on conjecture and probability alone.[4] And the probability is that already by 310 most of the major positions of 'Epicureanism' had been reached. Certainly Epicurus was already surrounded by much the same group of ardent followers who later formed the nucleus of his school in Athens. If his views changed, presumably

---

[1] De Witt, *Epicurus* 47, argues for this.

[2] De Witt, *Epicurus* 47; cf. Philod., *Rhet.* 2, pp. 51–2 Sudhaus.

[3] D.L. 10.4.

[4] It has sometimes been argued that the doctrine of the atomic swerve is 'late' Epicurus, and even that Epicurus did not hold it when he wrote the letter to Herodotus. Moutsopoulos ('Le "*clinamen*"'), however, seems to think that, even though the swerve is not present in our version of the letter, it is prefigured there. It is better to recognize that it was always a part of Epicurus' teaching.

8

theirs changed too. Yet we hear nothing of such changes in their case any more than in his. Nor can we argue that they could have disagreed with him, as members of the Academy, such as Speusippus and Eudoxus, disagreed with Plato. Epicurus did not tolerate such disagreements. As Philodemus tells us, it was the rule for members of Epicurean communities to take an oath of obedience to Epicurus and of acceptance of his precepts.[1]

In 306 Epicurus moved to Athens. It was an obvious move for two reasons: he himself was an Athenian and Athens was the centre of the philosophical world. A teacher with Epicurus' pretensions would wish to operate at the centre. In 307 Athens had come under the control of Demetrius Poliorcetes, and it has been argued that Epicurus secured protection there through the friendship of his disciple, the *hetaera* Leontion, with Demetrius' mistress Lamia.[2] The theory is unlikely – are we sure of the friendship between Lamia and Leontion? – and unnecessary. Leontion was an Athenian and therefore probably not a member of Epicurus' hitherto rather obscure circle before he himself came to Athens. In any case, even though Epicurus had made himself unpopular in Mytilene, which was part of the territory of Demetrius' father Antigonus, neither he nor his offence was important enough to make Antigonus wish to prevent him returning to the city of which he was already a citizen. Epicurus' fulsome letter to Leontion ('How you filled us with excited delight when we read your dear letter') need have no connection with this incident.[3] It was cited by critics of Epicurus as an instance of flattery of a mere *hetaera*; no one attributed political significance to it.

Apart from brief return visits to Lampsacus, Epicurus remained at Athens from 306 until his death in 271. He acquired a house in the Melite district, between the city and the Peiraeus, and a kitchen-garden not very far from the Academy. Lectures were given in the garden but the house was the centre of the society and the place where the close disciples lived. The institution which Epicurus built up over a period of years was hierarchically run. Epicurus himself was called the leader and

---

[1] Philod., Περὶ παρρησίας, p. 45, 8–11 Olivieri.
[2] Bignone, *L'Aristotele perduto* 2.134–43.   [3] D.L. 10.5.

9

held the title of 'wise man'.[1] The rest were searchers after wisdom and divided into various categories: associate leaders
(καθηγεμόνες) – these included Metrodorus, Epicurus' deputy,
together with Polyaenus and Hermarchus – assistants, and
pupils (κατασκευαζόμενοι). The same structure was apparently
repeated in other Epicurean communities as they developed.[2]
Epicurus kept in touch with these communities by letter, and
their subordination may have been marked by the payment of
dues to Athens.

As we have already noticed in Lampsacus, women were
members of the school from the start. They were mostly *hetaerae*,
such as Hedeia of Cyzicus, but also women of a higher social
class such as Themista, the wife of Leonteus. The famous
hetaera Leontion probably joined the school in the Athenian
period and took an active part in pamphleteering. Her treatise
against Theophrastus is praised by Cicero for its style; the fact
that it was the work of a *hetaera* is held to indicate presumption.[3]
There is no need to assume that the relations between the male
and female members of the school were platonic. Defectors
accused the Epicureans of orgies; that is a mis-stated exaggera-
tion. But, although the wise man will avoid passion (ἔρως),
Epicurus only forbids him sexual intercourse when it is illegal.[4]
In a fragment of Ionic Greek, perhaps quoted from Democritus,
he points out that intercourse never did anyone any good;[5]
but this should probably be taken to mean that the pleasure it
gives is only transitory and limited: it is not the pleasure that is
long-lasting absence of pain. When freed from passion, sexual

---

[1] For ἡγεμών see D.L. 10.20, Cic., *Tusc.* 3.37. Metrodorus was apparently
accepted as a 'wise man' by Epicurus (*De Fin.* 2.7; cf. Plut., *Adv. Col.*
1117c).

[2] For καθηγεμών see Philod., *De Ira* 45, 1–14 Wilke; cf. καθηγητής, Philod.,
Περὶ παρρησίας, fr. 45 Olivieri. Although De Witt's details of the Epicurean
hierarchy are apparently exaggerated ('Organization and Procedure'),
the attempt of Gigante ('Philodème: Sur la liberté de parole', 215–17) to
refute him *in toto* must be accounted a failure, except perhaps in the matter
of φιλόλογοι. Unhappily Gigante limits himself to a selection of the
evidence in the Περὶ παρρησίας alone.

[3] Cic., *Orat.* 151; *ND* 1.93; cf. Pliny, *NH* pref. 29.

[4] D.L. 10.118. Plutarch calls the Epicureans ἀνέραστοι (*Erot.* 767c).

[5] *VS* 51.

pleasure is natural but unnecessary. It may be enjoyed when not accompanied by the false belief that it is necessary.[1] Epicurus himself apparently enjoyed it. There is no evidence that he denied the widely-held view that he slept with Polyaenus' mistress Hedeia and with Leontion, the mistress or wife of Metrodorus.[2] Such relationships would not be of great importance in the context of Epicurean morality, and we should notice that in the school married women did not necessarily enjoy higher status than *hetaerae*. It was an occasion for reproach by a hypocritical public that Leontion was given pre-eminence over such 'respectable married ladies' as Themista. But for Epicurus philosophical ability was the basis of seniority.

Apart from its free women members the school also included slaves, both male and female. Within its confines a new kind of society was established – a sect with its own rules and its own standards of authority.[3] Epicureans appeared to outsiders as something of a clique, and the flattering epithets which the members of the school bestowed on one another and above all on the 'divine' Epicurus are hard to stomach.[4] Yet although Epicurus probably enjoyed the flattery of his associates as a compensation for the chronic illnesses he experienced for much of his life, it would be inaccurate to accuse the Epicureans of insincerity. They fawned on Epicurus because they thought he

---

[1] Cf. pp. 117–18 below.

[2] Plut., *De Occulte Viv.* 1129B; *Non posse* 1098B. I would read αὐτὴν with reference to intercourse with Themista at D.L. 10.5.10, following Froben, Bignone and Apelt. In his *Symposium* Epicurus discussed the right time for sexual pleasure. He thinks that we should 'use sex' at a time when our digestive processes will not be upset by it (cf. Plut., *Quaest. Conviv.* 653F–654B (Us. 61)).

[3] We should not however assume that this society included members from the lower classes or that it 'donnait un cadre à la solidarité des pauvres' merely because, according to Lactantius (*Div. Instit.* 3.25.4), Epicurus invited those 'ignorant of learning' to philosophy. Lactantius is probably only referring to Epicurus' well-known dislike for traditional Greek education. He does not say that workers and peasants (*opifices, rustici*) comprised a large group of the Epicurean brotherhood, as Tuilier suggests ('La notion', 325).

[4] Cf. Plut., *Adv. Col.* 1117AB. Epicurus' birthday was commemorated each year and the twentieth day of each month was celebrated in honour of Metrodorus and later also of Epicurus himself. Cf. De Witt, *Epicurus* 105.

had freed them from servitude to fate or to false views of the world and the gods.[1] The Epicurean school is not only an academy, it is a sect. But sectaries do not necessarily produce uninteresting philosophy, and we must judge the school not by its attitudes to the founder but by its thought.

Life in the Garden of Epicurus was as pleasant as possible; and in the spirit of the ethical teachings of the school, this meant in practice a fairly austere existence. The community's goods were not held in common; that, thought Epicurus, would suggest that his friends did not trust one another.[2] But the wealthier friends had to help finance the others; Epicurus requests money from Idomeneus for the support of 'my holy body',[3] and it seems that the communities outside Athens may have paid some kind of dues to the central organization. Within the sect the overall spirit was one of firm kindliness, typified by a famous letter to a child, perhaps the son of Metrodorus, written either by Epicurus himself, or, more probably, by Polyaenus.[4] 'Pythocles, Hermarchus, Ctesippus and I have reached Lampsacus safe and sound. We found Themista and the rest of our friends there in good health. I hope you are well too, and your mummy, and that you are obedient to daddy and Matro as before. Rest assured that I and all the rest of us are very pleased with you for being obedient to them in all things.' Friendships with one's own were most important, and the Epicureans constantly talked of gratitude and kindness to one another. The reverse of the coin was the disgust and loathing visited upon ideological opponents.

Epicurus died after a period of great pain in 271. He had arranged for Hermarchus to succeed, and in his will he bequeathed his property to the successive scholarchs. The will itself is preserved by Diogenes Laertius. Shortly before his death Epicurus penned a somewhat theatrical letter to Idomeneus, as an ethical testimony and to promote his own brand of

[1] Cf. Lucr., 5.81.
[2] D.L. 10.11.
[3] Plut., *Adv. Col.* 1117DE; cf. D.L. 10.20, Us. 184, and Philod., Περί παρρησίας, fr. 55 Olivieri.
[4] For the authorship of P. Herc. 176 (113 Arr.) see Vogliano, 'Autour du jardin d'Épicure'.

immortality: 'I am writing to you on this happy day, the day which will be my last. My pains from strangury and dysentery cannot increase their present intensity. Lined up against them are the pleasures in my soul at remembering our past discussions. As is worthy of your disposition towards me and towards philosophy from boyhood on, look after the children of Metrodorus.'

2

CANONIC

Introduction

In marked and deliberate contrast to Plato and Aristotle, Epicurus did not insist on a long course of preliminary education before a student embarked on his strictly philosophical work. All such unnecessary cultural background should be shunned:[1] at best it is a waste of time; at worst it encourages a false sense of achievement. Rhetoric, philology and mathematics are equally valueless.[2] Similarly for the student of philosophy himself formal problems are irrelevant and useless. It is not surprising, therefore, that Epicurus had no interest in most of the material which came in antiquity under the rather broad heading of logic. That the purely grammatical aspects of this science should have awakened no interest is hardly surprising, but Cicero, representing a tradition of hostile criticism, charges that Epicurus' ignorance of logic is such that he is unable to explain the reasoning behind any philosophical arguments, presumably including his own.[3] He abolishes definitions, Cicero complains. He teaches nothing about dividing and distributing; he has nothing to say on how reasoning is carried on and conclusions reached; he has nothing to say on how sophisms may be resolved and ambiguities cleared up. He places the criteria of reality (*iudicia rerum*) in the senses.[4]

This passage of Cicero is perhaps the best introduction to Epicurean canonic. It tells us what Epicurus was not interested in, and again what he thought important in the area of study traditionally called 'logic'. What is important is the *iudicium rerum*, the means of telling what the world is like. Since it is

---

[1] D.L. 10.6.

[2] Plut., *Non posse* 1093CD, 1094–5. Plutarch carries his repugnance to Epicurus' dislike of literary pursuits to great lengths: 'Who would get more pleasure out of going to bed with the most beautiful of women than in staying up with Xenophon's story of Pantheia' or with other literary ladies? (1093C).

[3] Cic., *De Fin.* 1.22; cf. Us. 242.   [4] Cf. D.L. 10.31; Aulus Gellius, 2.8.

14

essential for human happiness that we be able to understand
the physical world, if only to realize that death is not a source
of worry and that the gods are not to be feared, we must be able
to determine what the world is like; we need tools, reliable tools,
with the aid of which we can understand our surroundings.
Thus the only 'logical' study we need undertake is an investigation of our own means of knowing the world. And for Epicurus
our primary source of knowledge of the world is sensation.
That we do in fact acquire knowledge through the senses must
be defended against sceptics and Platonists.

Epicurean canonic, therefore, is an enquiry into the nature
of the tools we possess for knowing the external world and an
evaluation of the information with which these tools supply us.
As such, it is in the first instance an investigation of what the
Greeks were accustomed to call the criterion of truth or the
criterion of reality. The word 'criterion', Sextus Empiricus
tells us,[1] was used in two senses. In one sense it was used of that
in view of which we do some things and not others. In another
sense it referred to that in view of which we say that some things
exist and others do not (ὑπάρχειν), and that these things are
true and those are false. We notice immediately that the second
sense of 'criterion' has itself been divided into two separate
senses. The criterion is a criterion of the existence or of the reality
of particular things – this is probably what Cicero meant when
he spoke of the Epicurean *iudicia rerum* – but it is also a criterion
of truth and falsehood. This can only mean that the criterion
may be used not only to judge problems about the possible
existence or non-existence of objects in the world, but also to
settle questions about the truth-value of propositions about such
existent or non-existent objects. Throughout our enquiry,
therefore, we must try to discover whether Epicurus is talking
about the 'truth' or existence of objects in the world, or about
the truth or falsehood of propositions. We should be put further
on our guard by the supplementary evidence of Sextus that
Epicurus said that all sensibles (αἰσθητά) are true and existing
(ἀληθῆ καὶ ὄντα).[2] For he did not distinguish between a thing's

---

[1] Sextus Empiricus, *Adv. Math.* 7.29.
[2] Sextus Empiricus, *Adv. Math.* 8.9.

being true and its possessing existence (ἀληθὲς...ὑπάρχον).
Hence a proposition is true if it describes the state in which
something actually *exists* and false if it does not. How seriously
Epicurus took the theory that 'truth' must be associated with
the existence of the thing described is shown by his attitude
towards disjunctive propositions referring to the future.[1] As
Cicero points out, it was frequently argued that in every disjunctive proposition of the form 'either *p* or not-*p*', one of the
alternatives must be true. But Epicurus refused to accept this
because of disjunctive propositions about the future. He objected,
it seems, because he wrongly equated truth with necessity,
and perhaps also, more interestingly, because he would not
recognize the truth of any proposition which could not be
verified directly or indirectly by the senses. He may have
thought that, since in the case of disjunctive propositions about
the future neither alternative could be verified, therefore
'either *p* or not-*p*' cannot be accepted as true.

It is clear that Epicurus believed he needed 'criteria' which
could both inform him directly about the world and help to
evaluate thoughts and statements, if he was to be in a proper
position to conduct enquiries in physics. Thus we should be
aware of both these functions of the criterion when evaluating
and attempting to understand such notorious Epicurean
propositions as 'All sensations are true'. If we do not constantly
recall that Epicurus is concerned both with experience of the
world and with the linguistic expression of that experience, we
shall find his discussion of the criterion unnecessarily confusing.
Even if *we* do not think that problems about the existence of
particulars and problems about the truth-value of propositions
can always be solved by the same criteria, we must recognize
that Epicurus disagrees with us, and we must try to understand
why he thought as he did.

Before considering the criteria themselves, and first of all the
role of sensation, we must discuss the relationship between
propositions and objects in the world a little further. Epicurus
seems to have imagined that a kind of logical atomism would be
able to describe the world without ambiguity. Although in

---

[1] Cic., *ND* 1.70, *Acad. Pr.* 97; cf. *De Fato* 19, 21, 37–8.

fact his own philosophical style is intensely difficult and his language full of ambiguity, his expressed ideal was that each word should have a clear and unambiguous reference. According to Epicurus naming is an activity in which both nature and convention play a part. The original motivating force was a kind of natural instinct, moulded by sense-perception and modified by the different environment of different groups of human beings. When men needed to express themselves, they uttered a variety of sounds which came to refer to the various objects they knew and the various emotions they experienced.[1] Later, however, in order that communication should be facilitated, larger numbers of men began to make compacts about a convenient name for each particular thing they wished to identify. Now when we think philosophically about the world of nature, we must employ words in their ordinary senses.[2] It must be obvious what our terms refer to,[3] and we must realize that only if we accept words in their ordinary senses is it possible accurately to symbolize the object or event to which they refer.[4] Perhaps in an ideal world there would be a one-to-one relationship between words and things, and the structure of propositions would represent the structure of the world unambiguously.

Sensation

Modern writers on Epicureanism usually say that there are three criteria: sensation (αἴσθησις), general concepts (προλήψεις), and feelings, that is, pleasure and pain. In the spirit of *Basic Doctrine* 24, where Epicurus comes nearest to an unequivocal identification of sensation as the criterion, they usually also suggest that the latter two criteria are themselves dependent on sensation. This was also the common view in antiquity. We have already noticed a passage of Cicero in which it is suggested that the Epicureans relied on the senses as the *iudicia rerum*. It is easy to see, however, why the idea should

[1] D.L. 10.75–6; cf. Lucr., 5.1028–90. [2] D.L. 10.31.
[3] D.L. 10.37–8 (Herodotus).
[4] For the Aristotelian background of the idea of words as symbols see Düring, *Aristoteles* 67, note 101.

arise that to some degree Epicurus distinguished three at least potentially separable criteria. According to Diogenes Laertius,[1] in a work called *The Canon* he said that the criteria of truth are the sensations and general concepts and the feelings. Diogenes, however, does not speak of 'the sensations and *the* general concepts' (τὰς αἰσθήσεις καὶ τὰς προλήψεις), but of 'the sensations and general concepts' (τὰς αἰσθήσεις καὶ προλήψεις),[2] thus seeming to indicate that there are not two distinct criteria, but in some sense only one. By itself this evidence is of little value, but we should be at least aware of the possibility that the sensations and general concepts go together, and should look for further evidence pointing in that direction. The passage of Diogenes, however, is further complicated, for after describing the two (or three) criteria of Epicurus, Diogenes observes that the Epicureans in general added a further criterion, the image-making contact of the mind (φανταστικὴ ἐπιβολὴ τῆς διανοίας).

Leaving aside for the moment, however, the problem about 'contact' (ἐπιβολή), we can look at two further passages which may offer a little support on the linguistic level for the notion that sensations and general concepts are to be regarded as in some sense a single criterion. The omission of the article which we observed in Diogenes is also to be seen in a passage of Philodemus, where we find the phrase 'In accordance with the sensations and general concepts and the image-making contacts of the mind and the feelings' (κατὰ τὰς αἰσθήσεις καὶ προλήψεις καὶ τὰς φανταστικὰς ἐπιβολὰς τῆς διανοίας καὶ τὰ πάθη).[3] More direct evidence from Epicurus himself might be found in the letter to Herodotus, if an emendation proposed by Gassendi and more or less accepted by Giussani were acceptable.[4] This would make Epicurus say that the two criteria by which the world should be judged are the sensations and the feelings; but the manuscript readings should probably be retained, leaving the sense that we should judge everything in

---

[1] D.L. 10.31.　　　　[2] Cf. Furley, *Two Studies* 202.

[3] Philod., *De Sign.*, fr. 1, 12–14 De Lacy.

[4] D.L. 10.38. Gassendi wished to read ὁμοίως δὲ καὶ κατὰ τὰ ὑπάρχοντα πάθη. Giussani would omit the καί.

terms of the sensations. The sensations are then explained as *including* the 'contact' of the mind and the feelings of pleasure and pain which accompany every sensation itself. If then we are unable to use this passage, we must steer a cautious course, and admit that no further progress can be made by the use of purely linguistic criteria. We shall have to wait until we are in a position to offer an analysis of the philosophical significance of the term 'general concept' and have completed an enquiry into the epistemological relationships between 'general concepts' and sensations.

What then does Epicurus mean by a sensation? It is the contact between an object in the world, an effluent from such an object, or, in the case of sight, an image (εἴδωλον) emitted from such an object, and the organ of sense. If a sensation occurs, this contact must have taken place and it must have been a real contact, by which we mean a contact between an actually existing organ and an actually existing object or image, no matter from where the image came. This is what Epicurus meant when he said, as he seems to have said repeatedly, that all sensations are true.[1] When the contact between the organ of sense and its object occurs, there arises what Epicurus calls a presentation (φαντασία). The word is particularly appropriate to the sense of sight, but Epicurus seems to have used it of the results of the acts of each of the sense-organs. Hence he appears to have said not only that all sensations are true, but that all presentations are true. This needs further analysis and we must not forget that Epicurean 'truth' is not only a function of propositions. When Epicurus says that all sensations are true, he does not mean that all statements about the world are equally reliable and that, since the sense-organs are the criteria of truth, there is no need to relate what they report to the whole conglomerate of facts in our experience.[2] What Epicurus means when he says that all sensations are true is that a real event takes

---

[1] Plut., *Adv. Col.* 1121; Sext. Emp., *Adv. Math.* 7.203–16; 8.9; D.L. 10.31–2; etc.

[2] Cf. De Witt, 'Epicurus: All Sensations are True'; cf. 'The Gods of Epicurus' and *Epicurus and his Philosophy* 134–42. But De Witt's treatment of the subject goes far beyond the evidence.

place in the act of sensing. The actual organ contacts an actual image from some real object. What sensation does not report is the status of the real object. In fact far from doing any such thing sensation is irrational (ἄλογος).[1] As Sextus tells us, Epicurus held that sensation is able to grasp what comes within its range (ἀντιληπτική) and neither adds nor subtracts nor changes anything since it is irrational. Hence its 'reports' are always 'true' (ἀληθεύειν). The words of Epicurus himself, as reported by Diogenes, give the same account.[2] Sensation, says Epicurus, is irrational and has no memory. Since this is the case, it follows that the sensations and presentations cannot be 'refuted' by one another. It would be absurd to think that one sensation can refute another or that the sensations can be refuted by reason. There is nothing to refute; sensations do not involve reasoning of any kind, either true or false. They are simply what happens to the atomic components of the sense-organs of the body, and in Epicurus' view *all* reasoning depends on them. How he interprets these bodily happenings is another matter; the happenings themselves are true in the sense of being actual data through which we obtain contact with the external world. In two of the *Basic Doctrines* (23 and 24) Epicurus tries to show what will happen if this basic evidence is neglected or mistreated. If you fight against all sensations, he argues (that is, if you reject the evidence of the senses as a guide to the external world), then you will have no standard by which to measure even those sensations you say are false.[3] This implies what we have observed already, that all the data on which reasoning is based depend on the 'events' which occur in the sense organs. It also implies either that 'mind' (διάνοια), in virtue of which, for example, we may see the images of the gods in our sleep, is itself totally dependent on one or other of the five senses, or that it is itself a kind of sense. As we shall see, Epicurus has a consistent doctrine about mind, but he often expresses himself rather ambiguously. Although mind is in fact a kind of additional sense, the nature of its activity is such that Epicurus

---

[1] Sext. Emp., *Adv. Math.* 8.9; cf. 7.210.
[2] D.L. 10.31-2.
[3] Cf. Lucr., 4.469-79.

often has to give it separate treatment. In this chapter we shall only discuss his attitude to mind in so far as it affects the theories he propounds about the criterion.

Basic Doctrine 24 deals with purely *a priori* attempts to be selective in the acceptance of sense-data. Naturally Epicurus rejects this procedure. To adopt it would be to prefer untested opinion, itself of course derived from sense-data, to those data themselves. The result would be that even those sensations which we were prepared to trust would be distorted in the mirror of opinion, and total confusion would ensue.

It is clear that, when Epicurus says that all sensations and all presentations are true, he means that they all indicate something actual in the world. How we interpret that something actual is another matter. We are not given sufficient help by sensation to enable us to judge the truth or falsehood of the vast majority of propositions. In order to do that we have to compare our various sensations with one another and with our general concepts and feelings. We need to invoke what Epicurus calls the principles of 'supporting evidence' (ἐπιμαρτύρησις) and of 'absence of contrary evidence' (οὐκ ἀντιμαρτύρησις) in order to *understand* the 'true' evidence of our senses and formulate propositions whose structure accurately reflects the world as our senses describe it. But we must defer discussion of this until later in the chapter.

Two more points concerned with sensation itself must be noticed. It is a law of Epicurean physics that objects at a distance normally appear smaller than objects seen from close up.[1] The reason for this, according to Epicurus, is that, if we see an object in the distance, the 'images' it has thrown off have travelled a larger distance, before reaching our eyes. In the course of traversing the intervening space they have become worn away at the edges by other atomic bodies; thus the longer the distance they have to travel, the smaller they will become. And Epicurus assumed that if the images are smaller, they will

---

[1] Epicurus however regards the sun as an exception to this. His reason for thinking that the sun is more or less the same size as we see it is given in the letter to Pythocles, D.L. 10.91; cf. Lucr., 5.564–91; Philod., *De Sign.* col. 9, 15 ff. etc.

provide smaller presentations. Hence the object in the distance will seem smaller than the object close up.[1]

Bailey thought that this solution to the problem of different appearances was not that of Epicurus himself but that of his followers, and that it involves a disastrous admission, for, he argues, 'by the truth of a sensation Epicurus meant and could only mean its truth to the external object which it represented. If we have no guarantee of such correspondence, but are at the mercy of the accidents which may befall individual "idols" in their transit, then the "truth" of sensation is valueless not merely for scientific inquiry, but even for the most rudimentary requirements of practical life.'[2] This attempt to save Epicurus' logic is attractive but unhistorical. First of all there is no ancient evidence that the later Epicureans offered a different explanation of the fact that objects seem smaller at a distance from that offered by Epicurus himself. Indeed if Usener's conjecture παριδόντων is right in a passage of the letter to Herodotus[3] – and it certainly makes the best sense – we have Epicurus warning us not to overlook the matter of presentation over a long distance when we make judgments about the celestial bodies. And in the famous passage of the letter to Pythocles in which Epicurus argues that the sun is about the same size as it appears, we find a distinction between how things are 'in themselves' and how they are to us.[4] The distinction is an important one. The possibility is clearly envisaged that things 'in themselves' will be of a different size from the size they present to us through their 'images'. Naturally Epicurus says that as far as we are concerned the sun is as big as it seems; if he did not say this, he would be abolishing his axiom that all sensations are 'true', but he does not rule out the possibility that at different distances objects will appear (and therefore, as far as we are concerned, will *be*) of different sizes. Bailey would have been on safe ground

---

[1] Sext. Emp., *Adv. Math.* 7.209; Plut., *Adv. Col.* 1121.

[2] Bailey, *Greek Atomists* 256–7.

[3] D.L. 10.80 (OCT, p. 531, 21).

[4] D.L. 10.91 (Pythocles). It does not seem that the reasons sometimes advanced for denying this letter's authenticity have much validity, but even if it is not genuine, it is certainly an early document with philosophically correct (i.e. Epicurean) views.

if, instead of suggesting that Epicurus himself did not explain these variations by the wearing away of 'images', he had merely pointed out that Epicurus does not mention such an explanation in the writings we have; but he is going far beyond the evidence, and indeed beyond all probability, when he maintains that Epicurus did not hold such a view. Strictly speaking we do not know for certain whether he held it or not, but there is no *reason* to suppose that when Sextus attributes it to the Epicureans, we should deny it to the master himself.

Bailey's further claim that this doctrine is in fact fatal to Epicurus' system because 'by the truth of a sensation Epicurus meant and could only mean its truth to the external object which it represented' is also strange. It does not seem that this is what Epicurus meant by the truth of a sensation. What he meant was that the sensation marks a real relationship between the subject and the object sensed. He did not mean that it expresses any opinion about the nature of that object. If it did, then it would not be 'irrational' (ἄλογος). Epicurus' sensations give evidence not about the truth of judgments, but about the existence of objects sensed. Epicurus could only have understood the 'truth' of a sensation in terms of its truth to the external object in the sense that the presentation *represents* the object *in some way*; it does not exhibit the *manner* of the representation to the sensing subject. If this were not his opinion, it would have been pointless for Epicurus to caution Herodotus about the manner of *interpreting* representations from distant objects.

Bailey's thesis about the necessity for the 'images' to correspond with the object if sensations are to be true meets another fatal objection if we consider how the Epicureans tried to solve problems about our thinking of things which do not exist. The matter is raised in a number of texts.[1] When asked how we 'see' Centaurs or Scyllas or other creatures which never existed, the Epicureans replied that in the air are to be found a variety of 'images' which can form combinations looking like no creatures which ever walked the earth. Thus 'images' from men combined with 'images' from horses might produce the appearance of a

[1] Cic., *ND* 1.106–8; Lucr., 4.722–76; Philod., *De Sign.*, col. 31, 30–4.

Centaur. And again if we are asked how it can happen that a man can think of whatever he wishes, the answer is that there are all kinds of 'images' present in the air at all times and the mind can 'attend' to whichever of them it wishes and thus recall the past or imagine distant places and events. But how does it come about that two men can form a quite different mental image of someone whom they have never known or who, like Orpheus, perhaps never existed? A solution to this has been offered recently.[1] We recall that both in the writings of Epicurus himself and in Lucretius there is good evidence that the Epicureans held that 'images' can arise 'spontaneously' (*sua sponte*) in the air or be thrown off from all sorts of unlikely objects.[2] By a spontaneous image of a Centaur must be meant an image of a Centaur which is produced by atoms not emitted from a man and a horse. It is certainly true that this theory introduces a disturbing lack of continuity between sense-data and 'things in themselves', that is, the external world; but Epicurus would doubtless have said that false interpretations of the relationship between sense-data and the world have nothing to do with the value of sensation as a 'true' source of knowledge. The objection to that is that knowledge would seem to be of sense-data, not of the world itself; and that it must remain an open question whether the gap between the two can be bridged. Presumably Epicurus' reply would be that all incidences of images arising 'spontaneously' can be interpreted by the correct application of the principle of 'supporting evidence', that is, by comparing the sensations with one another. But, however that may be, little is left of the view that Epicurus insisted on the necessary correspondence of the image to the object. What Epicurus needed, of course, was a theory that the images are compressed in transit; all he offered – and it is a disappointing offering – was a theory that they are rubbed away at the edges.

Before leaving the direct sensations we should observe a final point. We are sensing things all the time without making a

---

[1] Kleve, 'Wie kann man ...?'

[2] Epicurus, Περὶ φύσεως (Pap. Herc. 1420), 32.[10] (Arr.). Kleve's text has some variations on Arrighetti's. Cf. D.L. 10.48 for a cryptic remark that there are other ways in which images come into existence. Cf. also Lucr., 4.736–7.

conscious effort to do so. But we also concentrate our sense-organs on particular objects to strain to see; we look rather than merely see. According to Bailey these activities of the sense-organs were what Epicurus called 'contacts' (ἐπιβολαί), but Furley has demolished the belief that 'contacts' are necessarily acts of concentration or deliberate attention.[1] Concentrated acts of sensation, of course, also provide presentations, and these presentations are equally 'true', though easily misread. Although a different psychological process is at work when we merely see something and when we look at it, when we hear something and when we listen to it, from the point of view of the criterion the two activities need not be differentiated. Hence when Epicurus said that sensation is a criterion, he referred both to the quasi-automatic processes of the five senses and to our deliberate use of them. There is no reason to believe that if we attend to a sensation, that is, if we concentrate upon it when we look hard, there is a necessary guarantee that the sensation or its presentation will correspond more exactly to the object from which the images flow. Certainly, as the letter to Herodotus makes clear, some presentations represent the objects from which they originate very accurately;[2] the difficulty is to know which ones do this and which do not. And we should always remember that in our peculiarly Epicurean sense all sensations are true. Hence in this sense all images, even those that arise spontaneously, in some way represent the object from which they come. Our difficulty is to understand the manner of this representation and hence to determine what kind of object is being represented. The whole problem will arise again when we consider the nature of the general concept (πρόληψις), the second kind of criterion according to Epicurus.

[1] Furley (*Two Studies* 208 on D.L. 10.50–1) argues that because some 'contacts' (ἐπιβολαί) are concerned with illusory visions and dream-images, we have incontrovertible evidence that 'contact' is not *necessarily* (my italics) an act of concentration or deliberate attention.

[2] D.L. 10.50. For discussion see Furley, *Two Studies* 206–8.

General concepts

As we have already noticed, there is some reason to think that general concepts are very closely tied to sensations. So far, however, we have not clarified the relationship. Basing themselves on the text of Diogenes Laertius the vast majority of scholars have argued that the term 'general concept' is used to refer to a correct general idea of an object that arises in the mind because of memories of constant sensory experience of that object. We need such general concepts in order to investigate the world, or to think at all, or even to name the data provided by the senses.[1] Diogenes' definition of them runs as follows: 'They say that a "general concept" is a kind of recognition (κατάληψις) or correct opinion or thought or general idea lying within the mind, that is, a memory of something which has frequently appeared from outside.'[2] That a 'general concept' is indeed some kind of *correct* idea is further indicated by a passage from the letter to Menoeceus,[3] where after explaining that our basic knowledge of the gods is transparently true and needs no further confirmation (ἐναργὴς γὰρ αὐτῶν ἐστιν ἡ γνῶσις) Epicurus goes on to say that many widely held opinions about the gods are not 'general concepts' but false suppositions (ψευδεῖς ἀποφάσεις), that is, false opinion. It is clear then that a 'general concept' is not a universally held opinion, a belief common to the whole of mankind; rather it is a general opinion which arises naturally in the minds of those men who do not allow themselves to be deluded by the intrusion of false opinions on the matter in question. The general concept of god is a common concept (κοινὴ νόησις), by which we mean not a concept held by all, but a concept of the most basic features of the objects conceived. As Epicurus puts it, it is drawn in outline

---

[1] Cf. Sext. Emp., *Adv. Math.* 1.57, οὔτε ζητεῖν οὔτε ἀπορεῖν ἐστὶ κατὰ τὸν σοφὸν 'Επίκουρον ἄνευ προλήψεως. For similar references see Us. 255; cf. D.L. 10.33.

[2] D.L. 10.33. All opinion is, of course, a movement of mind atoms, a movement that is 'in us', as Epicurus puts it (D.L. 10.51 (Herodotus)). By this Epicurus seems to mean that the atomic movement of opinion does not directly involve the images from outside. It is a reaction to the fact of sense-experience.   [3] D.L. 10.123 (Menoeceus).

(ὑπεγράφη) in the mind. It is an outline which will form a correct basis for the completion of the concept and the filling in of details later on.[1] Philodemus gives us a further indication of the notion we are looking for when he says that a general concept provides the basic definition of a particular thing (λόγος ἴδιος).[2] Thus the general concept of body is that it is something with mass and resistance, and the general concept of man is that he is a rational animal. Similarly in the letter to Menoeceus the general concept of god is that he is something possessed of blessedness and immortality.

According to Cicero, whose evidence we have no reason to reject in the matter, Epicurus was the first to use the term 'general concept' in this technical sense. But it was not only the Epicureans who used it. It was taken up by the Stoics and used in exactly the same way.[3] Sandbach has pointed out the curious coincidence that in our extant fragments from the Old Stoa the only general concept mentioned is that of the gods;[4] for other general concepts we have to go to Epictetus. But, as he also observes, this is certainly a mere coincidence, for Diogenes Laertius credits the Old Stoa, and probably Chrysippus himself, with the description of a general concept as a natural notion of the general characteristics of a thing (ἔννοια φυσικὴ τῶν καθόλου). If this is correct, there would be a great variety of general concepts. As Sandbach suggests, the coincidence that both the Old Stoa and Epicurus speak of general concepts of god in the fragmentary evidence we have available to us is probably because the nature of that particular general concept was in dispute between the schools. For Epicurus the general concept of god is that he is possessed of blessedness and immortality; the Stoics accepted this but added that he is also beneficent to mankind.[5] And we should not argue that there were *no* general differences between the Stoic and the Epicurean accounts of general concepts or rather of how general concepts arise. If we trust the passage of Diogenes Laertius, for the

[1] For ὑπεγράφη see Diano, *Epicuri Ethica* 103.
[2] Philod., *De Sign.*, col. 34, 5 ff.
[3] As has been shown by Sandbach, ᾽Εννοια and Πρόληψις', 49–50.
[4] Sandbach, *op. cit.* 47.   [5] Plut., *CN* 1075E; *SR* 1051F.

27

Epicureans general concepts arise only from the registration of sense-experiences as memories. The Stoics were not satisfied with this; they would allow them to arise from various other simple mental acts, such as comparisons. To the Epicureans this would smack of the intrusion of 'opinion' not based directly on particular sense-experience or the deposit (ἐγκατάλειμμα) of particular sense-experience. Needless to say, it follows from this account that there will only be general concepts of existent things. There is thus for Epicurus, as we learn from two of the *Basic Doctrines*, a general concept of justice, for there is an essential nature (φύσις) of justice, namely advantage.[1] On the other hand there is no general concept of time,[2] for, as Lucretius puts it, 'Time does not exist *per se*'.[3]

If we disregard the fact that in his definition of an Epicurean general concept Clement of Alexandria seems to think of it not so much as a concept but rather as the act of the mind which produces the concept, we can find a good summary of the theory in a passage from the *Stromateis*.[4] A general concept is defined as a contact (he should strictly have said 'the result of a contact') with something self-evident and with the self-evident thought (ἐπίνοια) of the object. The 'thought' clearly refers to the memory-image of the object recognized by the senses. The general concept is a concept arising directly from sense-perception and the memory of sense-perception with no intrusion of false 'opinion'. Thus with false opinion excluded it can be thought of as a concept which is, as the Epicureans put it, self-evident (ἐναργής); hence the general concept can be spoken of as a criterion. As the quotation from Clement might suggest,[5] 'self-evident truth' (ἐνάργεια) is a notion we must regularly associate with general concepts. According to Diogenes Laertius general concepts are self-evidently true (ἐναργεῖς),[6] and according to Sextus, Epicurus also called presentations 'self-evident truths' (ἐνάργειαι),[7] for he believed

---

[1] *BD* 37-8 (=D.L. 10.152-3). [2] D.L. 10.72 (Herodotus).
[3] Lucr., 1.459; cf. Sext. Emp., *Adv. Math.* 10.219.
[4] Clem Alex., *Strom.* 2.4 (Us. 255).
[5] Cf. Merbach, *De Ep. Can.* 51. [6] D.L. 10.33.
[7] Sext. Emp., *Adv. Math.* 7.203 (Us. 247).

that their evidence is unsullied by opinion. It is this quality which must be transferred from the presentations to the general concepts which arise from them, for we need general concepts to validate statements in ordinary discourse. Hence the general concept of an object must not only be expressed in terms whose sense is obvious, but will 'correspond' to the sense-data it describes so 'obviously' that it does not need verification by any further reference to these data. Thus when Epicurus says that presentations are self-evident, he means only that no opinion has intruded itself; but, when he says that general concepts are self-evident, he means that we have only to form them to recognize their truth and their correspondence with objective fact.

General concepts then are the direct derivatives of sensation. Before leaving them let us finally return to the passage of Diogenes in which we first met them, the passage where Epicurus is said to have spoken of 'the sensations and general concepts' (τὰς αἰσθήσεις καὶ προλήψεις). Now that we know more about general concepts, we can at least speculate that Epicurus may have deliberately bracketed them together with sensations in a single linguistic formulation, because they are closely associated philosophically. Furley goes too far when he suggests that 'the elevation of the general concept to the position of a third criterion along with sensation and feeling is the work of the doxographers';[1] after all, Diogenes claims that he is quoting from Epicurus' work *The Canon* to the effect that Epicurus himself listed general concepts along with sensation and feelings as a criterion. But although Furley's remark overstates the case, his emphases are correct. General concepts are used to check the validity of propositions, some of which cannot be *directly* tested against the evidence of the senses, but the general concept itself depends entirely on the records of sensation in the mind.

We may conclude this discussion by observing that there is one way in which a general concept is a criterion of 'truth' in a different sense from that which applies to sensations. As we have seen, sensations are guides to the existence of the object

[1] Furley, *Two Studies* 206. Furley modifies his position on p. 209, n. 6.

sensed. They indicate a direct contact between subject and
object. General concepts, of course, do not have this function.
We may have a general concept, say, of god, at a time when we
have no direct contact with god. Hence while sensations record
the existence of objects, general concepts are primarily useful
for evaluating the truth of propositions about such existents.[1]

Feelings

The third criterion (or the second if we bracket general concepts
with direct sensations) is feeling (πάθος).[2] Obviously all sensations are 'feelings' (πάθη) in the sense of experiences,[3] but when
Epicurus talks of feeling as a criterion he refers to pleasure and
pain.[4] Nevertheless these two uses of the word 'feelings' are not
totally disconnected. All our sensations, and indeed all the
sensations of animals also, are movements of the bodily atoms,
and these movements will always involve either disturbance, and
hence pain, or lack of pain, namely pleasure. Hence every
experience of the senses, every 'feeling' of the senses, will involve
the feelings of pleasure or pain. It has often been observed that
this doctrine is an atomist's transposition of the account of
pleasure given in the *Nicomachean Ethics* of Aristotle.[5] For
Aristotle pleasure accompanies activity. Epicurus will avoid
the technical term 'activity' (ἐνέργεια) in this context, and
will say instead that pleasure (or pain) is involved in the atomic
motions which result in sensation.[6] Thus pleasure and pain are
in a sense merely different ways of experiencing the effects of

---

[1] Further uses of the word πρόληψις are provided by Philodemus and may
be inspected in C. J. Vooys' *Index Philodemius*, but they add nothing more
to our understanding of the word. De Witt's views of πρόληψις are discussed in Appendix A.
[2] An unorthodox Epicurean view mentioned by Cicero (*De Fin.* 1.31) would
make the fact that pleasure is to be sought and pain avoided a kind of
general concept, since the mere feeling is inadequate. This is not Epicurus'
position.
[3] Cf. D.L. 10.52 (Herodotus) of the πάθος of hearing and 10.53 of the πάθος
of smelling.
[4] D.L. 10.34.
[5] Cf. most recently Düring, *Aristoteles* 455 and note 148 on Epicurus'
knowledge of the *Nicomachean Ethics*.
[6] Cf. the phrase τὰ ὑπάρχοντα πάθη at D.L. 10.38.

sensation itself, and it is easy to understand why Cicero, for example, discusses the Epicurean criteria in terms of the primacy of sensation. Of course, it is not only the acts of the five 'bodily' senses, seeing, hearing, touch, taste and smell, which will involve pleasure and pain. The acts of the mind, the mental sense, will involve them as well; indeed, as both Diogenes Laertius and Diogenes of Oenoanda tell us, they will involve them more acutely.[1]

The basic sensations are our guides to the existence of the objects sensed; the general concepts help us to describe our sensations properly and to formulate correct propositions; the feelings of pleasure and pain are the criteria of how we should act. Pleasure, Diogenes Laertius tells us, is appropriate to us (οἰκεῖον), while pain is alien (ἀλλότριον).[2] In the moral sphere, the sphere of choices and action, therefore, we refer to our feelings when we make our choices and decide what should be avoided. The reasoning behind this is straightforward enough. Since all animals are the products of nature, it is natural for them to direct themselves towards what is pleasurable and away from what is painful. Pleasure, which is appropriate to us, is appropriate in the sense that it indicates courses of action which will maintain us in an untroubled existence; pain is unnatural in that it indicates the road to non-existence and destruction. Hence if we say that the feelings are among the criteria of truth, we mean that they guide us along the path of a natural life in enjoyment of tranquillity. And for the Epicureans tranquillity of life involves an acceptance of the facts of nature as they are. By the constancy of our pleasures we can measure whether we are living this natural and hence good life. We should observe that many of our general concepts, such as that of the gods, are accompanied by pleasure.[3]

[1] D.L. 10.137; Diog. Oen. fr. 38, col. 1 Chilton; cf. Cic., De Fin. 1.55.
[2] D.L. 10.34.
[3] Cf. Cic., ND 1.49 and Philod., De Dis 1, col. 16, 19, p. 28 Diels; cf. Kleve, Gnosis 118.

Image-making contact of the mind

According to Diogenes Laertius the Epicureans, though not Epicurus himself, spoke of the image-making contact of the mind (φανταστικὴ ἐπιβολὴ τῆς διανοίας), as one of the criteria.[1] The word 'contact' is used by Epicurus with reference to the apprehension of an object by one of the senses. We have followed Furley in recognizing that it does not necessarily denote a concentrated act of attention. Now, as we have already observed, there is a kind of sensing which is achieved not with the sense-organs but with the mind. When we see images of the gods, we do not see them with our eyes but with our minds. There is, of course, no need to infer that for Epicurus all sensation is a mental operation. Indeed the opposite is true. As Lucretius tells us, the bodily organs of sense are not mere eyes of the soul. It is they themselves, not the soul in them, which see and hear and perform the other activities of sense.[2] But there is a kind of seeing in which the mind itself engages, as when we see the images of the gods. Does Epicurus not regard this kind of mental 'sensation' as a criterion of truth? We should recall, of course, that just as in the case of ocular vision we can both see something and look at it, so the same distinction can be made in thought. Hence there will be an ordinary mental 'sensation' as well as an act of attention by the mind. This attention of the mind may be directed not only to a sensible image,[3] but to a mental image such as the image of a god.

According to Diogenes Laertius (10.31), Epicurus did not describe mental 'sensation' or the contact of the mind as a criterion in *The Canon*. This at first seems surprising, since in the letter to Herodotus he speaks of the 'contacts of mind (διάνοια) or of any other of the criteria'.[4] This would naturally suggest that mind is itself a criterion. There is only one way to reconcile the two passages while remaining faithful to Epicurus' general theories about the atomic structure of the mind. If the text from the letter to Herodotus is to be taken seriously, we must assume

[1] D.L. 10.31.
[2] Lucr., 3.350ff. Cf. Solmsen, 'Αἴσθησις', esp. 252–5.
[3] *Pace* Vlastos, *Gnomon* 27 (1955) 71, note 1.   [4] D.L. 10.38.

that, when discussing the criterion in *The Canon*, Epicurus classified 'mind' as a sense. That our passage from the letter is not a mere piece of careless writing is proved by a repetition of the idea a few sections later. In chapter 51 Epicurus talks about contacts of the mind or of the remaining criteria, that is, the five senses.

The view that Epicurus treats 'mind' as one of the senses when discussing the criterion is strengthened when we consider that the reliability of the mind is no more and no less than that of the senses. We have already observed in what way we must understand the dictum 'all sensations are true'. And we have observed that Epicurus does not mean by this that any statements we make on the basis of unconfirmed sense-data will be true; opinion may intervene. Exactly the same situation pertains to mental perceptions. As Diogenes Laertius tells us, the Epicureans held that the visions (φαντάσματα) of the insane and the visions of dreams are both 'true', since they have the power to move us.[1] In more modern terminology we might say that neuroses and delusions are not to be dismissed as unreal; people are motivated by them. In the letter to Herodotus we find Epicurus himself arguing that contacts of the mind can produce deceptive images (φαντάσματα),[2] and Philodemus speaks of a false fear of the gods which may arise from the contact of our minds.[3] Indeed even the fact that we may think hard about our mental images does not guarantee that these images will not be delusory, though in one Epicurean sense they will also be true.

The doctrine of Epicurus becomes clearer when we realize that contacts of the mind are nowhere said to guarantee us the truth of propositions. We noticed in Clement's account of a general concept that it arises from one variety of contact, namely that directed towards something 'self-evidently true' (ἐναργές).[4] The implication is that there are other contacts which are directed to other things which are not 'self-evidently true', such as, for example, Centaurs. It is possible to think

[1] D.L. 10.32.
[2] Cf. D.L. 10.51 and the discussion of Furley, *Two Studies* 206–8.
[3] *De Dis* 1, col. 14, 8ff., p. 24 Diels. Cf. Kleve, *Gnosis* 112.
[4] Clem. Alex., *Strom.* 2.4 (Us. 255).

33

about a Centaur and conceivable that someone might believe in the existence of Centaurs even after thinking hard about them. What happens in such cases is that the mind is directed to actual mental images and forms false opinions about them. As Epicurus puts it in the letter to Herodotus, 'error would not have arisen unless we received within ourselves another kind of movement, linked to our image-making contact (φανταστικὴ ἐπιβολή) but differing from it'.[1] This other movement of our soul atoms is opinion (δόξα), and opinions (or suppositions, ὑπολήψεις) may be either true or false, according as to how they reflect the direct evidence of the senses and of the mind.[2] As for the data from the contacts of the mind itself, however, they are all 'true', but they are not all necessarily reliable. They indicate existent phenomena, just as do the data provided by contacts of the senses. Epicurus sums the matter up as follows: 'Everything that is thought about (θεωρούμενον) or received by the mind in contact is true.'[3]

Since then 'contact' (ἐπιβολή) seems to be some kind of general term for the relation between an organ of sense and its object, a contact of the mind must be the relation of the mind to sensible images or to images presented only to the mind itself, such as images of the gods. Contacts of the mind may, though not necessarily, lead to the formation of general concepts, since, if the mind is directly applied to remembered images, general concepts will naturally arise. However, before finally returning to the question of why in *The Canon* Epicurus himself did not speak of contact of the mind (or indeed of mind itself) as a criterion, we must consider one further point. Often the word 'image-making' (φανταστική) is used with 'contact', but sometimes it is omitted. Does the word 'image-making' indicate any special kind of contact? We recall that later Epicureans, who according to Diogenes called contact of the mind a criterion, spoke of this kind of contact as image-making. An answer to this problem has been suggested by Bailey. Following Giussani, he holds that all contacts are image-making, since all thought

[1] D.L. 10.51 (Herodotus).   [2] D.L. 10.34.
[3] D.L. 10.62 (Herodotus). For this sense of θεωρούμενον see Furley, 'Knowledge of Atoms and Void in Epicureanism', 615.

must be conducted with the aid of visual images.[1] However, this deduction does not seem to be correct. According to Diogenes the Epicureans held that thoughts (ἐπίνοιαι) arise from sensations – obviously visual images are involved here[2] – but Diogenes adds that there are other factors: coincidence, comparison, analogy (ὁμοιότης), combination, and calculation (λογισμός) come into play at this stage.[3] Some of the contacts which are not concerned with what is self-evidently true, those, for example, concerned with what is inaccessible to sense (ἄδηλον), such as the basic atoms or the void of which the world is composed, would seem to be hardly 'image-making' at all. In fact the word 'image-making' may be added to 'contact' to denote only those contacts which involve visual (or mental) images directly. It is possible, however, as Bailey also thought, that, where the epithet 'image-making' occurs, Epicurus often thinks of our attention to subtle presentations such as those from the gods.

It has often been observed that Epicurus recognized two kinds of things inaccessible to the senses (ἄδηλα): those like the heavenly bodies or the bodies of the gods which can be 'seen' by the eyes or by the mind, but which cannot be subjected to close inspection, and on the other hand the atoms and the void which, though existent, cannot be seen at all. At least it could be argued that it would be absurd to talk of an *image-making* contact of the mind providing us with data about the basic premisses of the atomic theory. We know of the existence of the void by inference. Void is necessary to account for movement.

---

[1] Bailey, *Greek Atomists* 573.

[2] For further discussion of ἐπίνοια, λογισμός (calculation) etc., see Diano, *GCFI* 20 (1939) 134, though his remarks about 'intuition' should be treated with great reserve. For ἐπιλογισμός, against Arrighetti's 'intuitionism', see De Lacy, *AJP* 79 (1958) 179–83. De Lacy rightly identifies ἐπιλογισμός as inductive inference based on empirically received information. Diano is right to emphasize that the ἐπί in ἐπιλογίζομαι stresses the spontaneously mental nature of the action.

[3] D.L. 10.32. Diano also disagrees with Bailey. He speaks of φανταστική ἐπιβολή as a species, ἐπιβολή as the genus (*GCFI* 20 (1939) 134). He draws attention to Περὶ φύσεως 28, 5, vi 1–5 (29.[15] Arr.), which seems to support his point, but though he is probably right, the meaning of the text is not transparent.

Nevertheless it appears that, although we cannot see the void or even 'mentally' see it, we recognize its existence by a contact of the mind. Cicero seems to be saying in the *De Natura Deorum* that it is by contact of the mind that we understand atoms and the void, and Lucretius tells us that it is by such contact that we know that atoms have no colour.[1] Epicurus himself uses the word 'contact' to refer to the appreciation of a philosophical system.[2]

Perhaps we can now understand why later Epicureans called the image-making contact of the mind a criterion. It is possible to direct the eye of the mind to other things than sense-data or mental-sense data. It can be directed at philosophical theories whether true or false. Even if true, such theories are not the primary components of experience. Epicurus probably thought that image-making contacts of the mind (whether mental seeing or mental looking) are most conveniently treated simply as acts of sensation. All those functions of the mind which correspond with those of the five senses, that is, those which involve direct contact with the physical world, can be regarded as sense functions. So far as these functions are concerned, mind is a criterion like the five senses and need not be listed separately in the canon. Perhaps this provides the correct interpretation of a part of section 38 of the letter to Herodotus. Epicurus says that we must check everything by the use of the senses. He then adds: καὶ ἁπλῶς τὰς παρούσας ἐπιβολὰς εἴτε διανοίας εἴθ' ὅτου δήποτε τῶν κριτηρίων. If the καί indicates an added explanation, we should understand Epicurus to be saying that we should refer to our senses, *that is*, to the contacts of the mind or of the five bodily senses. By 'contacts' we must understand 'image-making contacts'.

Yet it seems that Epicurus' use of the term 'contact' could be misinterpreted. A contact with a false philosophical theory should not be confused with a contact with the images of the gods. Perhaps the later Epicureans wished to clarify Epicurus' language. They wished to emphasize that only those contacts of the mind which are image-making, that is, which give us *direct* apprehension of the external world, are properly to be included in the criterion. Hence where Epicurus had said that

---

[1] Cic., *ND* 1.54; Lucr., 2.739–40.   [2] D.L. 10.35 (Herodotus).

the criterion is sensation, *including* under this heading *image-making* contacts of the mind, later Epicureans preferred to say that the five senses are a criterion and that the image-making contact of the mind is a criterion. Hence they can more clearly assert that, although there are other kinds of contact of the mind, these are not included in the criterion.[1]

True and false judgment

We can now see that for Epicurus sensation is indeed the guide to the world. General concepts are direct derivatives of sensation, feelings are the accompaniments of sensation, and much of mental perception is a special variety of sensation. To complete our study of Epicurus' canonic, therefore, it only remains to see how his criteria were used; and here the evidence is more straightforward. As the word 'criterion' indicates, sensation and its derivatives are to be used to help us make judgments. We use our criteria as witnesses to determine whether particular statements, aimed at understanding and interpreting the world, are true or false. Ideally we wish to make transparently correct statements, statements which do not distort what the Epicureans called the self-evident truth (ἐνάργεια) of sense-data, for that, as we have seen, is the 'foundation and basis' of all judgment.[2]

Epicurus divides objects in the world into two groups, those which can be seen, as it were, from close up (πρόδηλα), and those which are for different reasons more remote and obscure (ἄδηλα). Of these latter, some are objects in the heavens which can only be seen at a distance and which we cannot approach closely, others are those physical phenomena, such as atoms and the void, with which we cannot obtain direct contact through the senses or the mind. The first group can easily be dealt with.

---

[1] Further passages on ἐπιβολή are conveniently listed by Kleve (*Gnosis* 110 note 5 and 111, note 6). They include the following: D.L. 10.50 (Herodotus); *BD* 24 (D.L. 10.147); Cic., *ND* 1.54; Lucr., 2.739–45; 1044–7 and possibly 1080 if Lipsius' *inice mentem* is read. And from the Herculaneum papyri Kleve adds Περὶ φύσεως 28, 5, x 18 (29.[19] Arr.); Polystratus, *Lib. Inc.*, fr. 3, col. 4a, 13f. (p. 80 Vogliano); *ibid.* fr. 3, col. 4b, 5f. (p. 80 Vogliano).   [2] Sext. Emp., *Adv. Math.* 7.216 (Us. 247).

If we wish to make a statement about a tower, which is some distance away, we observe the phenomenon and make judgments about it. We think, for example, that the tower which is square is round. We then approach closer and observe the tower again. Each observation supplies us with evidence about the tower. We are checking the validity of our judgments by adducing supporting evidence (ἐπιμαρτύρησις). Each sensation provides us with new data. If a sequence of sensations adds further evidence in favour of our original judgment, then that judgment is confirmed and we may say that a proposition embodying it is true. If our inspection provides any counter-evidence, then the judgment is false. Of course the falseness of a particular judgment about the tower does not mean that our sensation was false, but that our thought about the sensation (our ἐπίνοια) was false.[1] False opinion has been added to the evidence of sensation.[2] It has not been tested by 'self-evident truth' (ἐνάργεια) and the underlying reality of things, and we are therefore in confusion.[3]

When we turn to what is 'remote and obscure' (ἄδηλον), the method of validating propositions and judgments is necessarily different. We cannot get a nearer view of the sun or of the atom. In these cases positive confirmation of a hypothesis by the direct use of the senses is out of the question. The method of testing is therefore to assure oneself that there is no sense evidence which positively opposes a particular belief, that there is no counter-evidence.[4] Epicurus seems to have proceeded in a somewhat different way in the cases of atoms and the void on the one hand and of celestial objects and gods on the other. In the case of things which cannot be seen at all, we proceed by inference.

[1] Evidence for ἐπιμαρτύρησις is to be found in Sextus Empiricus, *Adv. Math.* 7.212 and 215; D.L. 10.34; Plut., *Adv. Col.* 1121CD; Lucr., 4.462–8; Epicurus, Περὶ φύσεως 28, 3. ii (29.[7].4 Arr.).

[2] D.L. 10.50–1.

[3] *BD* 22 (D.L. 10.146). For the evaluation of φαντασίαι from a distance see also D.L. 10.80 (Pythocles), where Usener's reading παριδόντων, retained by Long (OCT), is correct.

[4] For ἀντιμαρτύρησις see Sext. Emp., *Adv. Math.* 7.215–16; Epicurus, Περὶ φύσεως 28 (29.[7].4 Arr.); cf. also 34.[2].1 Arr. We should notice that the term ἐπιμαρτύρησις seems to be limited to πρόδηλα, ἀντιμαρτύρησις to ἄδηλα.

Epicurus himself speaks of inference from signs in section 38 of the letter to Herodotus and uses it immediately to show the necessity of the void. Our senses point to the existence of bodies. If there were no void, these bodies could not move. Our senses tell us that they do move; therefore void exists. The form of the argument, as it was later formalized, is: if p then q, but p therefore q. The most important aspect of the argument is that p (e.g. there is movement) is, in the argument for the void, proved by direct observation. p is observed to be the case. Only if such observation takes place is this form of argument, later called argument by contraposition (κατ' ἀνασκευήν), acceptable to an Epicurean.

It seems that Epicurus was prepared to offer a variant of this empirical basis for inference: it is inconceivable that q should be the case, argues Philodemus, if p is not the case. Thus if Socrates is not a man, it is inconceivable that Plato should be a man.[1] That this type of proof is indeed empirically based is argued by Philodemus a little later. You can only object to an argument, he holds, if you start from the principle that something deprived of all similarity with appearance (τὸ φαινόμενον) is inconceivable.[2] It is unlikely that Epicurus himself formalized arguments about inconceivability, but he does argue against various possibilities as inconceivable (obviously on a basis of previously observed facts) in the letter to Herodotus and in the letter to Pythocles.[3] In the latter passage we read that we shall get into the position of postulating the inconceivable unless we explain meteorological phenomena in accordance with things in our own experience (παρ' ἡμῖν).

We have now, of course, shifted from things which cannot be seen at all (atoms and void) to those which cannot be seen clearly 'by near view' (meteorological phenomena). It seems that here too we must use the idea of inconceivability to construct our inferences, for certain explanations of the physicists or the mythologizers are completely out of keeping with anything we have ever observed. As in the case of atoms and

---

[1] Philod., *De Signis* 12, 19–31, p. 50 De Lacy.
[2] *Ibid.* 21, 27–9, p. 72 De Lacy.
[3] D.L. 10.47 (Herodotus), ἀδιανόητον γάρ; D.L. 10.97 (Pythocles).

the void, however, we get certain indications (σημεῖα)[1] about the nature of celestial phenomena. In the case of celestial phenomena, however, a number of theories may all be in accordance with the evidence of the senses and we may infer that they are all equally likely to be true. Obviously only one of them is true in our world, but others will be true in various other worlds which may exist or may have existed somewhere in space and time.[2] If we have no reason for accepting any one rather than another in a particular case, we should refrain from making a judgment. We should notice a difference, however, between the uncertainty with which Epicurus is content in offering explanations of particular phenomena in our world and the certainty with which he argues for one special theory, that of atoms and the void, as the only basis of reality. An explanation of this can perhaps be found: if atomism provides the explanation of the existence of any world, it must be the explanation of all worlds.

A basic defect in Epicurus' treatment of how we use the criteria to validate our opinions and judgments is obvious. There appears to be no good reason why confirmation should be the test for what is accessible to the senses, and lack of counter-evidence for what is not. It is merely that we are unable to see the stars or the void from close up. We can only surmise that Epicurus realized that some test is essential if knowledge of the world and the ensuing freedom from fear is to be attained. Since a test is necessary, he had to improvise one as well as he could.

[1] Epicurus uses the word σημεῖον several times in the fragments of the Περὶ φύσεως (27.[16].5; 29.[8].8; 29.[16].16; 29.[19].26). It also occurs in the letter to Pythocles (D.L. 10.87, 97). The verb σημειόω is also frequent; cf. D.L. 10.32 and 10.38 (Herodotus), etc. Philodemus' *De Signis* gives clear evidence that the doctrine of signs was formalized by later Epicureans in response to Stoic criticism and discussion, but we should recall that according to Sextus Empiricus it was not only Epicureans, but Epicurus himself, who said that the sign is 'sensible' (αἰσθητόν, *Adv. Math.* 8.177).

[2] Cf. D.L. 10.78–80, 86–8 and 113 (Pythocles); Lucr., 5.526–33.

3

PHYSICS

First principles

Epicurus regards the study of nature as a necessary evil; without it we are subject to delusions about the role of the gods in the ordering of the world and about the afterlife. We need to know the basic structure of the world of nature if we are to be happy.[1] Epicurus' physical theory is based on the atomism of Leucippus and Democritus, but he does not adopt their positions unchanged. For between Democritus and Epicurus is the work of Aristotle, and Aristotle had frequently attacked the atomic theory. Since we are concerned here to give an account of the positions of Epicurus and not to write a comprehensive history of ancient atomism, it will be necessary to recount many of Epicurus' theses which were in fact identical with those of his predecessors without describing their original purpose and scope. Yet although Epicurus owes much to Democritus, it is not only in ethics that he diverges greatly from his (unacknowledged) master. As we try to understand various Epicurean doctrines, the originality of his approach will become evident, and we shall see that, while both Democritus and Epicurus are atomists, the position of Epicurus is no mere copy, let alone the botched copy which some of his critics would have us suppose. We shall base our account on the letter to Herodotus, but other writings, both of Epicurus himself and of his followers, notably of Lucretius, have to be used to fill out the sketch which the letter provides.

Epicurus begins by accepting one of the canons laid down by Parmenides, as his predecessor Democritus had done. Nothing can come into existence from the non-existent (ἐκ τοῦ μὴ ὄντος);[2] the phrase is echoed repeatedly by Lucretius,[3] and Epicurus' basic argument is developed for over fifty lines: if something can come into existence from what has not previously

[1] *BD* 11.
[2] D.L. 10.38 (Herodotus). For 'seeds' see below pp. 58–9.
[3] Lucr., 1.150ff.

41

existed, there would be no need of 'seeds'. If creation were
spontaneous, therefore, there need be no permanent and
individualized species of things, such as the senses tell us there
are. Men could be born from the sea, birds from the earth and
cattle from the sky. And, Epicurus continues, just as nothing
can come into existence from what did not exist before, so no
existent can altogether cease to exist. If it could, all things would
have long since ceased to exist. Finally, concludes Epicurus, it
follows that, since the sum of things must be forever the same,
and has been the same for all time, the universe must always
have been fundamentally the same as it is now. We note the
importance of this immediately. When we describe the bases of
our world, namely atoms and the void, we must assume that
the behaviour of these components is the same now as it always
has been. Thus if atoms now swerve slightly from the downward
path, they have always done so; if they are now constantly
involved in collisions with one another, they have always been
so involved. We shall return to this theme later. It is sufficient
for the present to notice Epicurus' axiom. The state of the basic
components of the universe must remain unchanged, he insists,
because nothing else exists into which they could change.
That is, there are no other components than atoms and the void.
Since there are no other components, Epicurus continues, there
is nothing external which could vary the state of the components
which exist.[1]

Of what then does the universe consist? There is a lacuna in
the text of the letter to Herodotus, but it is easily filled from
what follows. The basic components are 'bodies' and void.[2]
We should notice first of all that void, empty space, is said to
exist. Parmenidean logic is rejected; it makes sense to say that
there *is* nothing between two objects. Epicurus here accepts the
standard atomist position,[3] and supports that position by an

---

[1] Lucr., 2.304 ff. elaborates on these principles and adds a further point:
that nothing completely new can come into existence *inside* the universe
since all possible combinations of atoms have already occurred. Cf.
Bailey, *Greek Atomists* 278.

[2] σώματα καὶ κενόν. This supplement of Gassendi's is, I think rightly,
accepted (e.g.) by Long and Arrighetti. Usener and Bailey prefer τόπος
to κενόν.   [3] Cf. Arist., *Met.* 985b.

appeal to the evidence of the senses. Everyone, he argues, is aware through the senses that bodies exist.

But the other basic constituent of the world is void, and here more difficulties arise. Obviously we cannot see void, for it is nothing. Indeed, as Epicurus says, it is a nature which cannot be touched (ἀναφὴς φύσις). When we discuss the Epicurean theory of sense-perception, we shall observe that all the senses are reducible to a sense of touch.[1] Hence if void cannot be touched, we cannot be aware of it through the senses. A correct calculation must therefore be employed to prove its existence, and Epicurus immediately introduces it: if there were no void, bodies would have nowhere to exist and no place through which to move. Yet bodies do exist somewhere – the senses tell us so – and are regularly in motion. Therefore void must exist.[2] That is all we find on this subject in the letter to Herodotus, but Lucretius goes into more detail, doubtless following a more elaborate writing of Epicurus. Lucretius considers the possibility that movement can be explained by the elasticity of a basic substance in which things exist. But, he continues, such elasticity can only be explained by the existence of void in the basic substance itself.[3]

Atoms: size and shape

Everything that exists is either body or void. There is no third possibility, for, as Lucretius argues, whatever can be touched is body and whatever cannot be touched is void.[4] If anything else is conceivable, Epicurus himself insists, it must be a property (συμβεβηκός) or an accident (σύμπτωμα) of bodies or void. All bodies, Epicurus argues, are either compounds (συγκρίσεις) or the components of compounds. The basic components of compounds are physically indivisible (ἄτομα) and unchangeable (ἀμετάβλητα). If there were no such basic and indivisible physical objects, then when compounds are destroyed, the

---

[1] See below p. 83.
[2] D.L. 10.40 (Herodotus).
[3] For this and other discussion of motion and void see Lucr., 1.329–97. If the discussion of 'elasticity' was in Epicurus himself, it was not aimed at the Stoics. But we cannot be sure if it was in Epicurus or not.
[4] Lucr., 1.432 ff.: cf. D.L. 10.40 (Herodotus).

process of destruction would either be endless, which is impossible, or bodies would be destroyed 'into that which does not exist', which is absurd. Hence the atoms must be strong enough to endure (ἰσχύοντα) when the compounds dissolve.[1] Lucretius adds a further argument to the same effect.[2] If there were no minimum bodies and the process of division could go on indefinitely, then all things would long since have perished, since we know that the processes of destruction work faster than those which lead to the formation of new compounds and hence new physical objects.

The basic components of physical objects are atoms. They must be completely solid, that is, they must have no empty space or void within them.[3] Since they are to remain firm when the compounds they form are dissolved, they must not only be solid; they must also be completely unchanging.[4] They possess in fact only three distinguishing features; they may differ in size, in shape and in weight. We will look briefly at each of these properties. It is obvious that, since the atoms are solid bodies, they will have a particular size, but Epicurus is rather cryptic about how many sizes there are. We must not suppose that every size of atom exists, he says; the evidence of the senses is against this. We must admit that there are differences in size, but it is not necessary to suppose that the different qualities we observe in physical objects require that the atoms be of every possible size. If that were so, he continues, we should be able to see some of the atoms, and that is impossible. The background of this argument is not easy to discern. According to Dionysius of Alexandria Epicurus held a view which differed from that of Democritus.[5] Dionysius says that Democritus accepted the existence of very large atoms, and according to Aëtius he envisaged the possibility that an atom could be as big as the cosmos.[6] The last statement is hard to credit, and it is likely that, if Democritus had only claimed that the atoms *admit* of infinite variety of size, people thought that this *implied* that some of

---

[1] Bailey's (and Bignone's) ἰσχῦόν τι is unnecessary.
[2] Lucr., 1.551–64.
[3] D.L. 10.42 (Herodotus), μεστά; cf. Us. 267.
[4] D.L. 10.54 (Herodotus).
[5] *Ap.* Eus., *PE* 14.23 (= DK 68A43).   [6] Aëtius, 1.12.6.

them would be visible, and even perhaps as large as the cosmos.[1] Indeed even in the letter to Herodotus it may well be that it is *Epicurus* who is claiming that if atoms were of every size some would be visible, not that it was Democritus who actually held such a view.

There are then a large number of different sizes of atoms, but all atoms are so small that we are unable to see them. But since the atoms differ in size, we might wonder whether we could distinguish their parts in some way, for if it were possible to place a smaller atom on top of a larger, we should obviously be able to 'see' a *part* of the larger one, while another part of it was obscured. But we must defer consideration of the question of 'parts' of atoms until we have discussed the other two properties which Epicurus himself tells us atoms possess, namely shape and weight. Obviously if the atoms have size they must have shape, but again we must be careful. At first glance one might assume that the number of shapes would be infinite, but Epicurus will not admit that. The number is 'incomprehensibly' large, he tells us. Lucretius gives the details.[2] Although the number of shapes is incomprehensibly large, it must be finite. If this were not the case, he thinks that we should again be faced with the possibility that some of the atoms would be infinitely large. It is true that in this passage Lucretius suggests another way out – but only to reject it. As we have seen, although the atom is physically indivisible, it might still admit of some kind of 'parts'. If these parts were themselves infinite in number, then the possibility of an infinite number of shapes would still exist; but, as we shall see, such 'parts' are not infinite in number. To this sophisticated argumentation we must add a point mentioned by the doxographers: some shapes are out of the question because the atoms would then be too easily broken![3] Yet although the number of shapes of atoms is limited (though incomprehensibly large), the number of atoms of each particular shape is infinite.[4] If that were not the case,

---

[1] Guthrie, *A History of Greek Philosophy* 2.394; cf. Furley, *Two Studies* 96. According to Aristotle (*ap.* Simp., *In De Caelo* p. 295, 5 ff. Heiberg) Democritus thought that all the atoms are so small as to be invisible, but still different in size.　　[2] Lucr., 2.478–99.
[3] Aëtius, 1.3.18 ff.　　[4] D.L. 10.42 (Herodotus).

Lucretius illogically argues, there could not be an infinite number of atoms.[1] The argument is illogical because an infinite number of atoms would be achieved if *any* single shape had an infinite number of representatives; but Epicurus also specifically says that *every* shape must be so infinitely numerous.

Atoms: weight and movement

Whether Democritus thought that the atoms have weight is still disputed; in any case Epicurus held that they do,[2] and the effect of the 'blow'[3] of their weight is that they move downwards through the void, unless they are hindered by collisions with other atoms or compounds.[4] Moreover, during this downward movement in the void the atoms, whether heavy or light, will all proceed at a uniform speed.[5] This atomic speed cannot be compared with the speeds with which we are familiar in our everyday world. An atom takes an incomprehensibly brief time to pass through every conceivable distance. It moves, says Epicurus himself, as quickly as thought. In section 62 of the letter to Herodotus Epicurus speaks of the movement of atoms in the smallest continuous time and again of their lack of movement in a uniform direction in the times which are distinguishable in thought. What this latter idea implies is that there are indivisible minima of time – times 'distinguishable in thought' – and that we cannot say that an atom *is moving* in any one direction in them. Themistius confirms that such an interpretation would square with Epicurus' general theory of motion.[6] According to Epicurus, he says, a moving object cannot be said to *be moving* (*scil.* at any continuous period of time) over each of the indivisible parts of a line, but rather to *have moved* over them. Naturally, to revert to the letter to Herodotus, it is

---

[1] Lucr., 2.522–31; cf. 1.1008 ff.
[2] D.L. 10.54 (Herodotus). For Democritus see Appendix B.
[3] Plut., *Plac.* 1.3.26 (= Us. 375).   [4] D.L. 10.61 (Herodotus).
[5] D.L. 10.61 (Herodotus); cf. Περὶ φύσεως 2, sections 23.[36–7] and 23. [42.]5 Arr., and Barigazzi, 'Cinetica'.
[6] Them., *In Phys.* p. 184, 9 Wallies, where we can compare Simp., *In Phys.* p. 934, 18 ff. Diels (ἐπάγει, etc.). That Epicurus' position is a reply to Aristotle's critique of earlier atomism is well argued by Furley, *Two Studies* 111–27. See also Merlan, 'L'univers', 259.

possible to say that the atoms *are moving* in a single direction in the smallest continuous period of time.[1]

If the atoms were totaliy unimpeded, they would be carried perpendicularly downwards by their weight, all travelling at a uniform speed.[2] Obviously if the atoms were always involved in such a progression, they would never have met and worlds would never have been formed. But before we consider this further, we must try to unravel what Epicurus meant in saying that in an infinite universe there is a perpendicular up and down. Section 60 of the letter to Herodotus gives us his explanation. He admits that strictly speaking one cannot talk of up and down as though there existed highest and lowest points.[3] 'Up' and 'down' must be used with reference to fixed points, and we, standing on the earth, provide such a fixed point. Our earth, Epicurus holds, is a round flat body resting on air[4] and lying in the centre of its world. The underside of this flat body gradually thins out and eventually becomes indistinguishable from the air on which it rests.[5] That the earth is in the centre of our world is important; it was the normal theory in Epicurus' day and was held, among others, by both Plato and Aristotle.[6] Epicurus did not say that the earth is the centre of the *universe*; indeed, if Lucretius is to be trusted, he expressly denied it,[7] but, as we shall see, he did not regard this as fatal to his account of 'up' and 'down'. If the earth is at the centre of our world, then obviously above our heads is 'up' and below our feet is 'down'. At least we can use the words that way and apparently Epicurus did so. He observed that, if we drop something from a tree-top, it falls in a particular direction. He calls that direction 'downwards'; and 'upwards' is its opposite.

[1] The problem is best discussed by Mau, *Zum Problem*.
[2] 'Perpendicularly' is a rendering of κατὰ στάθμην (Aët., 1.12.5 = Us. 280).
[3] Cf. Plato, *Tim.* 62D.
[4] Schol. to D.L. 10.74 (Herodotus), and Diogenes of Oenoanda, new Fragment 7, col. II, 12 (Smith, 'New Fragments', 367).
[5] Lucr., 5.534–63; cf. Epic., Περὶ φύσεως 11 (24.[43.]10ff. Arr.).
[6] Cf. Aristotle, *De Caelo* 2.293a15–293b33.
[7] Lucr., 1.1052–82 (*pace* Barigazzi, *SIFC* 24 (1950) 12). The theory here attacked that the earth is the centre of the universe was probably that of Aristotle, and possibly expounded particularly in the *De Philosophia*; see Furley, 'Lucretius and the Stoics', 16–23.

Thus Epicurus can say that all objects, because of their weight, fall in a particular direction in relation to himself when he stands upright on the surface of the earth, which is in its turn in the centre of the world. Since the earth is at the centre of the world, we should notice that the words 'up' and 'down' need have no relation to positions nearer or further from the edge of the world. Their meaning is entirely dependent on us as observers. In a sense we are a fixed point, or at least standing on a fixed point. That is the importance of the notion that the earth is at the centre of our world. But what about our world in the universe as a whole? We have seen that the words 'up' and 'down' are conventional terms referring to directions in relation to us. Heavy objects do in fact fall in a particular direction. We call that downwards. What is to prevent us applying these terms in the universe as a whole? Since physical objects fall in one direction, that is 'down' in our world, therefore atoms fall 'down' in our world. And if atoms fall 'down' in our world, then there is no counter-evidence to suggest that they do anything else anywhere else. Here Epicurus' canonic can come to the rescue of his physics. At any rate we know that as a result of some such argumentation Epicurus concluded that free atoms have one direction, 'downwards'.

Now we have already observed that, if there had been a time at which all the atoms were falling perpendicularly downwards at uniform speed, worlds could never have formed since the atoms would never have met. But worlds in fact exist and atomic speed does not vary; therefore, Epicurus held, the atoms cannot all have been constantly moving perpendicularly downwards. Hence arises the need for a minute swerve of atoms in the atomic rain.[1] This swerve, as Lucretius tells us, takes place at no fixed time and at no fixed place.[2] Its existence is necessitated by the evidence of the senses that there is a world and that therefore all atoms cannot always have been falling perpen-

---

[1] The swerve is not mentioned in the letter to Herodotus. There may be a lacuna in chapter 43 (or 61). But cf. Lucr., 2.216–93; Aët., 1.12.5; 1.23.4; Cic., *De Fin.* 1.18, *De Fato* 22, 46, *ND* 1.70; Diog. Oen., fr. 32 Chilton, and many other references listed in Us. 281. For the importance of the swerve in Epicurean psychology see below pp. 92–9.

[2] Lucr., 2.293.

dicularly downwards. Obviously in some sense the rain of atoms is prior to the swerve, but that priority need not be a temporal priority. We shall return to this later. For the time being we can observe that, once the swerve has occurred, the swerving atoms will collide with other atoms and a third type of atomic movement will be set up. The atoms will be jolted from their downward paths by blows from all sides. We should notice that Epicurus rules out another way in which the downfalling atoms could meet. He rejects the idea that the heavier atoms might catch up the lighter. For, he believes, in the void all atoms must travel at the same speed.[1]

We must now consider the third type of force that affects the motion of atoms, the 'blows' (ἀντικοπαί) which arise when the atoms collide, in the first instance because of the swerve. At this stage we should recall that we are still dealing with the the movements of individual 'free' atoms, not of atomic compounds. It should be clear that as a result of the swerve atoms floating in the void may be subject to blows from any direction and their own direction correspondingly varied. Of course, the weight of the atom is still also affecting its motion and will come entirely into its own again if the pressure of blows happens to be relaxed. But in the case of very light atoms the effect of weight will be so far nullified by that of 'blows' that if a light atom is trapped between two heavy ones and they clash together, it can be driven in an 'upward' direction.[2]

Despite all the blows which an atom experiences, however, its speed is not affected. In whatever direction it goes, it will be travelling through void 'as quickly as thought'. Epicurus probably believed that the speed of atoms, even if deflected, is uniform for the same reasons that he believed that in the void the downward speed of two atoms of different weights is the same. It has been argued that he made this assertion because otherwise he could not have replied to Aristotelian criticism of earlier atomists and would have had to abandon his thesis of indivisibility,[3] but we need not assume that he found his

---

[1] Cf. Furley, *Two Studies* 122, note 9.
[2] Simp., *In De Caelo* p. 569, 5 ff. Heiberg.
[3] See above p. 46, n. 6.

solution to this problem difficult to swallow. In the world of atomism there is no reason why 'free' atoms should not move at uniform speeds in the void. What is to stop them?, Epicurus might have said. We can certainly afford to give him the credit of thinking along these lines.

We can now return to a question which we had to defer until we had outlined all the factors which contribute to the infinitely complex movements of Epicurean atoms: weight, the swerve, and the collisions of the atoms with one another. The question is that of the origin of disorderly motion. Was there ever a time when there was no universe? All the atoms were raining downwards because of their weight. No swerve had taken place, and hence no collisions. According to a recent critic, who finds the idea of the logical, rather than the historical priority of the perpendicular fall of the atoms to their swerve attractive, there are no Epicurean texts to guide us on this point. 'We do not know', concludes Merlan, 'whether Epicurus was aware of this problem, nor, if he was, how he solved it.'[1] Earlier, others have been bolder. Both Liepmann[2] and Krokiewicz[3] argued that the priority of the downward fall is only logical, and Krokiewicz went on to draw the proper inference that, if the priority of the downward fall due to weight is only logical, there must always have been a series of worlds in existence. And despite Merlan the position of Liepmann and Krokiewicz is substantially correct. Lucretius provides the evidence. In one passage he tells us that the processes of generation and destruction have existed from infinite time (*ex infinito tempore*);[4] in another we read that the atoms have been driven both by blows and by weight from infinite time, so that every possible combination of atoms has already come into existence.[5] Kleve has added an *a priori* argument which points in the same direction. Since the Epicureans have no doubt that time has no beginning, and since time can only be understood in relation to the existence of physical compounds of atoms, these compounds themselves

[1] Merlan, *Studies* 58.　　　　　[2] Liepmann, *Mechanik*, 47 ff.
[3] Krokiewicz, *Nauka Epikura*; cf. the review by Merlan, *Gnomon* 10 (1934) 607–8.　　　　　[4] Lucr., 2.574.
[5] Lucr., 5.187–91; cf. Kleve, 'Die Urbewegung'.

must always have existed. There seems to be no reason to suppose therefore that the cosmological processes had a beginning in time. There have always been worlds and there always will be. The priority of the downward fall of atoms to the swerve is a logical priority only.[1]

The causes of atomic motion, therefore, are weight, the swerve, and the collisions of atoms. But, as has often been noticed, Epicurus and the Epicureans sometimes talk about chance (τύχη) as a cause, or at least appear to do so. Particularly in the ethical writings we find exhortations to endure the rebuffs of chance and fortune. Sometimes this means little more than that we must be prepared to meet unexpected, though not uncaused events.[2] We may similarly discount such phrases as Lucretius' *fortuna gubernans* in a passage where the poet is hoping that the end of the world will not occur in his own lifetime. *Fortuna* here is a personification of what will happen; the Stoics talked of Fate in similar ways.[3] But in the letter to Menoeceus (133–4) there are more serious problems. Epicurus seems to be saying that the causes of events are either necessity, chance, or human action. We can postpone an enquiry into the origins of human behaviour until we treat Epicurus' psychological theories in more detail;[4] and by 'necessity' Epicurus obviously refers to the observable and definable laws of nature, the *foedera naturai*, as Lucretius calls them. What then does he mean by chance? Two possibilities are immediately ruled out. Chance is not a god, as the general public may believe. Nor is it an unstable cause (ἀβέβαιος αἰτία). It is not clear whose views Epicurus is attacking here. He may have Democritus in mind (rightly or wrongly), or he may be thinking of the 'errant' cause in Plato's *Timaeus*. Unfortunately in the letter to Menoeceus he does not develop his own view of chance in physics. He contents himself with saying that human behaviour does not depend on chance circumstances. It is not a matter of chance whether we behave well or ill. Rather chance may provide us

---

[1] This conclusion would not need argument if we accepted Bailey's treatment of D.L. 10.43 (Herodotus). But his suggested filling of the lacuna, even if true, must be admitted to be question-begging.

[2] *VS* 47 Metrodorus.

[3] Cf. Rist, *Stoic Philosophy* 112–32.   [4] See below pp. 90–9.

with opportunities which we can use as we wish. Since in this
whole section Epicurus is contrasting the effects of 'chance'
both with those of formulable natural laws and with acts which
are 'in our power' entirely, he must be thinking neither of the
effects of the weight of the atoms nor of the swerve in the atoms
of the soul. What he is concerned with is the effect of the swerve
in nature, that is, with those collisions of atoms which are not
to be explained in terms of any mathematical formula or
comprehensible law. There are some atomic movements which
can in no way be forecast. Obviously the *general* behaviour of
complexes of atoms can be forecast, but 'free' atoms are not
susceptible to the necessity which must largely apply to atoms
in groups; and even within a group there is always the limited
possibility of random atomic behaviour. As Plutarch puts it,[1]
'an atom swerves to the very smallest extent in order that the
heavy bodies, living things and chance may come into existence
and that what is in our power may not perish'. This passage is
not isolated, as is sometimes suggested.[2] It fits into Epicurus'
account of the movement of atoms. The swerve is necessitated
by the fact of the existence of worlds, but the swerve must of
necessity be random. There is no reason to distrust Plutarch's
suggestion that Epicurus associated 'chance' with swerves. His
rejection of the 'Democritean' or 'Platonic' notion that chance
is an 'unstable cause' need have nothing to do with this
question. In the letter to Menoeceus Epicurus is at pains to
point out that the existence of chance does not militate against
the achievement of the good life.[3] There is a random element,
an element of chance in nature, and Guyau was probably right
in holding that Epicurus attributed it to the swerve of atoms.[4]

'Parts' of atoms

We have now considered the basic qualities of the Epicurean
atom and the factors which keep it in constant motion at

---

[1] *De Soll. An.* 964c. [2] Bailey, *Greek Atomists* 327. [3] Cf. *BD* 16.
[4] Guyau, *La Morale d'Épicure* 85–91. The details of Guyau's view need not
be accepted, even if his general thesis is largely correct. On chance in
Epicurean physics see now a new Fragment of Diogenes of Oenoanda
(7, col. III, 8–14 and Smith, 'New Fragments', 367–70).

uniform speed. Before considering the void, the other primary constituent of the Epicurean universe, we must return to a question which had to be deferred. By definition the atoms are the basic *physical* constituents of matter. By definition they are physically unsplittable. But although the atom cannot be physically divided, it is 'theoretically' divisible.[1] Modern scholars are gradually coming to a consensus that the atoms of Democritus were theoretically as well as physically *in*divisible,[2] and Furley has argued convincingly that it was because of Aristotle's critique of this position that Epicurus developed the idea that, although the atom is physically indivisible, it can be theoretically divided, though only into minimal parts. It is not even theoretically divisible to infinity.

That Epicurus argued that the atoms are 'theoretically' divisible is borne out both by the letter to Herodotus and by Lucretius.[3] That the atoms should have such 'theoretical' parts must, of course, follow from the fact that they are of different sizes. With his new theory Epicurus can correct an obvious mistake of Democritus, though he does not point the mistake out in any fragment we possess. Some have wished to argue that the number of such parts is infinitely large, that is, that the atom is theoretically divisible to infinity; but that is almost explicitly contradicted by the evidence. Epicurus himself talks about the smallest part in the atom[4] – an odd phrase if the atom is in fact theoretically divisible *ad infinitum* – and he seems to envisage that atoms are built up of such quasi-physical, though not actually separable, parts. Lucretius is even clearer. He argues that the number of shapes of atoms is limited, as we have seen. This is intelligible, he holds, if the minimal parts of the atom are limited in number but not otherwise.[5] If these parts are limited in number, then of, say, four minima only a

---

[1] I adopt the terms 'theoretically divisible', 'theoretically indivisible' from Furley, *Two Studies*. For a more detailed discussion of the whole problem Furley's work is indispensable.

[2] Cf. Mau, *Zum Problem* 24–7; Furley, *op. cit.* 97–101; Guthrie, *Greek Philosophy* 2.503–7.

[3] D.L. 10.56–9 (Herodotus); Lucr., 1.599–634; 746–52; 2.478–99. See Furley, *op. cit.*   [4] D.L. 10.59 (Herodotus).

[5] Emphasized by Furley, *op. cit.* 41–3, against Vlastos, 'Minimal Parts'.

limited number of shapes can be imagined, for the parts must be arranged in such a way that there is no possibility of our forming the concept of a part of a minimal part. But if there were an infinite number of theoretical parts to the atom, then an infinite number of shapes would also occur. And an infinite number of atomic shapes would allow the possibility of infinitely large atoms – which the Epicureans reject. Such then is Epicurus' view of the minimal parts of the atom, formulated in reply to Aristotle's critique of earlier atomism. But it might be suggested that, while Epicurus has faced some of the difficulties which arise for Democritus, his solution is open to the criticism that the same problems will occur all over again. Democritus thinks that the atoms themselves are theoretically indivisible; they are so small that internal distinctions cannot be made. And yet they differ in size. Epicurus recognizes difficulties about theoretically indivisible atoms. He posits minimal parts of the atom. Does the same problem arise? Granted that such minimal parts are the smallest thing conceivable, does it follow that they are the smallest thing that could exist? Now if Epicurus' theory is to avoid a regress, it is clear that the minimal parts must all be of the same size and shape. And it has been pointed out that Lucretius does indeed assume that the shapes of the minimal parts are invariant;[1] his argument would not work if this were not the case. Obviously this is how Epicurus understood minimal parts; he tells us in the letter to Herodotus that the minimal parts provide the standard of measurement of their own lengths for larger and smaller things.[2] Any two smallest conceivable parts must by definition be exactly equal. Lucretius adds further details: of themselves they have no weight and no motion.[3] Clearly this follows from the fact that they are theoretical and not physical minima. So it seems that Epicurus has indeed avoided the problems facing Democritus.

But there is a peculiarity in Epicurus' *argument* for minimal parts which cannot be completely passed over. In the account in the letter to Herodotus Epicurus describes the theoretical

[1] Vlastos, *op. cit.* 147, note 114; cf. 139, note 87.
[2] D.L. 10.59 (Herodotus).   [3] Lucr., 1.632–4.

minima by analogy with the smallest parts of physical objects which we can recognize with the senses.[1] Just as there must be such a minimum sensible part of an object, so there is a theoretically minimal part of an atom. But the analogy is odd. Epicurus thinks that the minimum sensible part of an object, in order to be sensible, must be three-dimensional. Similarly, he seems to argue, since we can think of theoretical minima, they too must exist, also in three dimensions. But he has not shown by this analogy why the atoms themselves should not be theoretical minima. We can thus see why Epicurus needs minimal parts of atoms without being happy about the reasons he offered to explain their existence. If he had stated that, if atoms differ in size, they must have minimal parts, all would be clear. Yet although he does not say it, perhaps we can suppose that he assumed it.

Secondary qualities

We have now listed all the qualities and described all the possible motions of an Epicurean atom. But, it may be objected, physical objects which we experience in the world have a wider variety of differences than those of shape, size and weight. But, for Epicurus, as for his atomist predecessors, all other qualities of physical objects – let us call them secondary qualities – depend on the size, shape, weight, position and arrangement of the atoms of which they are composed.[2] These secondary qualities are subject to change; that is because the arrangement of the atoms is subject to variation – the atoms are of course always in motion – and because the number of atoms forming a particular physical object is itself constantly changing. It is right to emphasize that one of the 'secondary qualities' of which the atoms are devoid is that of sensation.[3] Lucretius makes a point of saying that this is due to particular movements of various combinations of atoms and is not a permanent function of any single atom.[4]

1 D.L. 10.59 (Herodotus).
2 Cf. D.L. 10.54-5 (Herodotus); Lucr., 2.730-864.
3 Bailey, *Greek Atomists* 292; cf. below pp. 80-8.
4 Lucr., 2.865-990.

Void

We have now completed our account of the atom and must look at the other basic 'existent' in the Epicurean world. This is called 'the void' (τὸ κενόν) or 'space' (χώρα),[1] and, if we believe the doxographers, 'place' (τόπος). As we have already observed, Epicurus has no hesitation in saying that this void exists. Earlier atomists had run into logical puzzles by calling the void non-being (οὐκ ὄν or μὴ ὄν),[2] thus bringing down on themselves the wrath of Aristotle, who remarks in the *Physics* that some people gave in to the Eleatic arguments and said that non-being (τὸ μὴ ὄν) exists.[3] To escape this objection, which he would have regarded as merely semantic, Epicurus avoids the term 'non-being' and speaks of void as though it were a substance. But it is a substance of a very peculiar kind; its differentiating mark is that it cannot be recognized by the senses, for it is an 'untouchable substance' (ἀναφὴς οὐσία).

There is a slight difficulty associated with Epicurus' terminology about the void, as has often been observed. The terms 'void' and 'space' suggest that Epicurus is talking about the empty spaces between atoms and groups of atoms. The term 'place' might suggest that he is concerned with the area occupied by such atoms or groups of atoms; this somewhat looser term is partly explained by a passage from the letter to Pythocles, where we read that worlds may be found in a place with a lot of void in it (ἐν πολυκένῳ τόπῳ) but not in 'pure void' (εἰλικρινεῖ καὶ κενῷ).[4] Here the word 'place' seems to have a wider meaning than 'void'. Some 'places' contain atoms and others void! But a 'place' can only be defined in relation to atoms or groups of atoms; it is, as Simplicius tells us, the distance between the limits of the enclosing object.[5]

---

[1] D.L. 10.39–40 (Herodotus). Bailey follows Usener's probably false supplement τόπος at D.L. 10.39. It is not justified by Lucr., 1.420, where the reading is *inane* (= κενόν) or necessarily even by Plutarch, *Adv. Col.* 1112E (τόπος), for Plutarch's quotation is not from the letter to Herodotus.

[2] See especially Bailey, *Greek Atomists* 118–19.

[3] The atomists are certainly among those attacked by Aristotle in *Phys.* 187a. There may be other victims as well.

[4] D.L. 10.89 (Pythocles).

[5] Simp., *In Phys.* p. 571, 22 ff. (= part of Us. 273).

The point seems to be that all void is potentially place and all place is potentially void. If this were not so, then motion, as we have seen, would be impossible. This might seem to be reading Aristotelianism into Epicurus, but that is not the case. 'Potentially' must be used solely with reference to time. At any indivisible moment of time the universe consists of atoms or groups of atoms arranged in a particular way, and a large number of empty spaces between them. These empty spaces are what Epicurus calls 'the void'. We notice that, when talking about physical objects, Epicurus will speak of the 'intervals' (διαστήματα) or spaces between the atoms which compose them. At any other indivisible point of time, of course, the atoms will be arranged differently. They will have moved into different places. The places of some atoms will be what was previously empty space. However at the second point of time we should observe that the universe will still formally consist of the atoms and empty space or void. Thus any part of the whole universe is potentially void at any time. And there is a further point to be noticed. According to Simplicius some of the atomists held that the void exceeds bodies in infinity (ἀπειρία);[1] yet it is not clear how far Epicurus, even if he held this view, would have understood its implications. Perhaps he would have understood 'infinite' as 'boundless'. At least his argument in the letter to Herodotus points in that direction: neither atoms nor void can be the limit, for if they were they would have to be limited by something else.[2] If you stand at the edge of the universe and throw your spear, says Lucretius, it will either be stopped by something else or it will go on farther. Either way you cannot be at the edge after all.[3]

The difficulty of Simplicius' remark about the void exceeding atoms in 'infinity' is more obvious when we recall that Epicurus distinguished different senses of 'infinity' or 'boundlessness' for atoms and the void. Atoms are 'infinite' in number, the void in extent. But it is hard to see how these can be compared

---

[1] Simp., *In Phys.* p. 618, 16–18 Diels (= part of Us. 273). Simplicius speaks of οἱ περὶ Δημόκριτον ἀρχαῖοι φυσιολόγοι as holding this view, but he does not say that they were the only ones to hold it.

[2] D.L. 10.41 (Herodotus).   [3] Lucr., 1.960–7.

for 'degrees of boundlessness' or 'degrees of infinity'. Presumably if Simplicius' account is to be trusted, Epicurus held that more of the universe is void than is occupied by atoms, but if the number of atoms is infinite, this still seems difficult.

Compounds

Let us now consider the formation of physical objects, the furniture of the world revealed to us by the senses, from their component parts, the atoms. The general outlines of Epicurus' position are clear. As a result of the constant collisions of the atoms, all of which are moving constantly at a uniform speed, groups of atoms are constantly being flung together. Some of these atoms become interlocked – the Epicurean term is περιπλοκή.[1] Thus a kind of cover (τὸ στεγάζον) begins to be formed.[2] Other 'free' atoms may find themselves shut in by the atomic shell forming around them. It should be remembered, however, that both the enclosed atoms and those forming the shell are still all moving in an infinitely complicated series of individual directions at the same 'atomic' and inconceivable speed. Obviously among these compounds (συστάσεις, συστήματα, concilia) some will be more and others less close-packed. The most compact will form the hardest, most solid kinds of substance.[3] None, however, will be so closely packed that each of its component atoms cannot move constantly in the intervals (διαστήματα) of the compound itself.

Naturally compounds of atoms are of different sizes, and many of the smaller ones are not recognizable by sense-perception. Nevertheless it is from groups of such smaller compounds that the larger compounds, the visible physical objects, are formed. Some small compounds are particularly suited (though not for any teleological reason) to join with others to make particular physical objects. Thus compound A is suitable, if joined with compounds B and C, to form a drop of water. Epicurus seems to have referred to such basic compounds as the 'seeds' of the substances which they may later

[1] D.L. 10.43 (Herodotus).   [2] D.L. 10.65 (Herodotus).
[3] Lucr., 2.98–108.

form. Everything cannot be created out of everything, Epicurus argues; if that were so, there would be no need of seeds.[1] The notion of a seed is not very prominent in Epicurus' own writings and the picture has been obscured by Lucretius, who, while frequently using the word *semina* (seeds), allows it to have two meanings. For Lucretius a seed is either an individual atom or a small group of atoms suitable for the production of a visible and therefore more complicated compound.[2] But for all that there is no doubt that the doctrine is genuinely Epicurean. We proceed at random from individual atoms to seeds and from seeds to physical objects. These physical objects are not new substances formed by processes analogous to those of chemical change, as has sometimes been argued; they are combinations of seeds. Nor on the other hand are they mere collections of seeds or collections of atoms. Thus when soul atoms and body atoms are combined in such a way as to produce a living being, that living being is a new object which exists in the strict sense of the word. While it lasts, the compound is as real as the atoms of which it is composed. We shall consider this departure from Democritean atomism in more detail when we investigate Epicurus' theory of properties or qualities, but the reason why Epicurus took up the new position is clear. Physical objects exist, are real, because our senses tell us that they exist. And our senses not only tell us that they exist; they tell us they are not atoms or seeds, but men, plants, trees, rocks and stars.

At this point we must consider a further difficulty. We have already observed that in every compound, in every visible substance however hard, the atoms are in constant movement in every conceivable direction at uniform speed. This produces an internal vibration which Epicurus, in good atomist tradition, calls a παλμός.[3] But if this vibration is constant, we may wonder how it affects the movements, and even perhaps the continued existence, of the compounds themselves. To understand this we shall have to consider the account of the movement of com-

---

[1] D.L. 10.38 (Herodotus), cf. 74 (Herodotus) and 89 (Pythocles).
[2] For *semina* as atoms see Lucr., 2.755, 773, 988 etc. For *semina* as simple compounds see 6.160, 200 etc. In certain passages where the word occurs (e.g. 4.1036ff.) it is very hard to be sure which sense is intended.
[3] D.L. 10.43 (Herodotus).

59

pounds in more detail. We begin with the collection of atoms all moving at the same speed in a confined space. For atoms to fit together at all, we read, it is necessary that their movements have some kind of similarity. Lucretius speaks of an atom joining its movement to that of a compound.[1] To some extent this must be a 'harmonizing' of its movement, at least if the compound is in motion, for as Furley neatly puts it, 'a compound will move, if all its component atoms move in the same direction *over a period of time*'.[2] Obviously all the atoms will not move in the same direction in one of the indivisible minima of time; if they did, the compound would be travelling at inconceivable (i.e. atomic) speed. As it is, the actual speed of an object depends on the length of time required for all the atoms in the compound to be moved in the same direction. This means that at any particular continuous period of time some atoms are trying to move in one way, some in another. If a majority are pushing in one direction – and except in the case of downward movement this must involve overcoming the downward pull caused by weight – they will pressure the others and the whole object into doing the same thing. Obviously if contrary pressures external to the compound are brought to bear, the object will slow down, but if we leave such pressures aside, the speed will depend on the degree of resistance of the minority of atoms to those moving in the dominant direction. And since the atoms are travelling at the same speed, this would seem to mean that, if the number of atoms trying to move at a particular time in a different direction from that of the compound itself is large, then the speed will be slow. As Bailey puts it, 'anticope' (the check on the direction of the object due to collision) is the inverse determinant of speed.[3] In Epicurus' words, 'check and absence of check take on the appearance of slowness and speed'.[4] It seems that Epicurus thought that the words 'fast' and 'slow' indicate greater or lesser approximations by compounds to the unattainable speed of the atoms themselves.

[1] Lucr., 2.111.
[2] Furley, *Two Studies* 123; cf. D.L. 10.62 (Herodotus).
[3] Bailey, *Greek Atomists* 335.   [4] D.L. 10.46 (Herodotus).

What then are we to say about compounds which are at rest?[1] The internal vibration of the compound, due to the incessant motions of the constituent atoms, continues. Presumably in such cases the atoms never all move in the same direction; there are equal and opposite pressures, and therefore equal and opposite atomic movements which thus keep the compound at rest. Finally we should consider what happens when objects increase in speed. When talking about the speed of a thunderbolt Lucretius offers a variety of explanations of the fact that the speed increases. But one in particular is relevant to our general discussion. The thunderbolt is travelling at less than atomic speed. Therefore 'free' atoms which are travelling at atomic speed in the same direction as the bolt will catch up with it; they will hook on to it and drive it along faster.

We have now considered the formation of compounds and their movements. Of the destruction of these compounds little need be said. All the time they are being subjected to blows both from the free atoms and from other compounds. Eventually they will succumb. The atoms within the compound itself are under constant pressure and after the initial period of growth the compound will gradually go into decline. The *coup de grâce*, however, will normally be delivered from outside. Lucretius discusses the process in detail in the second book of his poem; he draws a picture of the rise and fall of substances both at the level of individual physical objects and of the individual worlds themselves.

Qualities of physical objects

When we look at a compound, we do not see atoms and the void. We see shape, size, colour. When we test its other qualities, we may find that it smells and has a recognizable taste; it may be hot or cold. We must now consider the Epicurean account of these 'qualities', some of which are possessed by the atoms as well as by the compounds, others by the compounds alone. The atoms, as we have observed, are distinguishable by their size, shape and weight, as well as by their arrangements and by their differences of motion. These basic qualities of the atom are

[1] Lucr., 6.335–9.

permanent features of it. Here we immediately notice a difference between the atom and the compounds. The atom is permanent, hence its qualities are permanent. Compounds are subject to decay and all, except the gods, will in fact decay sooner or later. Hence their qualities, even the basic ones which they share with the atoms themselves, their size, shape and weight, are subject to change. Thus we cannot say that a compound is possessed of weight, for example, in the same way as an atom is possessed of weight. Epicurus seems to distinguish in this matter by using the very general word 'quality' (ποιότης) for the characteristics of an atom,[1] but adapting a more technical term for analogous 'qualities' of the compound. When size and shape are predicated of a compound, he uses the word 'characteristics' (συμβεβηκότα, coniuncta).[2] It will perhaps be convenient here to refer to these characteristics as the primary qualities of physical objects.

Epicurus is much exercised to dispel false theories of what these primary qualities are – and among primary qualities in addition to size, shape and weight he mentions colour. They are not independent realities; this is presumably a dismissal of Platonic forms. Neither are they immaterial existents accompanying bodies; this seems to be a reference to Aristotle's account of the relation between quality and substance. Nor are they material parts of bodies; this is perhaps a dismissal of the tendency apparent in many of the pre-Socratics to think of qualities such as 'the hot' (τὸ θερμόν) as substances.[3] Rather they are, as Lucretius puts it, things which cannot be separate from the substance without the substance being destroyed. Perhaps this is not quite clear. Many objects may to some extent change their shape or size without being destroyed. What Lucretius means is that all objects must have a shape and size, not that they must have a particular shape and size. The ranges of shapes and sizes will obviously vary from object to object and from time to time. Lucretius gives further examples of primary

[1] D.L. 10.54 (Herodotus).
[2] D.L. 10.68–73 (Herodotus); Lucr., 1.449–82.
[3] It has often been suggested that Epicurus' opponents here are Stoics. This is possible, since we do not know the date of the letter to Herodotus, but Epicurus seems to be alluding to rather more long-standing positions.

qualities: stones have weight, fire has heat, water is wet, all bodies can be touched, void cannot be touched. Epicurus adds a further point of importance which at first sight looks obvious. It is not true, he holds, to say that in an absolute sense (ὅλως) these qualities do not exist. This curious comment is a rebuttal of Democritus, who took the view that qualities such as colour, sweetness, bitterness, heat and cold are objects of belief only. In reality there are only atoms and the void.[1]

This position would be anathema to Epicurus because it is contradicted by the evidence of the senses. We taste what is sweet; we feel cold. Therefore sweetness and cold are just as real as atoms. Epicurus' departure from the Democritean position must be given great emphasis; it means that the changing substances of the physical world are during their period of existence as real as the basic elements, the atoms, of which they are composed. This is Epicurus' attempt to dispose both of the scepticism of Democritus, which he may have thought must logically lead to the end of all knowledge, and of the hesitancy of the Platonists to admit that changing realities really exist. Epicurus' position was easy to misunderstand. He apparently argued against Theophrastus that colours are not intrinsically present in bodies but depend on particular arrangements and positions of the object relative to the eye. Plutarch interprets this as a sceptical position. According to him it means that the particular body is no more coloured than uncoloured.[2] Yet that is not Epicurus' position. The body looks coloured when viewed from a particular place. That means it *is* coloured. If it were not coloured when looked at from that place it would not be the same body.[3] It looks coloured because the shape and arrangement of its atoms make it look that way. And as for colour, so fairly similarly for taste, sound and smell.[4] Tastes, sounds and

---

[1] Democritus, *ap.* Sext. Emp., *Hyp. Pyr.* 1.213–14; *Adv. Math.* 7.135–6; cf. Diog. Oen., fr. 6, col. 2 Chilton; D.L. 9.72, 106; Plut., *Adv. Col.* 1108F–1111D; Guthrie, *Greek Philosophy* 2.440.

[2] Plut., *Adv. Col.* 1110C.

[3] Lucretius points out that if the light is different the colour will also be different. Light provides blows on the object, which naturally affect the movement of its atoms (2.799–809).

[4] Cf. Lucr., 2.381–477.

smells are due to the different shapes of the atoms which form the particular compounds. Sweet tastes come from smooth atoms. Naturally this theory was bitterly attacked in antiquity. How can a compound be hot, asks Plutarch, if its constituents are not?[1] But Plutarch misreads the Epicurean position.[2] According to Plutarch Epicurus' first principles are atoms and the void, but in epistemological matters Epicurus relies in the first instance on the evidence of the senses. It is the senses which tell us that objects are hot or cold. Temperatures are given. It is the existence of the atoms which has to be worked out. And the balance of evidence is, the Epicureans think, overwhelmingly in their favour.

In addition to the primary qualities there are also secondary qualities, called συμπτώματα (*eventa*) by Epicurus. They are, as Lucretius describes them, qualities which may come and go without affecting the nature (*natura*) of the object. Lucretius lists as secondary qualities slavery, poverty, wealth, freedom, war, concord. Presumably what he means is that these are secondary qualities of a subject if they exist in a subject from which they may be removed without the subject's necessarily being destroyed. 'May be', however, is important. It appears that Epicurus is prepared to say that in fact some secondary qualities are always present to the things they qualify. Thus 'action' and 'suffering', according to Epicurus, are secondary qualities of the soul.[3] This means that, although all souls 'act' and 'suffer', action and suffering are not *physical* qualities of the soul without which it would not be a soul.

The ontological status of the secondary qualities, however, is rather peculiar. Naturally enough Epicurus dismisses the notion that they might be *per se* entities in a quasi-Platonic sense. Nor are they 'among the things unseen' or possessed of some incorporeal reality. They have of themselves no position (τάγμα) in nature; that is, apparently, their position depends on other things which do not depend on them. But they are nevertheless real and have the peculiar characteristics (ἰδιότης) which sense-perception can recognize. To speak of a secondary quality,

[1] Plut., *Adv. Col.* 1111D.   [2] Cf. Bailey, *Greek Atomists* 356–7.
[3] D.L. 10.67 (Herodotus).

therefore, must be merely to describe certain inessential features
of a subject. One is describing reality because the senses
recognize the secondary qualities, but the reality is that of the
object, not of the quality itself.

The doctrine of primary and secondary qualities has been
slightly obscured in Bailey's account.[1] According to Bailey
critics of Epicurus have not realized that Epicurus would not
have said of any quality 'this is always an accompaniment'
(primary quality) or 'this is always an accident' (secondary
quality). The same quality might according to Bailey be a
primary quality of one thing, a secondary quality of another.
But this is misleading if primary qualities are such that their
disappearance would physically change the object they qualify.
Thus weight will *always* be a primary quality of its subject.
Bailey claims that slavery (a secondary quality according to
Lucretius) is a secondary quality in relation to Epictetus but a
primary quality 'in relation to "a slave"'. But this is to misinterpret the whole Epicurean idea. Strictly speaking 'a slave'
has no qualities. It is a mere word. What is real are atoms, the
void and compounds. Thus Epictetus is real. And if he is a slave,
slavery is one of his secondary qualities. This is the only sense
in which Epicurus and Lucretius talk of qualities at all. They
are qualities of specific physical objects.

Bailey's mistake arose out of an attempt to defend Epicurus
from the complaints of Brieger and of other early critics.
According to these critics Epicurus is inconsistent in that he calls
colour an accompaniment (primary quality), although it is not
always a primary quality of bodies. As Bailey points out, colour
is only an accompaniment of visible physical objects, not even
of those 'same' physical objects in the dark. But when we say
that an object is coloured, we mean that it is such that we can
see it as coloured in the light. To point out that if we look at it
in the dark, the colours have disappeared, is unhelpful. We
should only have to worry about whether colour was a primary
quality if, when we put the object back in the light, it still
appeared uncoloured.

Before we conclude this discussion, we must consider briefly

---

[1] Bailey, *Greek Atomists* 308–9.

a single special case – that of time. This is, as we have seen, to be viewed as a series of indivisible minima, but it is also a special kind of secondary quality. It is a secondary quality of secondary qualities.[1] Events in time are, as we might expect, secondary qualities of the people and places with which they are concerned. We envisage these secondary qualities as themselves occurring in a certain context. This context is what we know as time. Obviously it does not exist apart from events, and for the Epicureans events are the actions, not the nature, of those who participate in them. As Epicurus puts it, we know by inductive reasoning that time is connected with particular days and nights, feelings, movements and states of rest.[2]

Such then are the basic elements of Epicurus' physical theory. It remains to see how they are applied to cosmology and to the question of the development of man.

[1] D.L. 10.72–3 (Herodotus); Lucr., 1.459–82. For the Platonic–Aristotelian background see Barigazzi, 'Il concetto del tempo'.
[2] See p. 35, n. 2 for ἐπιλογισμός.

4

MAN AND THE COSMOS

In the previous chapter we examined the basic principles of the universe and the nature of its physical constituents. We shall now look at two further features of Epicurus' physical theory: his account of the world in which we live – and in particular its growth and decline – and the development of human institutions in it.

As we have observed, the universe as a whole is boundless. It has no limits either of time or space. Within this universe there is our own world, which came into existence at a particular time in the past and has a lengthy, though still limited, life expectancy in front of it. Like all other worlds our world (κόσμος) is a 'circumscribed portion of sky'[1] which contains the stars, the earth and all the other phenomena of the heavens. These larger atomic compounds are enclosed, as we would expect from our discussion in the previous chapter, by interlocking atoms. If they were not, the smaller atomic compounds which form parts of the world would separate from one another and the world would disintegrate into the infinite void. The number of such worlds is infinite; some of them are like and some unlike our own. That the number of shapes of worlds is infinite seems unlikely, though perhaps Epicurus did not make up his mind on this question. In the letter to Pythocles it is suggested that all shapes are possible;[2] a scholion to the letter to Herodotus gives the opposite opinion:[3] the number of shapes is limited. Perhaps the latter view is more likely to have been the normal opinion of Epicurus himself.[4] We know that the number of shapes of atoms is limited, whereas the total number of atoms is not. Parallel argumentation would suggest that, although the total

[1] Bailey's translation of the phrase in D.L. 10.88 (Pythocles).
[2] D.L. 10.88 (Pythocles).
[3] Schol. to D.L. 10.74 (Herodotus).
[4] If the letter to Pythocles is not from Epicurus' own hand, the problem of squaring it with the scholion disappears. It is certainly possible, however, that Epicurus' position was not fixed.

number of worlds is unlimited, the number of shapes which worlds may take has a term. But certainty is unattainable.

Worlds can be created both in predominantly empty space (ἐν πολυκένῳ τόπῳ) between existing worlds,[1] and in gaps, if they are large enough, within an existing world-system. This marks a denial of the position of Leucippus – whom Epicurus alludes to but does not name – that a world comes into existence in totally empty space. Democritus apparently also disagreed with Leucippus on the question of void, but his own views are equally unsatisfactory to Epicurus. The idea of Democritus that atoms collect together and form a vortex by necessity (ἀνάγκη) is ridiculed.[2] Epicurus would urge that for the formation of a world the right shapes of atoms and the right positions of atoms are required, and that the notion of a vortex is unnecessary. If a sufficiently large number of atoms of the appropriate sizes and shapes fit together, a world would be formed. In a sense a world is nothing more than an enormous atomic compound. No special procedures or laws are required to explain its coming into existence other than those which will explain the existence of any other compound. Yet there is a slight caveat to be added. Epicurus talks about the 'foundations' of the world being susceptible of increase and of the world's being susceptible of growth within fixed limits. He speaks of the 'watering' (ἐπάρδευσις) of the compounds, as though he were speaking of some kind of plant or primitive living thing. He seems to have the idea that the world can 'grow' up to a fixed term and then, being unable to receive material to make up for the losses which it constantly experiences, begin to decline. This declining appears to be analogous to the decline of living things after they have passed their acme.[3] Democritus' idea that growth can continue indefinitely unless one world collides with another is rejected. The principles of canonic are involved here. Such unlimited growth is in contradiction with what the senses observe. Yet the process of growth, attainment of maximum development and decline, is, we must always remember, a random product of the chance meetings of atoms. All teleological concepts must be excluded.

[1] D.L. 10.89 (Pythocles). [2] D.L. 10.90 (Pythocles). [3] See further Appendix C.

68

We have noticed the concept of the 'watering' (ἐπάρδευσις) of compounds. We must now look at three other terms used in the account of the formation of the world in the letter to Pythocles. As has always been recognized, the obscurity of the letter can be illumined by reference to Lucretius' poem.[1] The relevant words are 'additions' (προσθέσεις), 'articulations' (διαρθρώσεις) and 'changes of place' (μεταστάσεις ἐπ᾽ ἄλλον τόπον). As Lucretius explains, when a group of atoms which will form a world are first hooked together, they rush about in all directions in complete chaos. Eventually they begin to function together (προσθέσεις). Then sets of atoms separate from one another, thus starting to form the individual 'members' of the world (διαρθρώσεις). Finally the new compounds begin to react on one another, light compounds being forced upwards, heavier compounds downwards (μεταστάσεις). Eventually the finished 'product' appears. We should recall at this point that the rule of heavy compounds sinking does not always apply. Presumably some are simply piled on others. At any rate the underside of the earth is not all composed of heavy material. Rather the earth gradually thins out and gradually merges with the air around.[2] Presumably this is dictated by the principles of canonic. If it were not so, the earth would be constantly sinking, and there is no reason to believe that that is the case. Rather it is at the centre of the world.[3]

In many Epicurean sources, particularly the letter to Pythocles and the poem of Lucretius, we can find details of Epicurus' descriptions of physical phenomena: thunder, lightning, rain, clouds. We shall not discuss this material here since our primary concern is with Epicurean philosophy. We shall only observe that rather than using the evidence of physical phenomena to aid his philosophical enquiries, Epicurus employed the principles of canonic as a key to specific problems in the area of the natural sciences. A notorious example of this is his assertion that 'in itself' the sun is not much larger than it looks. The 'reason' is that as on earth we notice that fires feel less hot (and look less bright) before they seem smaller, therefore since

[1] D.L. 10.89 (Pythocles); cf. Lucr., 5.432–48.
[2] Lucr., 5.534–9.
[3] See above p. 47.

69

nothing could be hotter than the sun, it cannot be much larger than it looks.[1] Similar arguments about brightness are applied to the moon and the stars. Their principal effect is to highlight the weakness of Epicurean arguments from analogy.

Of more relevance to our present enquiries is the Epicurean account of the later stages of the development of our earth and the development of civilization upon it. For this our chief source is the fifth book of Lucretius, but there is no reason to doubt that, in general, apart from the question of the old age of the present world, the poet is recording genuinely Epicurean teachings.[2] After the world had become a recognizable entity, we read, the physical features of the earth began to take shape. And after the rocks and hills and seas there appeared trees and plants. Next came the animals (*mortalia saecla*), primitive forms of which grew out of the earth by spontaneous generation; and later human beings appeared by a somewhat similar process. Lucretius talks of wombs in the earth from which men were born. All this is in line with certain pre-Socratic tenets and little argument for it is offered by Lucretius. In detail it has the interest of a fairy-tale, but there is an important general principle involved in the psychological domain. We shall touch upon the question of the nature of the life of living organisms in a later chapter, but we may notice in Lucretius' account here that no new 'vital' factor is added to the ingredients of a living compound to distinguish them from those of an inanimate one. It is, as we shall see, a matter only of the arrangement, shape and size of the atoms of which the compound is made up.

All kinds of creatures appeared before the coming of man, and their appearances were at random. There is no goal towards which living creatures are striving; survival is incidental to the chance possession of the means of survival. Yet at the same time Lucretius denies that such creatures as are told of in legends, Chimaeras, Scyllas and the rest, ever existed. Such creatures,

---

[1] Cf. D.L. 10.91 (Pythocles); Lucr., 5.564–91.

[2] Much of this material may go behind Epicurus to Democritus. For a strong restatement of Democritus' role in the development of anthropology, see Cole, *Democritus*. Cole rightly emphasizes Epicurus' selective attitude to his sources, 170–3.

he maintains, have 'discordant members'. Their constituent
parts could not co-exist.

It is not clear at what stage human beings appeared.
Certainly after the plants and birds, but whether we are contemporaries of the animals that walk the earth is not made
explicit. The first men appeared from the earth in the same
spontaneous fashion as the animals. It is a mark of the old age
of the earth, Lucretius tells us, that the process of spontaneous
generation, once frequent, is now beyond its power. At any rate
men appeared, and they were much stronger than those of
Lucretius' own time. Originally they depended for their food
on what they could collect. They lived in caves in the woods
and knew nothing of fire or clothing. They had no notion of
justice or of any social laws. It has been much disputed whether
Lucretius regards their life as that of a Golden Age, whether he
is a primitivist or a partisan of human progress, but to see his
account in these terms is misleading.[1] Lucretius is not interested
in the question of whether the human race progresses or retro-
gresses in any theoretical or ideological sense. He is trying to
describe in what ways early men were similar and in what ways
they were dissimilar to the men of his own day. Hence he is able
to say that while in the past men feared the attacks of wild
animals, they were luckier than his contemporaries in other
ways: they had nothing to fear from pitched battles or ship-
wrecks. They might die of starvation, but had no need to worry
about death from overeating or poison. Above all they had no
fears springing from the dogmas of religion. Primitive men
made covenants among themselves in order to protect themselves, but although these covenants, and in general the growth
of 'civilized' behaviour, alleviated the human lot in face of the
dangers of life 'in the raw', they also gave more scope to greed
and folly, thus ushering in catastrophes on a larger scale. Yet
we should always remember that the evil effects of such apparent
catastrophes can be readily overcome. Happiness, thanks to the
teachings of Epicurus himself, is within our grasp.

[1] See Merlan, 'Lucretius – Primitivist or Progressist?'. Though we agree
with Merlan's attitude to Lucretius' thought, there is no need to accept
his views on the text of the poem.

One aspect of the development of civilization is worth special attention. In the letter to Herodotus, Epicurus suggests that originally men were only capable of reacting to events.[1] Only later did they begin to reason in advance in order to anticipate the impact of nature. A particular area where this process can be seen is the development of language. Names for particular objects arose at random in different communities of men. Hence in its origins language had nothing to do with convention. But as time passed, covenants began to be made in the area of language also, and when the question of naming a new object came up, reasoned decisions were taken so that the new name should fit into the previous patterns of naming. Hence for Epicurus language is produced by a combination of natural and artificial factors. Human reason takes a hand in processes which began spontaneously and, it should be noticed, in a certain sense its procedures are random. Sometimes, to avoid ambiguity, a special name may be given by agreement, as it were, between the parties. Such names, although coming into existence because of a need to clarify a given situation, represent more or less arbitrary acts of the reason. Thus they are both natural, in that they answer a natural need, and conventional, in that they arise by a determination of the human mind.

The Epicureans seem to have been in some doubt as to how far they could call this whole process 'natural'. Lucretius seems to contrast the sounds that are produced by nature (*natura*) with the names that are the product of need (*utilitas*).[2] Diogenes of Oenoanda appears to take a slightly different view when he denies that names are attributed to their objects by allocation and teaching (κατὰ θέσιν καὶ διδαχήν).[3] But Diogenes' view may not differ very much from that of Epicurus and Lucretius. All wish to emphasize that the *origin* of language is to be sought in the random use of sound by human beings: in other words that originally names are a natural growth. Thus Epicurus would agree with Diogenes that originally naming was not a matter of decision and teaching. There never was a 'name-maker' in the

---

[1] D.L. 10.75 (Herodotus).   [2] Lucr. 5.1028–9.
[3] Diog. Oen., fr. 10, col. 3, 10 ff. Chilton. Diogenes is quoting Epicurus (D.L. 10.75 (Herodotus)) in his use of θέσις.

sense suggested by Plato's *Cratylus*. And Diogenes does not necessarily deny Epicurus' later assertion, namely that after words had thus appeared naturally, human beings 'naturally' began to exercise their reason in accepting some sounds and discarding others. Diogenes' purpose is probably polemical. He is so concerned to emphasize that language did not *begin* either historically or logically by convention that he passes over the use of convention at a later stage of linguistic development. The correct interpretation of the position of Epicurus seems to be that he rejected the traditional antithesis of nature and convention. Convention in naming, as in the formation of concepts like justice, is itself a natural process which arises at a certain stage in the development of the human race. In other words for human beings the formation of conventions is an advanced stage of 'natural' development. And there is thus little need to talk of the master (Epicurus) outstripping the pupils in his theory of language.[1] As in other areas, the pupils diverged from the master more in presentation than in doctrine.

---

[1] As does Bailey, *Greek Atomists* 382.

5

SOUL, MIND AND BODY

The atomic composition of the soul

The first principle of Epicurus' theory of the soul is that it is a material substance. As we have seen, for the Epicureans the whole cosmos consists of atoms, the void and the compounds of atoms. The soul is a compound of atoms. In the fragments of Epicurus himself no reasons are given for the assertion that soul is a body (σῶμα),[1] that is, a substance, but Lucretius supplies us with two:[2] the soul, he argues, has the power to move the body. Since the body is material, it must be moved by a material object. Therefore the soul is material. Similarly when the body suffers, the soul suffers also. Pain can only be transferred from body to body; therefore the soul must be material. Modern materialists have sometimes proposed variants of a view current in the ancient world also, and attacked both by Plato in the *Phaedo* and Aristotle in the *De Anima*, that the soul is not itself material but an epiphenomenon of the material constituents of the body. Lucretius, believing that the soul is a substance, has to reject this position,[3] and he probably used the same arguments as Epicurus himself. Speaking of the two 'parts' of the soul, which he calls *anima* and *animus*,[4] Lucretius rejects for each of them in turn the theory that they might be 'harmonies' (epiphenomena) of bodies. The word 'harmony', he concludes, is a musical term; those who apply it outside the field of music can only be confused. It is often said that Lucretius is aiming at Aristoxenus and perhaps Dicaearchus, but the theory is older than these pupils of Aristotle.[5] Perhaps Epicurus attacked Aristoxenus specifically, but in rejecting his position he is rejecting a traditional version of the materialist theory of the soul.

[1] D.L. 10.63 (Herodotus).   [2] Lucr., 3.161–76.
[3] Lucr., 3.94–135.   [4] For these terms see below.
[5] For Aristoxenus and Dicaearchus see Sext. Emp., *Adv. Math.* 7.349 and Cic., *Tusc. Disp.* 1.19.

All souls, then, those of gods as well as those of men, are composed of atoms. According to the letter to Herodotus the soul is a body which can best be compared with breath (πνεῦμα) blended with heat.[1] One of its parts, Epicurus continues, is composed of exceptionally smooth and fine particles, though all the soul atoms are comparatively smooth and fine. It has usually been supposed that Epicurus is saying that souls consist of three kinds of atoms: those resembling breath, those resembling heat and the third, exceptionally fine, variety to which he gives no name. This interpretation becomes easier if we read the word 'third' (τρίτον) in the text and make Epicurus speak of the unnamed atoms as comprising a *third* part of the soul. But 'third' (τρίτον) is an unwarranted and question-begging emendation of Diels. All that the letter to Herodotus tells us about the composition of souls is that, as well as being something like breath and heat, they include atoms of an unnamed type.

This brings us to the question of the number of types of soul atoms. It is often said that Epicurus himself only mentions three in the letter, though he may have mentioned more elsewhere, but it now appears that the letter only mentions one – the type of atoms which have no name. He does not tell us directly how many varieties are required to produce a soul or, and this is most important, whether souls have further physical characteristics which he has not mentioned. We may perhaps suppose from the account in the letter that in addition to 'unnamed' atoms, atoms like those of breath and of heat are needed to complete the soul's nature, but we do not know whether these three types comprise the sum total of its components. According to Lucretius, whose account is in this respect identical with those of Plutarch[2] and Aëtius,[3] they do not. Disregarding the minor detail that Lucretius forgets to say that some soul atoms are *like* the atoms of heat, some *like* the atoms of breath, we notice that he offers us not three but four varieties of atom. In addition to atoms of heat (*vapor*, *calor*) and of breath (*ventus*, *aura*) he mentions air (*aer*) as well as the ultra-fine

[1] D.L. 10.63 (Herodotus).   [2] Plut., *Adv. Col.* 1118.
[3] Aët., 4.3.11 (Us. 315).

unnamed element.[1] Most commentators have recognized that
in one respect this is unimportant. Lucretius could not have
diverged from Epicurus on so fundamental a matter. Either a
reference to air has dropped out of our texts of the letter to
Herodotus, or, more probably, Epicurus did not think it
necessary to mention it in a preliminary treatise; for similar
reasons he fails to mention the division of the soul into the
anima and the *animus*. But perhaps the cases are different. It is
understandable that Epicurus might decide against discussing
the subdivisions of the soul, but it would at the least be curious
if, when he had intended to catalogue the kinds of atoms in the
soul, he should have left us with the erroneous impression that
there are only three. But we are now in a position to see that
he does not attempt such a catalogue in the letter to Herodotus.

Before leaving the question of the number of elements of the
soul we should pay closer attention to the evidence of Aëtius.[2]
According to Aëtius, Epicurus thought that there are four
varieties of soul atoms. The nameless element is particularly
concerned with sensation (αἴσθησις), air contributes quiet,
heat the apparent heat of the body, and breath (πνεῦμα) motion.
We can now see that a theory of four types of soul atoms is not
inconsistent with Epicurus' words in the letter to Herodotus,
despite the fact that in the letter air is not mentioned. However
we should notice that Aëtius associates breath with motion,
and it is certainly possible that Epicurus did so himself in a
work now lost. But in Lucretius' account, while heat is associated
with ferocious animals and cows live 'by calm air', breath is
particularly connected with the 'cold minds' of stags; and the
only motion associated with it is trembling caused by fear.[3]
In other words we have to admit that the evidence which points
to the existence of four kinds of atoms in the soul may not be
entirely consistent in other details. It is possible that Aëtius'
association of breath (πνεῦμα) with motion in general is a piece
of Aristotelianism which has slipped into the tradition. Bailey's
acceptance of his account may be premature.[4] We shall be safe
if we conclude that Lucretius, Aëtius and Plutarch need not

---

[1] Lucr., 3.234.   [2] Aët., 4.3.11 (Us. 315).
[3] Lucr., 3.293–322.   [4] Bailey, *Greek Atomists* 390.

conflict with the letter to Herodotus with regard to the number of kinds of soul atom, but that we cannot be sure of the precise functions of all of the types.

Let us now consider the unnamed variety of atoms in more detail. Epicurus deemed it necessary, he says, because such atoms, being finer in texture, are better able to 'sympathize' with the rest of the living organism. By this he seems to mean that, if the soul were only 'like heat' and 'like breath', its atoms would be too 'like' other atoms to be able to record the more subtle movements of the bodily frame which we are in fact able to perceive. Hence there must be something else, something 'finer still', which, as Lucretius tells us,[1] is able to convey the sense-bearing movements, that is pleasure and pain, first to the other soul atoms and then to the body.[2] This nameless element, Lucretius continues, is deepest down in the body and acts, as it were, as the soul of the soul.[3] Clearly this theory contains remnants of the non-atomist doctrine that the soul is separate from the body. There is a slight tendency to treat the nameless element of the soul as an entity in itself; Lucretius' phrase *anima animae* is evidence of the fact.

Before leaving the different varieties of soul atoms, we should notice a further point. The atoms of all souls are similar in kind; they are all smooth and fine and round.[4] Since atoms differ only in shape, size and position, all the dispositions of men and of animals of the same species must be due to such variations. Now since all human soul atoms are unusually smooth and fine,[5] differences of shape will presumably be minimal. They may exist in small degree, but the essential differences of character in different individuals will be due primarily to the number of atoms of each kind and to their arrangement. Furthermore, when the character undergoes training, such as learning Epicurean philosophy, the numerical ratios between the types of atom in a man's soul will not change. Their arrangement, however, will presumably be modified. Furley says that

---

[1] Lucr., 3.245.
[2] For this interpretation of *sensiferos motus* (cf. 1.251) see Solmsen, ' Αἴσθησις ', 16 (254).　　　　　　　　　　　　[3] Lucr., 3.274–5.
[4] For these ideas see scholion to D.L. 10.66 (Herodotus), Lucr., 3.186.
[5] Lucr., 3.244.

'learning cannot diminish the sum of "hot" atoms in a passionate man's psyche, but perhaps it can push them away into less effective regions (or something like that)'. And the point of pushing them away is that the position of the atoms is altered; thus the individual's character is presumably modified.[1] It would be interesting to know how Epicurus would have explained character changes due to physical injury or loss of limbs. The pattern of the soul atoms throughout the body need not be immediately changed by an amputation, but is presumably modified when the news of the amputation reaches the mind and is telegraphed back to the rest of the body. Perhaps this will become clearer when we have discussed the division of the soul into *anima* and *animus*.

Before doing that, however, we should give further consideration to the fourth, 'nameless' element, the element which is the 'soul of the soul', the first instrument of perception and the first to experience the feelings of pleasure and pain that accompany touch in the living organism. It has been generally held, since Giussani,[2] that Epicurus' concept of this nameless element and his association of it with the most sensitive part of the soul is influenced by Aristotle's fifth element in the cosmos, or by his *quinta natura* which, at some stage of his career at least, he supposed is present in the soul. This Aristotelian influence on Epicurus *could* still be present even if the *quinta natura* was intended by Aristotle as an *immaterial* substance;[3] Epicurus' point could be that Aristotle was right to introduce a new substance but wrong to make that substance immaterial. It seems probable that Giussani was right to suspect Aristotelian influence here; certainly in Plutarch's account of the Epicurean 'nameless' element we find attributed to it many of those capacities which Aristotle in the *De Anima* allots to our 'intellectual faculty'. This nameless element, says Plutarch, is that by which the soul judges, remembers, loves, hates. On it in general hang all the powers of practical reasoning and calculation.

[1] Furley, *Two Studies* 200. Of course, others are not hot (Lucr., 2.842–6). Furley means the atoms that are like those of heat.
[2] Giussani, *Studi lucr.* 187.
[3] See the interesting article of Easterling, 'Quinta Natura', *Mus. Helv.* 21 (1964) 73–85.

Indeed we should add that not only does this fourth (or third) element in the soul bear certain marks of Aristotelianism, but that it also has similarities with the 'ruling part' (ἡγεμονικόν) of the Stoics. Lucretius says that it lords it over the whole body.[1]

Anima and animus

We can now tackle the problem of the division of the soul. Although a basic division into a rational and an irrational 'part' is not described in the letter to Herodotus, it is mentioned by a scholiast to the letter as follows:[2] the irrational part of the soul is distributed through the remaining parts of the body, while the rational part is in the chest, as is clear from our fears and joy. The word 'part', we should notice, does not occur in the Greek text of this sentence. It is a convenient translation, but it is important to recall that a literal translation would speak of 'something irrational' and 'the rational'. There is nothing here to support any idea that the two 'parts' are composed of different atomic constituents.

Throughout book three of *De Rerum Natura* Lucretius divides the soul; he calls the irrational part *anima* and the rational *animus*. In the discussion to follow, the Latin terms will be kept to avoid confusion. Presumably *anima* represents the Greek ψυχή ('soul'), used in something like its restricted Homeric sense of 'mindless life', while *animus* more certainly represents διάνοια ('mind'). Be that as it may, there is no evidence, as we have seen, that the *anima* and *animus* are composed of different elements. Both are made up of the four (or three) types of soul atom, but the *animus* is localized in the chest.[3] A further difference is that while the *anima* is distributed throughout the body – soul atoms are thus intermingled with body atoms – the *animus*, being concentrated in one place, is the largest grouping of soul atoms and hence the most receptive to 'sense-bearing' motions. It is also possible that the proportions of the types of soul atoms

---

[1] Lucr., 3.281; cf. 3.95, *consilium regimenque*.
[2] Schol. to D.L. 10.66 (Herodotus).
[3] Lucretius (3.140–2) rejects the scholiast's reason for the localization: we feel pleasure and pain in the chest!

differ in the *anima* and *animus*, though this need not be so and is not mentioned in the sources.

The soul then is identical in its physical components throughout. The distinction between *anima* and *animus* is a distinction of faculties in a quasi-Aristotelian manner, not a distinction between different types of physical body. This is presumably the reason why it is not mentioned in the brief sketch of the soul in the letter to Herodotus. In this case there is no question of Lucretius' offering a variant on the doctrine. There is nothing in Epicurus' account which does not square with the version of Lucretius (or of the doxographers), and nothing in Lucretius' account which would be inconsistent with what Epicurus says in the letter. That being so, we can now proceed to a more detailed description of the soul's various operations.

Sensation

The soul is a material entity. But, since soul atoms are unusually fine and rounded, they do not cling together firmly. They need to be held in place by the larger and more tightly assembled atoms of the body. That is why, if the body is destroyed, the soul atoms cannot survive as a sentient compound. On the destruction of the body the soul will fly apart into its separate components. Conversely, since in the first instance it is the soul atoms which are capable of feeling, though only when penned together in a bodily structure, if these atoms are dispersed, there is no feeling left in the remaining parts of the body. Hence at death, when the soul atoms are scattered, the body loses all feeling. And death will normally occur when the 'nameless' atoms of the soul are affected by 'pain or evil',[1] since these atoms are, as we have seen, deeply hidden throughout the soul, which is itself dispersed over the whole body. Thus to touch the fourth element is to touch the whole bodily structure and to throw it into chaos.

Democritus had held the simplistic view that throughout the living organism soul and body atoms exist alternately.[2] Lucretius deals with the matter somewhat cavalierly.[3] He

---

[1] Lucr., 3.252–3.   [2] Cf. Lucr., 3.371.   [3] Lucr., 3.370–95.

answers Democritus from an Epicurean standpoint, but seems to lose sight of his own distinction between *anima* and *animus*. His point seems to be that soul atoms in general are much less frequent throughout the organism than atoms of body. Hence it happens that we do not feel everything which touches us. The impact of an object may be only on body atoms, with the result that in regard to that object the living creature is insensate. Objects of this kind are very small, such as specks of dust or chalk or mist at night or spiders' webs. They are able to touch the body so lightly that no trace of movement is communicated to the atoms of the soul. This passage of Lucretius helps us understand some of the implications of the remark of Epicurus himself in the letter to Herodotus that the soul is the principal cause of sensation (αἴσθησις).[1]

A good deal of confusion about sensation has been generated by another passage of Lucretius.[2] Lucretius rejects the view that the body cannot feel. It is obviously wrong, he holds, to think that the body is a kind of window of the soul, and that it is 'really' the *anima* which feels.[3] The difficulty arises with all the organs of sense. But while it is true that the body has powers of feeling, the problem is only rendered more puzzling if we present it (with Furley) as follows:[4] 'The question is whether the body or only the soul has sensation. The Epicurean doctrine is that the body has sensation, though only when in conjunction with "soul".' But all that Lucretius says in the passage in question is that it is absurd to suppose that the body does *not* have the power of feeling. Clearly what he means to say is that it is not true that only the soul has feeling; the body also has the power to feel. And by feeling he means here the feeling of pleasure and pain.

After explaining that the body has the power of feeling, in circumstances which we will shortly investigate, Lucretius goes on to explain how the sense-organs work: in particular he is concerned to refute the view that it is not the eyes but the *mind* (the *animus*) which sees. But we know that in the eye itself

---

[1] D.L. 10.63 (Herodotus). [2] Lucr., 3.350–8.
[3] Cf. Aët., *Plac.* 4.23.2 (Us. 317).
[4] Furley, 'Lucretius and the Stoics', 26.

SOUL, MIND AND BODY

there are mingled the atoms of the *anima*. Hence to deny that the *animus* in the chest is capable of seeing does not involve denying that the *soul* (in its function as *anima*) is involved in seeing. Lucretius wants to deny that the mind sees through the eyes. It is the eyes and the eyes alone which see. But it must be remembered that within the eyes themselves, as in all the other organs of sense, are mingled the *anima* atoms. Hence when Lucretius argues that the *mind* does not see or feel, he does not exclude the possibility that in some way the soul sees and feels. For in a living organism sense-organs are inseparable soul–body complexes. Solmsen is right to draw attention to the fact that Lucretius uses the word *sensus* to denote both feelings (pleasure and pain) and sensation (sight, touch, etc.).[1] But when he says that 'the account of the perceptions (sight, touch, etc.) in Lucretius' *fourth* [his italics] book is entirely consonant with the principle enunciated in III, 359 ff.', and that 'the individual senses and their functions are explained without reference to an activity or participation of soul or mind', he is misleading us. It is true that in book four, when dealing with the individual sense-organs and their operations, Lucretius does not discuss the *anima*, but book three indicates that, when discussing the acts of our sense-organs, we are discussing *anima*–body complexes. There is no need for Lucretius to point this out each time the subject comes up. His discussion of our not feeling specks of dust because they do not affect the *anima* makes it clear that as for feeling pleasure and pain, so for sense-perception, the first impact is on the soul atoms. Indeed in the beginning the impact is on the 'nameless' atoms in the *anima*–body complex.

In brief then the phenomenon of sense-perception can be described as follows. Like all atomic complexes the soul–body complex is continually involved in internal movement. New movements, originating from outside, are set up whenever anything strikes the body in such a way as to affect the *anima* atoms present in it. All such effects are both sensations (one meaning of *sensus* and αἴσθησις) and also feelings of pleasure or pain (the other, related meaning of *sensus* and αἴσθησις). Naturally, since individual atoms have no power to feel or sense,

[1] Solmsen, 'Αἴσθησις', 19 (257).

feelings and sensations will only occur when a soul atom is part
of a larger organism. They are, as Bailey says of sensation,[1] a
kind of accident of compounds containing at least one 'nameless' atom. The next step in our enquiry therefore must be to
give an account of the activities of each of the sense-organs in
turn; some brief remarks of Epicurus, together with Lucretius'
fourth book, will be our guide.

It is necessary to grasp at the outset that for the Epicureans
all sensations are reduced to the contact of material objects,
in fact to different varieties of touch. Touch, Lucretius emphasizes with an oath, is the sense of the body (*sensus corporis*).[2]
But although all sensations are varieties of touching, we shall
best understand the theory if we consider the most important
of the particular senses first, and that is the sense of sight.
Epicurus' theory of sight differs from that of Democritus.
It is not true, he holds, that the objects of vision make impressions on the air between themselves and the eye and that these
formed air-impressions then enter the eye. That, Epicurus
seems to think, is unnecessarily complicated.[3] Rather, because
of their internal movements, all objects are constantly giving off
exact replicas or images of themselves. These images (εἴδωλα)
strike the eye of the beholder. Apparently Epicurus went so far
as to say that they enter into (ἐπεισιόντων) the eye of the
beholder, and we read of the passages through which this entry
takes place.[4] The actual entry of the images is confirmed by
Lucretius,[5] but it leaves us with several difficult problems.
Obviously if thin films, made up of various atoms, enter the eye
of the beholder, that eye is constantly receiving new material.
Hence it must be constantly undergoing drastic changes, since
the images are of the same shape and colour as the objects
which emit them. But Epicurus speaks in the same passage of
the impact of images on the *mind* and we know that most kinds
of atomic images cannot remain in the mind, which is always
composed of four and only four types of atom. The solution

[1] Bailey, *Greek Atomists* 393. [2] Lucr., 2.434.
[3] D.L. 10.49 (Herodotus).
[4] Lucr., 4.344, 350. For further references see Kleve, *Gnosis* 18, n. 2.
[5] Lucr., 4.331, 339.

suggested by Lucretius (4.341) seems to be that images enter the eye (and the mind) and then pass out, or are pushed out, at the other side. What happens to them then is quite unclear. As for the atoms of the eye itself, they are presumably re-patterned in the form of the image which has struck them. Of course a single image cannot achieve this. Seeing only occurs when a succession of similar images, thrown off the same object, enters the eye.[1]

Let us look at the emission of images in more detail. The images are originally the same size, shape and colour as the objects from which they come, but unlike these objects they are hollow. Since they are thus ultra-fine, they travel from the emitting objects at near-atomic speed, for very few atoms will impede their progress by colliding with them.[2] When the images strike the eye, they produce a 'presentation' (φαντασία) of their sender.

But although the presentations which arise in this way are all 'true', in the special sense of 'existents' that we recognized in Epicurean canonic, we do not immediately know when we see a presentation how large the object producing it is. When we see a tower in the distance, it looks small. We have discussed this also in an earlier chapter. Here we should only notice the physical phenomena connected with images which produce such 'subjective' effects in our sense-organs. Although images are fine, not easily impeded, little subject to the slowing effects of internal vibrations and easily able to pass through one another, they do not necessarily represent the objects of vision as they are 'in themselves' for a number of reasons. Images may coalesce in passing from the object to the eye and a compound, deceptive to the facile mind, may be formed. Thus the image from a man may coalesce with the image from a horse and we shall seem to see, indeed in a sense we shall see, a 'non-existent' object, in this case a Centaur.[3] Secondly when images travel over great distances, they experience a certain buffeting from

---

[1] D.L. 10.50; Lucr., 4.89.   [2] D.L. 10.47.

[3] Images of non-existent objects like Centaurs may also arise 'sponta-neously' in the air. In such cases atoms neither from men nor horses may combine to form a Centaur-image. Cf. Lucr., 4.131; D.L. 10.48. Cf. pp. 23–4.

other atoms in the air, and their corners are worn down. Hence a square tower may appear from a distance to be round.[1]

This does not seem very satisfactory. Since the images of the tower are originally as large as the tower, yet by the time they reach the distant eye they are only able to produce a small presentation, have we really accounted for the enormous decline in size? A few corners chipped off in transit is not a sufficient explanation. Bailey supports the ingenious suggestion that the effect of the constant stream of blows on the image is to make it gradually collapse – we remember that it is hollow – but that its rate of diminution is uniform and that the amount of diminution is proportionate to the distance travelled.[2] But although this proposal is attractive, it runs up against the difficulty that the appearance of square towers as round does not suggest the idea of uniform diminution. Furthermore it should be pointed out that a theory that images are battered into collapsing during their journey through the air between the object and the eye does not easily harmonize with the undoubtedly Epicurean doctrine that because of the fineness of images they travel at nearly atomic speed and are only very slightly hindered by external objects. For want of a better solution we must concede the remote possibility that Bailey is right; but it is more likely either that Epicurus did not notice this kind of problem or that it failed to interest him.

A further objection to Epicurus' theory of the emission of images is that, if this process is constant, and images are constantly being emitted from all solid objects, these objects will quickly melt away. To a limited degree Epicurus admits this; indeed, as we shall see when discussing Epicurean theology, it is a distinguishing characteristic of the gods that they can totally replenish the atomic wastage which they, like all other compounds, are constantly experiencing.[3] Unlike the gods, however, other compounds will eventually be destroyed and many of them are in fact gradually diminishing in size through the loss of images. But this phenomenon, even when it is occurring, is not visible.[4] For there is a constant accretion of

[1] Lucr., 4.353 ff. [2] Bailey, *Greek Atomists* 412–13
[3] See below pp. 149–51. [4] D.L. 10.48 (Herodotus)

atoms to solid objects as well as a constant subtraction. We should note, however, that Epicurus indicates that the process of diminution is invisible, not that it does not occur.

Before leaving the phenomena of vision we should consider what happens when we look hard at an object, when we look at something rather than merely see it. Here it is important to recall that the physiology of sensation does not involve the emission of anything from the eye to catch, as it were, particular atoms outside the eye itself. Any such theory, a version of which is to be found in Plato's *Theaetetus* (156DE), is specifically ruled out in the letter to Herodotus.[1] Rather acts of attention must involve acts of selection. When a whole range of images strikes the eye, only some of them are retained. The process may have been envisaged as something like an instant act of the memory. Particular images, those to which we are attending, are constantly recalled, and thus their impressions are renewed, while others around them are ignored, just as when we remember a particular mathematical formula we may not at the same time recall any other related formulae which we know. Lucretius refers to this selection process in the case of the mind as a self-preparation to receive,[2] and presumably he would say the same of the eye, but he offers no explanation of the specific physiological processes involved. Presumably, however, there is a directive from the ruling-principle, the *animus*. Looking will thus be an act of the will, and we shall understand its operations better when we consider how Epicurus thinks acts of will take place. For the time being we may content ourselves with observing that, since 'attending' with the eyes involves selecting from among the presentations before us, we have additional confirmation of our earlier insistence that the sense-data we 'look at' are no more reliable as a safe guide to reality than the sense-data we 'see',[3] for it is obvious that 'opinion' is involved in the process of selection. Strictly speaking, all the evidence of the senses is true, in the Epicurean sense of true (=real), but objects 'looked at' may still be misleading; we shall often misinterpret such evidence more easily than the evidence of

---

[1] D.L. 10.49 (Herodotus). [2] Lucr., 4.804.
[3] See above pp. 24–5.

simple sensation, for in our process of attending, we are liable to introduce false judgments.

It is clear from our discussion of vision that Lucretius' enthusiastic acclamation of touch as 'the sense of the body' is justified. The Epicurean treatment of vision makes it a matter of the images striking (touching) the eye. Little time need be spent on the remaining senses. Taste is not mentioned in the letter to Herodotus, but Lucretius has a lengthy description.[1] Essentially it is a matter of squeezing the 'juices' out of food. The atoms thus squeezed affect the tongue and palate. Smell, like sight, is the result of effluences – called particles (ὄγκοι) by Epicurus[2] – striking the sense-organ. These particles come, according to Lucretius, from deep within the objects which emit them. Hence they have a hard time reaching the surface. That is one reason why they do not carry very far. The other reason is that the particles move rather slowly and are thus easily dispersed in the air. The slowness is to be explained by the comparatively large size of the particles, when compared with the particles of sound. That is also why smells, unlike sounds, cannot penetrate stone walls. As for the fact that some animals have better powers of smell than others, that is because the shapes of the smell-particles are better suited (*aptus*) to some noses than to others. By this Lucretius presumably means that smell-particles fit more easily into some noses than into others. Finally we come to sounds. These too are caused by a flow of particles (ὄγκοι) from the object.[3] The particles are all similar to one another even if travelling in different directions – that is why several people can hear the same sound – and while moving away from their source they maintain some kind of common character which can usually be identified by the hearer who, as in the case of sight, is continually assailed by them. Again as in the case of sight Epicurus denounces the account given by Democritus. It is not true, he says, without mentioning Democritus by name, that the sound-particles mould the air between the subject and the object. Rather they strike the

[1] Lucr., 4.615–72.
[2] D.L. 10.53 (Herodotus); cf. Lucr., 4.673–705.
[3] D.L. 10.52–3 (Herodotus); cf. Lucr., 4.524–614.

sense-organ directly, thereby producing the sense of sound. Different kinds of sounds are produced by particles of different shapes striking the ear.

Operations of the mind

As we noticed in the chapter on canonic, mind (*animus*, διάνοια) functions in the first instance as a kind of sense. Hence atoms, too fine to affect the sense-organs, are able to penetrate as far as the mind and produce mental pictures. Thus we are able to see the gods, as well as the products of chance meetings of images of unrelated objects. Hence our visions of Scyllas or Centaurs,[1] when seen in sleep or in waking dreams. In general, Epicurus speaks of the 'contacts' of the mind and of the other senses as though they arise in a similar manner.[2] As with the five senses, so also with the mind-sense, we can 'attend' to the evidence presented to us – or we can merely register it. Since the operation of the mind is a kind of seeing, it generates few new problems for the Epicurean psychologist.

But as we have already noticed when discussing the origin of error, the mind has other functions besides that of recognizing subtle images. It concerns itself with the evaluation and interpretation of both mental and sensible presentations. We have discussed one of these activities, the formation of general concepts (προλήψεις), in our chapter on canonic. General concepts accurately reflect the sensible or mental *presentations* on which they depend. Physiologically they arise from the movement of the atoms of the mind. But the mind is able to perform other mental operations besides the formation of general concepts. Epicurean psychological terminology, despite Epicurus' own strictures on the matter, does not seem to have been

---

[1] For a discussion of the 'errors' we are liable to make about these chance combinations see above pp. 23–4. It is worth noting the remark of Lucretius (4.765–7) that in sleep our memory is suspended. Hence, because we do not remember what is true, we are more easily misled into believing what is false, e.g. that so and so long dead is visible to us. Diano's view (*RAL* (1943) 265–70) that *dissentit* (l. 766) is a translation of διαισθάνεται used in a technical sense, is attractive and hopefully correct.

[2] D.L. 10.51 (Herodotus).

completely technical, but its broad import can be discerned. When the mind receives information from the sense-organs about sense-experiences and feelings of pleasure and pain, it is able to make judgments about them. We must remember that the mind does not *itself* experience these sense-perceptions as feelings: as Aëtius puts it, Epicurus holds that the feelings and sensations (τὰ πάθη καὶ τὰς αἰσθήσεις) occur in the sensitive places; the ruling part does not experience them directly.[1] But information is conveyed from the sources of sensation by a movement of atoms to the mind, and the mind is stirred to make judgments. Some of these, as we have seen, involve correct general concepts, others are false. All of them, if they are based on sensation and not on the perception of the mind itself, are apparently called acts supervening on a sensation (ἐπαίσθησις, ἐπαισθήματα).[2] Such an act is the comprehension, the understanding of a particular sensation, and probably, as Bailey suggests, includes such things as recognizing that the man in the distance is Epicurus.[3] This recognition, Diogenes tells us, takes place when the mind is able to compare the present sensation with others stored in the memory. 'Comparing' is a general term; it would include, according to Diogenes, the occurrence in the mind of coincidences, analogies, similarities, and combinations. These would, as it were, be put together by a reasoning process (λογισμός) and the result would be an act of comprehension (ἐπαίσθημα).[4]

Such acts of comprehension are themselves related to the class of mental acts to which the Epicureans gave the general name 'after-thoughts' (ἐπίνοιαι). 'After-thought' seems to be a word used to describe an idea which arises primarily from data already available to the mind, and deriving only remotely from sense-experience. It is true that all knowledge ultimately depends on the senses or on the mind functioning as a mental sense, but we do not *see* such 'inaccessible realities' (ἄδηλα) as atoms and the void. We calculate their existence on the basis of

[1] Aët., 4.13 (= Us. 318).
[2] D.L. 10.32 and D.L. 10.52, 53 (Herodotus).
[3] Bailey, *Greek Atomists* 420; cf. Aët., 4.8.2 (Us. 249).
[4] D.L. 10.32.

knowledge already assimilated, for example about the fact of motion. We then grasp that motion requires a void. The *process* of reasoning here is in most general terms called 'calculation' (λογισμός); its result is the formation of an 'after-thought'.[1] Epicurus hopes where possible to base his reasoning on clearly observed data, but obviously with atoms and the void this is impossible. In such cases the senses and the mind-sense provide us with indications (σημεῖα) from which we have to make inferences, while referring these inferences back to the evidence of the senses whenever we can.

Finally we come to memory; this appears to be the permanent impression left on the mind by a constant series of events. The mind atoms are re-formed to take account of the new data. Presumably forgetfulness is caused by the eventual obliteration of the patterns and alteration of the movements. But when we consider the question of the act of memory, and of how we recall, that is, choose to recall, a particular fact, we enter upon a new range of problems.

Will and action

The mind is capable of initiating action. We have already observed that the Epicureans argued from the fact that the emotions are felt in the chest to the theory that this is the location of the *animus*.[2] Lucretius tells us explicitly that some of the pleasures and pains of the mind are felt by the mind alone, while others are communicated to the *anima* and the body. The vehicles of communication are the nameless atoms, present

---

[1] Other ἐπίνοιαι are formed by περιλήψεις, which seem to be inductive appreciations of a general nature, particularly of size and quality. See Diano, *GCFI* (1939) 135–7 with references there given. Diano's description of περίληψις as having a 'carattere intuitivo' is unwarranted. A further source of ἐπίνοιαι is the ἐπιλογισμός. This is an inductive process, opposed to deduction by Epicurus (D.L. 10.73 (Herodotus)). Presumably it is a variety of λογισμός or a later calculation based on a λογισμός. At any rate it is ultimately based on empirically received information. For its various (but all inductive) uses see De Lacy, *AJP* 79 (1958) 179–83 where the evidence is listed.

[2] Schol. to D.L. 10.66 (Herodotus); cf. Lucr., 3.136–60; Plut., *Adv. Col.* 1118D.

both in the mind and in the *anima*–body complex. In the case of pleasure and pain there are incidences of bodily movement, such as trembling, sweating, and so on, initiated by the mind. In Lucretius' and Epicurus' terminology the origin of such movements is 'in us'. A good example of this is provided by false fears about punishments after death. Since such punishments do not exist, our fear of them is generated by our own opinions, false opinions which do not represent correctly the evidence available to us through the senses. Such fears originate from our own error; hence their causes are 'in us'. As we shall see, neither Lucretius nor Epicurus pays sufficient attention to the problem of whether we can avoid such false opinions being 'in us', in other words, to the problem of the degree to which we are 'determined' by our environment.

Lucretius explains in some detail how human acts take place. The theory he offers – which is undoubtedly the theory of Epicurus – seems to be an atomist's version of the Aristotelian theory of action;[1] Lucretius uses the Aristotelian example of starting to walk.[2] The mind first needs images of movement. These *simulacra meandi* are, of course, derived from sensation. They strike the mind, says Lucretius, and thence decision (*voluntas*) arises.[3] The form of this decision is that the movement of the mind stirs the atoms of the *anima* and ultimately those of the body. We should not be misled by the Lucretian phrase 'the mind stirs itself so that it wants to go forward'.[4] This is not a 'spontaneous' act, requiring explanation in terms of the swerve of atoms – which is not mentioned in book four of Lucretius at all – or of any other unusual physical event. It occurs when and only when the mind is struck by the relevant images and 'chooses' to react. On this occasion, the *animus* moves the *anima*, which strikes and moves the body. Lucretius tells us that bodily movement is aided by the opening of the bodily pores. Thus air is let in and this helps the object along; it is rather like the action of a sail.[5] Lucretius does not say exactly why the pores

---

[1] Furley, *Two Studies*, esp. 217–18. For Stoic use of the same theme see Rist, *Stoic Philosophy* 33–4.
[2] Cf. *De Motu Anim.* 701a4–6.   [3] Lucr., 4.881–3.
[4] Lucr., 4.886–7.   [5] Lucr., 4.892–906.

so conveniently open at the appropriate moment, but presumably the *anima* atoms are in some way responsible.

We said that action occurs when and only when the mind is struck by the relevant images. Does this mean that whenever we think of walking, we walk? Clearly if that were the conclusion to be drawn from the Epicurean theory, its absurdity would be patent. But Lucretius does not claim this; apparently whether we act on the basis of the images before us, indeed whether we even choose to focus our attention on them and hence *think* about them at all,[1] depends on what kind of people we are at the moment when they are presented to us. Action then depends on character.

The Epicureans were anxious to show that human action is not dependent on what they think of as 'external causes'. In the atomic world such external causes are the blows of other atoms upon our atoms; the tendency of all atoms to move downwards is an 'internal cause'. Lucretius says that because of the existence of weight all things are not determined by blows.[2] But the atoms of the mind might still seem to be ultimately governed by their weight.[3] Lucretius refers to the blows as an external force and the weight as an internal necessity. Internal necessity, however, must also involve the first arrangement of the atoms at birth. To prevent the domination of this internal necessity over the mind Epicurus introduces the atomic swerve.

[1] Lucr., 4.802–17.
[2] Lucr., 2.287–93. For a more detailed discussion see Furley, *Two Studies* 178–82.
[3] My interpretation depends on reading *mens* (the emendation of Lambinus) for the MS *res* in line 289. Virtually all editors read *mens* and it is ably defended by Furley (*Two Studies* 179–80), though Furley retains a few doubts. It is further supported by a parallel passage in the *De Fato* of Cicero (section 23) which Furley does not mention. Cicero says that the reason why Epicurus introduced the swerve was that he was afraid that if the movement of the atom is always governed by weight, the movement of the mind would be governed by the movement of the atom. Furley's position and the reading *mens* are strengthened by this passage, since Cicero is saying that the swerve is to prevent the dominance of the mind by *internal* necessity, that is, by weight, and that is exactly Furley's point. Furley observes (p. 182) that, if *mens* is the right reading, the function of the *clinamen* 'is to save the mind not from external force but from internal necessity'—which is what Cicero says.

Were it not for this 'minute swerve of atoms, occurring at no set place or time', the mind would be totally subject to internal necessity.

In the second book of Lucretius we find two kinds of 'necessity' threatening the *voluntas* or decision of the mind, that of weight and that of blows. In any individual instance these pressures can be understood in two ways. First the mind could be so constituted at birth that all our actions are determined by a fixed weight of atoms in a fixed position. Hence we would be congenitally irreformable. Lucretius specifically denies that this is the case.[1] Secondly, and this is the instance we considered earlier, we could be such as to react inevitably to atomic blows on our minds. We could walk every time we see the images of movement (*simulacra meandi*). Epicurus mentions both kinds of pressure in a passage of his work *On Nature* and indicates why he is worried about them. If our acts were totally dependent on the weight and blows of atoms, he suggests, then many of us would be morally irreformable. No reprimands would ever reach us.[2] This moral concern is echoed by Diogenes of Oenoanda, who says that the Epicurean swerve saves us from the fate and moral determinism which beset the atomism of Democritus.[3] Cicero too contrasts Epicurus and Democritus on this point,[4] and it is at least certain that the Epicureans believed that the swerve must be introduced into atomist psychology for moral reasons. Whether we agree with most of the modern critics that Epicurus is consciously attacking a genuinely Democritean thesis, or whether we hold that he believed fatalism to be the logical *conclusion* of Democritus' position, and perhaps the position of Nausiphanes, is comparatively unimportant.[5] What matters is that Epicurus clearly thought that without the swerve fatalism could not be avoided in an atomist's world. As for Democritus, we know too little of his ethics to be sure.

[1] Lucr., 3.307–22 with Furley's comments, *ibid.* 198–200.
[2] Cf. Περὶ φύσεως 31.[27.]3–9 Arr.
[3] Diog. Oen., fr. 32, col. 3 Chilton.   [4] *De Fato* 23.
[5] Furley's best evidence for this (*op. cit.* 174–5) is the use of the term at D.L. 10.134 (Menoeceus). But this need not refer to other atomists.

According to the Epicureans, and here they have much in common both with Aristotle and the Stoics, actions are in our power if we are not subjected to overwhelming pressures. It cannot be overemphasized that Epicurus treats us as free if we are not so pressured. These pressures take the form, for Epicurus, of atomic movements, each affecting the next. As Furley has admirably shown,[1] 'the *voluntas* must be saved from a succession of causes which can be traced back to infinity. All (Lucretius) needs...is a break in the succession of causes, so that the source of an action cannot be traced back to something occurring before the birth of the agent.' It is to secure this break in the causal chain that the swerve is introduced. The power of external necessity is overcome, as is clear from Lucretius, by internal necessity; internal necessity is overcome by the swerve. It does not matter how many swerves take place in the soul. There is no evidence in any Epicurean text for the view that every 'voluntary' action or any *particular* 'voluntary' action is preceded by an atomic swerve. Lucretius, who has often been held to suggest this, merely remarks that *voluntas* requires a swerve, not that every or any specific act of *voluntas* requires one of its own.[2] It is our mind in general that must be freed by the swerve, not each separate decision.[3] One swerve would be strictly sufficient to ensure that the pattern of the soul is not wholly determined before birth. Too many might make behaviour entirely random, but an indeterminate and small number would be both plausible and effective for Epicurus' purposes. Thus the swerve ensures that our actions are not predetermined from eternity; the varying patterns in our minds, partially generated by the swerve and affected by the downward tendency of our mind atoms, ensure that we are not certain to react in specifiable ways to specific *external* stimuli, that is, to external necessity. This explains why different men react differently when faced with similar circumstances.

We can now see what happens when, as Lucretius puts it, the mind arouses itself so that it wishes to move. First of all the images of movement are received; then the mind *decides* whether

[1] Furley, *op. cit.* 232.   [2] Lucr., 2.257-8.
[3] Lucr., 2.289.

to walk or not. The outcome of the mental 'debate' depends on the pre-existing pattern of the mind atoms. If these are arranged in one way, not of course determined at birth, then there is the decision to move. If they are arranged differently, the decision is to remain at rest. Thus the decision, which for Epicurus is 'in our power', depends on our characters. Like Aristotle, and indeed following Aristotle, Epicurus persists in disregarding the question of how far 'we' may be said to be determined by that part of our character formation – above all in childhood – over which we have been able to exercise little or no control. In favour of Epicurus, however, it should be pointed out that, since every act of advising and exhorting to virtue involves the striking of the mind by new atoms of speech, presumably themselves patterned in particular ways, then even if good advice is ignored, it does beat on the mind and must exercise some influence, however slight. Epicurus does not argue that water-drops at last will wear away a stone, but at least it may be said for his theory that no mind can become completely programmed in childhood, completely set in its ways, or completely unresponsive to moral exhortation if it is understood atomically. It is always liable to some degree of modification.

We now see how Epicurus explains acts like walking, acts in which a decision determines the movement of the limbs. Peculiar problems seem to arise, however, with certain kinds of purely mental activities, such as remembering. We recall that before we decide to walk or not walk, we are presented with the images of movement. What happens when we decide to recall what is the sum of 2 and 2? Our answer '4' need not be an act of calculation; it could be pure memorization, parrot-fashion. What does Epicurus imagine happens in such a case? Clearly the images of a set of numbers, or even of 4, are not presented to our minds for *selection*, for we do not 'look at 4' and decide whether or not it is the sum of 2 and 2. Rather we 'know' the answer because we have memorized it. Once we have 'remembered' 4 no further mental operation is necessary. It is not certain what answer Epicurus would give to the problem of such mental acts, though perhaps he would say that the images of the problem somehow 'imply' the images of the answer, our minds being patterned to react in that way.[1] And it is not only memorization that is difficult to explain. How do we know whether to 'attend' to a particular piece of data? Do we need images of attending to object A if we are to attend to object A? Here, however, Epicurus' solution is more obvious. There is little doubt that we attend to those objects which we have become conditioned to attend to. When we attend to an object of vision we are already 'seeing' it – thus we have a presentation at hand. And we still react to our presentations, as we have seen, according to our characters.

That the explanation of action which we have offered is generally correct, is supported by further passages from Epicurus' work *On Nature*. Both the text and the meaning of the text are difficult to decipher, but it is clear that Epicurus is discussing the original constitution of the soul (its σύστασις) and certain states which arise in it later. He calls these ἀπογεγεννημένα, which seems to mean 'acquired dispositions'.[2] This indicates that such dispositions arise in a man on a base of the atomic pattern of his soul at birth. Thus dispositions are nothing more than the effects of blows on the original atomic structure. Since this is the case, action is also the product of the original constitution of the soul (its original σύστασις) and the sequence of incoming blows. Thus without a swerve, 'fate' could not be avoided.

But there is a section of the work *On Nature* to which we should give special attention.[3] Epicurus is distinguishing between human actions and the actions of wild animals (τὰ ἄγρια τῶν ζῴων). We do not give warnings to wild animals, says Epicurus, because we treat the original constitutions of their souls and their 'acquired dispositions' as a single entity. In the first place this suggests that wild animals are entirely governed by the

---

[1] Cf. Diano, *RAL* 4 (1942–3) 267: 'La memoria ... è un' ἕξις, la quale si forma grado a grado nell'anima per effetto delle modificazioni ch'ella subisce da parte degli εἴδωλα o simulacri ...'

[2] Cf. Περὶ φύσεως 31.[21.]17; 31.[24.]24 and 29; 31.[25.]6; 31.[25.]27 Arr. The pioneer work on these difficult texts was done by Diano; cf. *Epicuri Ethica, ad loc.* and *GCFI* 30 (1949) 220–2. There is further discussion by Arrighetti (notes *ad loc.*).

[3] Περὶ φύσεως 31.[25.]22–34 Arr.

combination of their atomic movements at birth and the movements induced in them by the blows from external atoms. But more than this must be implied. In the case of wild animals the original constitution of the soul (the σύστασις) involves a set of movements. These movements are not of such a kind as to permit the development of a moral character; they can be varied only by external atomic pressures, and even in men external pressures alone cannot explain actions 'in our power'. Now Epicurus thinks that in the case of wild animals we must treat their original nature at birth and their developed nature with its new movements and new dispositions as one (non-flexible and non-moral) thing only. We can only conclude from this that the original nature of wild animals is rigidly determined and that wild animals do not possess any mind atoms whose *swerves* could allow 'freedom of the will'.

At first sight this conclusion is puzzling. It is true that it seems to be in line with our interpretation of the role of the swerve in human psychology and to mark out men from animals. But if his text is correct,[1] Lucretius attributes a swerve of atoms, and therefore the possibility of some kind of 'choosing' dependent on a power 'in them' to race-horses. It is through the swerve, Lucretius begins, that *libera voluntas*, freedom from the causal nexus of fate, exists for living creatures over the earth. We note that he says living creatures (*animantibus*), not just men.[2] And, as we have said, the example he chooses to illustrate the power of *voluntas* is the race-horse, eager to dart forward when the barriers are raised. But Lucretius may not be contradicting Epicurus here. As we have seen, Epicurus speaks of wild animals, while Lucretius is talking of horses, which are tame or at least tameable. If the Epicureans drew a distinction between tameable and untameable animals, they may have accounted for it by allowing a measure of *libera voluntas* and hence a swerve of mind atoms, to the tameable. That would explain why they are tameable.[3] We should remember, of course, that the swerve of

---

[1] The emendation *equorum* in line 264 seems certain and has been universally accepted.   [2] Lucr., 2.256.

[3] Mrs Huby (*Apeiron* 3 (1969) 19), who entertains this idea about wild and tame animals, is slightly worried by the fact that in *BD* 32 Epicurus *may* be denying to all animals the power of making agreements. But, as she says,

atoms is not limited to the 'minds' of men and (perhaps) tameable animals. Any atom may swerve, but only the swerves of certain types of mind atoms produce the conditions in which the phenomenon called 'freedom of the will' can occur.

Before we leave Epicurus' attempt to save men from fate by his theory of the effect of the swerve on character, we should consider a passage from the letter to Menoeceus.[1] Here, if the restoration of Bailey is basically correct, we find mention of three causes of events: necessity, chance, and 'ourselves'.[2] The three are mentioned again in a section of Aëtius, but in place of 'ourselves' there is a reference to our character (προαίρεσις).[3] The use of this word is instructive; in some Stoic writers, especially in Epictetus, it means our moral personality. That is certainly the sense we should expect the Epicureans to be interested in. Acts which are in our power are above all those mental acts which determine whether we shall enjoy tranquillity or live in perpetual but misplaced fear of death and the gods. And 'character' (προαίρεσις) in the Stoic Epictetus has much in common with *voluntas* in the Stoic Seneca.[4] And we have found Lucretius talking about the *voluntas* whose 'freedom' is preserved for us by the swerve of the atoms of the mind. Whether Aëtius is accurate in assigning the *word* 'character' (προαίρεσις) to Epicurus may be doubted, but the idea he seeks to convey is the same as we find in Lucretius and in the letter to Menoeceus.

What then occurs when we act? An image is presented to the mind. The arrival of that image will generate feelings of attraction or repulsion according to the nature of our formed dispositions. If the act seems appropriate and likely to induce

the text of Epicurus does not rule out the possibility of tame animals and social insects making 'agreements'. And in any case even if no animal can make an 'agreement' not to injure and be injured, it does not follow that *libera voluntas* is totally ruled out.

[1] D.L. 10.133 (Menoeceus).
[2] The Epicureans wished to de-emphasize the importance of chance in the life of the wise man. Cf. *VS* 47 (Metrodorus), *BD* 16. In a fragment of the Περὶ φύσεως (31.[33.]3–4 Arr.) Epicurus describes motion as (a) δι' ἡμᾶς, (b) διὰ τὴν φύσιν καὶ τὸ περιέχον.
[3] Aët., 1.29.5 (Us. 375).   [4] Cf. Rist, *Stoic Philosophy* 223–32.

pleasure, a desire will arise to accomplish it. According to our dispositions once again we shall accept or reject that desire. If we accept it, the decision to move is conveyed from the mind through the *anima* to the limbs.

'Materialism' in psychology

We have completed an outline of Epicurus' doctrines of the soul. We should draw one important general conclusion. Although sensation is a matter for the organs of sense, the constant involvement of the *anima* and its atoms (which are identical in kind with those of the mind) means that Epicurus' account of sensation, feeling and behaviour is to some degree psychosomatic. Epicurus does not go as far in this direction as the Stoics. His comparative dissociation of the mind prevents this. But it should be noticed that in Epicurus we do not find a strong form of the body–mind dualism with which ancient thought has often been saddled. Nor do we always shed the most light on Epicurean psychology by emphasizing that it is materialist. The term 'materialism' is often defined by contrast to 'idealism', 'doctrine of immaterial substance' and so on. This tends to make us think of Epicurean materialism as blind to the problem of the difference between animate and inanimate objects. It would be going too far to say that Epicurean materialism is a vitalism. That would be to assimilate the doctrines of Epicurus to those of the Stoics. But Epicurus has at least taken over from Aristotle the concept that a single substance can explain living and non-living, 'material' and 'immaterial' substances. This single substance should not be misinterpreted in the light of other varieties of materialism. We should forget neither the 'sympathy' of the nameless element in the soul nor the fact that despite this 'sympathy' it remains a material object.

6

PLEASURE

The concept of pleasure

When we were discussing Epicurean canonic, we noticed the role allotted to pleasure. We observed that our senses feel pleasures and pains and that these pleasures and pains indicate what is appropriate and inappropriate to our human natures. Since then pleasure is the guide to a certain aspect of reality, and since pain indicates what is hostile to our existence as human beings, Epicurus held both that in some way we direct our lives in accordance with these criteria, and that it is right that we should so direct them, thus seeking pleasure and avoiding pain.[1] So far the canonic leads us, but it is not far enough to see our way forward clearly. We need to understand what Epicurus means by pleasure and what he means by pain; and this is not transparent. To the casual observer it might appear that Epicurus' theory of pleasure is riddled with inconsistencies.

We read, for example, in a very well known passage that Epicurus cannot conceive what is the good if we discount the pleasures of taste, of sex, of sound and of the sight of sweet movements.[2] Elsewhere, however, when explaining what he means by claiming that pleasure is the end of life, Epicurus comments that he is not talking about the pleasures of sensuality, but rather of freedom from bodily pain and mental affliction. It is not eating, drinking and sex, but sober reasoning which produces the happy life.[3] In recent times, at least, interpreters of Epicurus have explained his ethical theory more in terms of the second of these passages than of the first. Thus Epicurus appears as the teacher of an ascetic quietism who is easily contented and seeks only to be left in peace and untroubled. Epicurus' tenet that the highest

---

[1] D.L. 10.128 (Menoeceus), τὴν ἡδονὴν ἀρχὴν καὶ τέλος λέγομεν εἶναι τοῦ μακαρίως 3ῆν. Cf. Sext. Emp., *Adv. Math.* 11.96 (Us. 398) and Cic., *De Fin.* 1.30.

[2] D.L. 10.6 (Us. 67).   [3] D.L. 10.131-2.

pleasure is to be identified with the absence of pain is thus emphasized strongly.[1]

Basically this picture is correct, as we shall see, but those who have adopted it have not always found it easy to interpret the more outrageously 'sensualist' passages and have sometimes explained them away as over-exuberant polemic. In line with the view of Epicurus as a quietist we now frequently meet the assertion that the word 'pleasure' gives a misleading impression of Epicurus' ideal. With a certain degree of justice behind their claims, scholars wish to call Epicurus the teacher of joy or of *Freude*, rather than of pleasure.[2] But no word is entirely satisfactory, and when talking about the more obvious pleasures of food, drink and sex it would be misleading to use the word 'joy'; that might be to foist on Epicurus a too spiritualizing approach.[3] No word is entirely adequate. We must select an English term and recognize that Epicurus would give it a technical sense, not a sense immediately recognizable from ordinary speech. It seems the least confusing alternative to stick to the word 'pleasure' and see how Epicurus would interpret it.

On many questions in Epicurean thought modern scholarship has taught us to look back to Plato and to Aristotle, as well as to the earlier atomists, if we wish to understand the philosophical scene at a more than superficial level. In our examination of pleasure we shall find Epicurus using both Platonic and Aristotelian ideas while working out a position which is obviously neither Platonic nor Aristotelian. In the *Nicomachean Ethics*, and in particular in book seven, we see Aristotle suggesting *both* that pleasure is in a sense a single concept, of which a single definition can be given,[4] *and* that there are two kinds of pleasure: pleasure in rest (ἡδονὴ ἐν ἠρεμίᾳ) and pleasure in motion. Pleasure in rest is the higher form and enjoyed by god;[5] some at least of the

---

[1] See the classic formulation at Cic., *De Fin.* 1.11; cf. Plut., *Non posse* 1087D (ἡδονή/μὴ ἀλγηδών) and D.L. 10.137.

[2] Mewaldt, *Epikur: Philosophie der Freude*; Merlan, *Studies* 15.

[3] Merlan (*Studies* 18–19) defends *Freude* by reference to Schiller's ode, but the context of Epicurus' 'sensualist' utterance is hardly parallel to this.

[4] *NE* 1153a14–15.

[5] *NE* 1154b27. For the Aristotelian background to Epicurus' theory of pleasure see especially Merlan, *Studies* 7–10, 19–24.

pleasure we derive from change is due to the inadequacy (πονηρίαν τινά) of the human race.

There is little doubt that these distinctions of Aristotle form at least part of the background for the distinction between what Epicurus calls 'katastematic' pleasures and 'kinetic' pleasures or pleasures in movement (ἐν κινήσει, κατὰ κίνησιν).[1] Now it is obvious that for Epicurus, as an atomist, *all* pleasure must involve the movement of atoms, for atoms are constantly in motion. Thus even katastematic pleasure could not easily be defined as 'pleasure in rest' (ἐν ἠρεμίᾳ) in the Aristotelian manner. What Epicurus needed was a word which would describe not the rest of atoms during the experience of pleasure, but their steady, harmonious and orderly motion. The phrase 'light and gentle movement' used by Plutarch perhaps describes katastematic pleasure.[2] The phrase 'katastematic pleasure' itself must mean the pleasure deriving from a well-balanced and steady state of the moving atoms in a sensitive organ.[3] And perhaps kinetic pleasures are pleasures deriving from a steady, though limited and temporary, change in the state of those atoms. Epicurus' position is described by Diogenes Laertius as follows: there are two kinds of happiness (that is, of pleasure), the one enjoyed by god, which cannot be increased (ἐπίτασιν οὐκ ἔχουσαν)[4] and is the highest possible (τὴν ἀκροτάτην), the other which is associated with the addition and subtraction of pleasures. The passage is slightly misleading in that it might seem to suggest that the gods do not enjoy kinetic pleasures. That, as our discussion of the gods will show,[5] would be a faulty conclusion. But Diogenes' meaning can be discerned. The gods can enjoy an unvarying kind of pleasure which cannot be sur-

---

[1] The word καταστηματική is rare but used by Epicurus (D.L. 10.136). Our fragments do not contain the word κινητική. However we may conveniently follow modern scholars in referring to pleasures κατὰ κίνησιν as 'kinetic'. Cicero uses the word *movens* (cf. *De Fin.* 2.31).

[2] Plut., *Adv. Col.* 1122E (Us. 411).

[3] Cf. Plut., *Non posse* 1089D (Us. 68), εὐσταθὲς σαρκὸς κατάστημα. Cicero speaks of pleasure *in stabilitate*, *De Fin.* 2.16, but when he contrasts *voluptas stans* with *voluptas movens* he may mislead (*ibid.* 2.31). He might give the impression that a *voluptas stans* does not involve movement of atoms. This is impossible, but the movement must be regular, unvarying (*ibid.* 2.75). [4] D.L. 10.121. [5] See below pp. 154–6.

passed; but there are other pleasures, the greatness of which is not discussed, which come and go.

We have already noticed in Aristotle the distinction between 'pleasure in rest' and 'pleasure in motion' (or change). But it was not only Aristotle and Epicurus who discussed pleasure in these terms. The Cyrenaics, a hedonist group originating with Aristippus, one of the associates of Socrates, were apparently aware of the distinction, but rejected it.[1] For the Cyrenaics katastematic pleasures are not pleasures at all. Such so-called pleasures, they claim, are the experiences of a corpse.[2] Epicurus however is here nearer to Aristotle, as he is also when he regards pleasures of the mind as greater than those of the body. Naturally he recognizes both kinds as pleasures, and he holds that both mental and bodily pleasures can be either katastematic or kinetic. We should notice, however, that he uses the negative terms 'untroubledness' (ἀταραξία) and 'lack of hardship' (ἀπονία) for the katastematic pleasures of the mind and of the body respectively, while reserving the positive terms 'joy' (χαρά) and 'good spirits' (εὐφροσύνη) for the pleasures which are kinetic.[3] Although both these positive terms apply to kinetic pleasures of the mind, we know from countless other sources – as well as from the obviousness of the matter itself – that Epicurus did not neglect the kinetic pleasures of the body.

According to Epicurus the striving for pleasure is our first natural impulse, an impulse which we share with the animals. It is not an impulse which arises from anything we have been taught, but is part of our very nature as sentient living beings.[4] We must be careful, however, not to jump too readily to conclusions from this. When Epicurus makes remarks of this kind, he does not mean that a search for thrills, even of a moderate kind, is our first natural impulse. What he means is explained in one of the *Vatican Sayings*.[5] What the flesh cries out for is not

[1] D.L. 10.136.   [2] Clem. Alex., *Strom.* 2.21.
[3] There is a textual problem and a slight inconsistency in Diogenes' account of pleasure in 10.136, but the meaning is clear enough. For discussion of the text and other matters see Merlan, *Studies* 3–7.
[4] D.L. 10.137, εὐαρεστεῖσθαι (cf. Diano, *GCFI* (1941) 20, 27); Sext. Emp., *Hyp. Pyr.* 3.194, *Adv. Math.* 11.96; Cic., *De Fin.* 2.31, etc.
[5] *VS* 33.

to be hungry, not to be thirsty, not to be cold. For a man who has these things and expects to continue having them would rival Zeus for happiness. Viewed in the light of this saying, Epicurus' doctrine about first natural impulses is readily intelligible and can be seen to be empirically based. What the new-born child wants is the quietness and untroubledness produced by food and clothing; basically that is what all men want throughout their lives. We should notice that these are simple bodily wants; we are here introduced to the Epicurean thesis that in some sense all mental pleasures depend on and are to be referred to the pleasures of the body.

We are now at the point where we can consider one of Epicurus' most notorious sayings, which has come down to us from many ancient sources and has been much misunderstood. The beginning and root of every good is the pleasure of the stomach, says Epicurus. Wisdom and the refinements (τὰ περιττά) are referable to this.[1] The paradoxical nature of this claim is obvious, and its startling appearance was exaggerated by the Epicureans themselves for polemical reasons and to dramatize their differences with other schools. I was delighted, claims Metrodorus, when I learned from Epicurus about the proper way of gratifying the stomach;[2] and the infuriated Plutarch denounced the Epicurean school as people who describe a circle with the stomach as centre and radius, including in it the whole range of pleasure. But whether through being misled by the polemical character of the language used by the Epicureans, or through wilful misunderstanding of the Epicurean position, Plutarch and many other ancient critics suppose that, when talking in this way about the pleasures of the stomach, Epicurus is only thinking of kinetic pleasures, which they wrongly interpret as the transitory delights of eating and drinking. But, as Diano has shown,[3] this is not the case. Our passage about the pleasures of the stomach being the basis of the

[1] Athen., 12, 546F and see Us. 409. As will appear from the discussion, this text should be compared with D.L. 10.129 (we say that pleasure is the ἀρχή and τέλος of the blessed life).
[2] Ap. Plut., Non posse 1098D; cf. Metrodorus, frr. 39–42 Körte.
[3] See Diano, RAL 12 (1936) 850–2.

pleasure of wisdom and of other sophisticated pleasures is best
taken in conjunction with the theme that the cry of the soul is
not to be hungry and not to be thirsty. Thus when Metrodorus
says that Epicurus showed him the proper way of gratifying
the stomach, he means that Epicurus showed him what the
stomach needs, that is, not to be hungry. And when Epicurus
says that the beginning and root of all good is the pleasure of the
stomach, he means not that eating is fun, but that the beginning
and root of all good is not to be hungry and not to be thirsty.
When a man is not hungry and not thirsty and not cold he
enjoys freedom from the hardships of the body (ἀπονία). And, as
we shall see, if he enjoys and *is satisfied* with such freedom, and
if he has the right attitude to his desires, hopes and fears, he is
in the best position to secure the supreme pleasure of the mind
which the Epicureans call untroubledness (ἀταραξία). We can
recognize one of the senses in which the pleasures of the mind
are to be referred to the pleasures of the body.[1] Epicurus does
not mean that the mind cannot be happy unless the body is
free from pain; but mental pleasures depend on a right attitude
to bodily feelings.

According to Epicurus, the first natural impulse of children
and animals is to pleasure. Disagreeing with Plato and Aristotle,
who looked to the behaviour of adult human beings as an aid
to the formulation of what is naturally human, Epicurus preferred the presumably uncorrupted impulses of the very young.
But what kind of pleasure do the young strive for? If our view
that it is katastematic pleasure is right, Cicero, attempting to
refute Epicurus, misrepresents him grossly.[2] According to
Cicero it is only kinetic, not katastematic pleasure which is
naturally desired by children and animals. Now there is no
reason to think that Epicurus denied that children and animals
desire kinetic pleasure – in the case of children at least this may
be because opinion, often false opinion, is one of the motivating
factors in their behaviour – but all that he says is that the *first*
impulse, in both the temporal and the ontological sense, is to

[1] For this 'referral' see Cic., *De Fin.* 1.25, 55; Clem. Alex., *Strom.* 2.21, etc.
For the idea that the pleasure of the flesh is reported to the mind see Plut.,
Non posse 1087B.   [2] Cic., *De Fin.* 2.32–3.

pleasure; and by pleasure he means in the first instance the pleasure of not being hungry and not being thirsty. Cicero tries to establish that, although it is obvious that the Stoics are right in thinking that the first natural impulse is to self-preservation, Epicurus perversely held that it is not merely to pleasure, but to kinetic pleasure, or rather, as he polemically puts it, to thrills derived from sensation. Hence he claims that the Epicurean argument is in the following absurd form: since the natural impulses of children and animals are directed towards *kinetic* pleasure, therefore *katastematic* pleasure is the *summum bonum*. If Epicurus held that kinetic pleasure is the beginning and root of all good and the object of our basic desires, Cicero's polemic might have something to be said for it. But Epicurus nowhere presents such a view.

All the ancient sources agree that Epicurus identified unsurpassable pleasure, the fullness of pleasure, which he called a stable condition of the flesh and a confident expectation for the future on this score,[1] with a complete absence of pain and anxiety. Speaking of bodily pleasure in *Basic Doctrine* 9, he says that pleasure in the flesh is not increased but only varied (ποικίλλεται) when the pain of want is removed.[2] In other words, when the body is enjoying complete absence of pain, it is already enjoying the greatest pleasure. That does not mean that it cannot alternate its katastematic pleasure with the pleasure that is kinetic. However, in the course of such alternation, the 'amount' of pleasure is not increased; all that happens is that the senses are tickled or soothed.[3] What Epicurus means by saying that the amount of pleasure is not increased is made clearer by the scholiast to *Basic Doctrine* 29, who tells us that there exist natural but unnecessary desires which only vary pleasure and do not remove pain. The satisfaction of these desires can only involve kinetic pleasure. Thus we conclude that, even when such desires are satisfied in such a way as not to involve us in accompanying pain, the pleasure already available to us katastematically is not 'increased' because our

---

[1] Plut., *Non posse* 1089D.   [2] Cf. *varietas* (Cic., *De Fin.* 2.75).

[3] γαργαλισμός (Plut., *De Lat. Viv.* 1129B), *mulcet* (Lucr., 2.422), *permulcet* (Cic., *De Fin.* 2.31), *titillaret* (*De Fin.* 1.39). Cf. Diano, *SIFC* 12 (1935) 256.

pleasures have become kinetic. Clearly Epicurus employs the concept of the 'increase' of pleasure in an unusual way which needs elucidation. Diano has already shown us how to set about the job.[1]

There is no doubt that Plato as well as Aristotle has contributed to Epicurus' theory of pleasure. Diano has discussed the relationship of Epicurus' positions to those of the *Philebus* in detail, and we shall limit ourselves here to Plato's concept of a pure pleasure and to how that concept relates to Epicurus' idea of a katastematic pleasure. For Plato a pure pleasure is a pleasure unmixed with pain. The corporeal nature of the metaphor should be noticed; it is as though we were concerned with mixing wine with water. This should be borne in mind especially when we consider a curious passage from the *De Dis* of Philodemus,[2] in which there seems to be a comparison between (pure) pleasure and pure whiteness. The argument seems to be that if any *part* (μόριον) of an object is black, however small that part may be, then the whiteness of the whole object is 'defiled'. If the simile is pressed, Philodemus is saying that, if any part of something experiences 'less' pleasure, then the pleasure of the whole is diminished. The suggestion seems to be that the greatest pleasure is the pleasure of a sentient object none of whose parts feels any pain. This squares admirably with Epicurus' idea of the greatest pleasure. If absence of pain is complete, then in a quasi-Platonic sense the organism is experiencing pure pleasure,[3] the greatest pleasure, the fullness of pleasure. Hence no ensuing kinetic pleasures, which cannot take away pain since there is now no pain to take away, can do anything to 'increase' the pleasure we feel; they can only vary it. The role of the kinetic pleasures which supervene upon the 'greatest pleasures' is to supply variations on a theme. It follows that, if a whole human being, both body and mind, is enjoying complete katastematic pleasure – Epicurus calls this

[1] In his articles in *SIFC* (1935), *RAL* (1936), and to a lesser degree *GCFI* (1939–42).
[2] Philodemus, *De Dis* 3, Pap. 152, fr. 1, 19–25 Diels.
[3] The notion of a 'pure' pleasure occurs. We should notice the appearance of the word ἀκεραίους in *Basic Doctrine* 12.

fulfilment (πλήρωμα)[1] – his pleasure cannot be increased, and that in his case at least all kinetic pleasures are variations on the existing katastematic pleasures *and dependent on their prior existence*. In such a case we can easily see how the dependent kinetic pleasures contribute nothing to happiness, that is, to the absence of pain. The more fundamental problem is whether Epicurus thought that *all* kinetic pleasures contribute nothing to the absence of pain and whether they *all* depend on individual katastematic pleasures in those parts of the organism in which they occur.

Before examining this, however, we must return to a text we mentioned earlier, where Epicurus says that he cannot conceive the good apart from the obviously kinetic pleasures of taste, sex, hearing and sound. This text can now be explained precisely. Epicurus says that without these kinetic pleasures he cannot *conceive* what is good; it is assumed that he is thinking of such pleasures as existing without accompanying pains. Often, however, he points out that kinetic pleasures (like Platonic impure pleasures) frequently *are* accompanied by such pains. Thus we can say that, if kinetic pleasures are unaccompanied by pain they are obviously good, but that it is important to discover when they are so unaccompanied, and what the existence of such unaccompanied kinetic pleasures tells us about katastematic pleasures. Secondly we should notice that Epicurus is discussing a *concept* of the good, not enjoyment of the good. Clearly in our human life we are not always in possession of every possible katastematic pleasure of body and mind. If we were, we should be gods and should need nothing. But since we are not, we feel the lack of certain of the basic pleasures; and lack begets need and desire.[2] If we had no desire of a good, we should not form a concept of anything good. It would never occur to us to do so, unless perhaps we were aware of the *theoretical* possibility of losing what we were already enjoying. Since then we experience an actual lack (and the gods are aware of a possible lack) of katastematic pleasures, we feel desire for them as goods. And the process of obtaining what we desire

[1] For πλήρωμα see Diano, *SIFC* 12 (1935) 245 and the references given.
[2] D.L. 10.128 (Menoeceus).

will frequently involve kinetic pleasure. Thus if we are hungry and get food, we enjoy the kinetic pleasures which occur when we eat. It is natural then that we should be very conscious that kinetic pleasures are in fact pleasurable; it is more immediately obvious that they are pleasurable than that katastematic pleasures are pleasurable. Hence when we begin to form a *concept* of pleasure, it is natural that the first pleasures which spring to our minds are kinetic pleasures. This may be all that Epicurus meant – apart from the polemical value to be attached to putting things in an offensive way – when he said that he could not conceive of the good apart from the (kinetic) pleasures of the senses. If these things are not pleasures, what is?

The subsidiary role of kinetic pleasure

It is certain that for Epicurus the greatest pleasure is a complete absence of pain, both from the body and from the mind. The existence of such a pleasure, if the Epicurean view is explained in terms of their atomic theory, means that the person enjoying it experiences no rough movements among the atoms composing his organs of sensation and mental perception. He will be like a calm sea with no disturbing breezes.[1] But what is the position of all actual human beings, none of whom regularly enjoys such absolute tranquillity? What is the relationship in us between kinetic and katastematic pleasures? What are we to make of the thesis that even in us ordinary mortals the existence of kinetic pleasures *always* presupposes the prior existence of katastematic pleasures in the same organs? As has frequently been observed,[2] the strongest text in favour of this thesis is from Lucretius. It runs as follows:[3]

> Deinde voluptas est e suco fine palati;
> cum vero deorsum per fauces praecipitavit,
> nulla voluptas est, dum diditur omnis in artus.

[1] For γαληνίζειν see Plut., *Non posse* 1088ε; D.L. 10.83 (Herodotus). Cf. Cic., *Tusc.*, 5.16. The opposite of γαλήνη is the storms and gusts of passion (Plut., *Non posse* 1090β and generally Us. 413).
[2] Merlan, *Studies* 12.
[3] Lucr., 4.627–9; cf. Diano, *SIFC* 12 (1935) 260 and *RAL* (1936) 852.

Diano interprets this to mean that, when we eat, our palate, which is already in a state of katastematic pleasure since it experiences no pain, comes to feel the kinetic pleasure of eating. Later, when the food has passed through the mouth into the body, this kinetic pleasure ceases; then the various parts of the body are restored by the food and katastematic pleasure accompanies the restoration. This interpretation is a little difficult, but it is hard to see what else Lucretius could mean. He specifically says that after the food has left the mouth there is no pleasure, and since he has been talking about the kinetic pleasure of taste, it is natural to assume that he means no kinetic pleasure.

It has been argued that this text of Lucretius is the only evidence which favours the theory that all kinetic pleasure supervenes on katastematic pleasure, but this is imprecise. It may be true that it is the only evidence which favours it *directly*, but indirect support from elsewhere is strong.[1] Diano has drawn attention to one of the *Basic Doctrines* which states that, whenever something which brings pleasure is present (obviously to a sensitive organ), then there can be no pain simultaneously present to that organ.[2] Or, as Olympiodorus put it, pleasure is not mixed with pain.[3] We know that Epicurus held that all sensation is felt in the organs of sense themselves, and that the mind (ἡγεμονικόν or *animus*) is without sensation (ἀπαθές).[4] This, when viewed in the light of the texts from Lucretius and Olympiodorus, means that, when we enjoy a taste, the particular group of atoms in the mouth which enjoys it is completely free from pain, that is, in a state similar to that of katastematic pleasure. Similarly when Epicurus said on his last day that, although his bodily pains were now intense, yet he was still enjoying happiness, he must have meant, in terms of the atomic theory, that, although he was suffering in some of his bodily structures, yet the atomic compounds in his mind and in the rest of his body, the vast majority, that is, of his atomic struc-

[1] The problem is discussed further in Appendix D.
[2] Diano, *RAL* (1936) 834, *SIFC* 12 (1935) 266. See *Basic Doctrine* 3.
[3] Olymp., *In Plat. Phil.*, p. 225 Stallbaum (Us. 421).
[4] Aët., 4.23.2 (Us. 317).

tures, were free from pain and thus enjoying the supreme happiness.[1] The same explanation accounts for the Epicurean paradox that the wise man is happy on the rack. Insufficient attention has been paid to the fact that, although the wise man is said to be happy on the rack, it is also Epicurus' opinion that he will groan and lament under the torture.[2] The two statements can be fitted together only if we realize that the happiness of the wise man is the happiness of the largest groups of his bodily and especially of his mental constituents, while the pain is experienced in atomic structures composed of smaller numbers of atoms.

The limit of pleasure

Epicurus maintained that all pleasures and all pains have clearly defined limits. The 'flesh' is liable to produce the false opinion that its pleasures are unlimited in intensity and in duration, but the trained mind knows that such an opinion is false.[3] It is not the stomach that is insatiable, says Epicurus, but there is a false opinion that the stomach needs unlimited filling.[4] And just as pleasures have their fixed limits, so also do pains. All bodily suffering can be despised, argues Epicurus, for if it is acute (that is, if it affects a large number of atoms) it cannot last long without being followed by the relief of death. On the other hand, if it is of longer duration, it can be borne without much difficulty, since it must therefore be comparatively mild.[5] In the case of such long-lasting illnesses and pains the amount of pleasure is always greater than the amount of pain,[6] that is, more components of the body are enjoying pleasure than are feeling pain.

In a passage of the *Tusculan Disputations* Cicero spells out the basis of Epicurus' theory that pleasure and pain do not mix and that, since the organs are the parts which experience the actual pleasure and pain, then in any living creature which thinks rightly there is always a predominance of pleasure.[7] The pain of Philoctetes, runs the argument, is certainly great (*plane*

[1] D.L. 10.22.   [2] D.L. 10.118.   [3] *BD* 20 (D.L. 10.145).
[4] *VS* 59.   [5] *VS* 4; cf. D.L. 10.133 (Menoeceus).
[6] *BD* 4.   [7] Cic., *Tusc.* 2.44; cf. Diano, *RAL* (1936) 862–3.

magnus) but it is not the greatest possible (*summus*). The only
thing that pains him is his foot; his eyes, his head, his lungs and
the rest of his body are in a proper state of good health. Therefore every day he experiences more pleasure than pain. The
discussion continues in terms of a pain 'greater by ten atoms'.
It is clear that each sentient component of a living being feels
either pleasure or pain, but not both at once.

According to Diano, when the Epicureans talk about the
intensity of pleasure or pain they mean the amount (or area)
of pleasure or pain, for we know that they held that pleasure
and pain are to be measured not by quality but by quantity.[1]
This was thought to follow from the fact that both feelings are
homogeneous *qua* feelings, that is, that they are simply the
absence or presence of pain in a particular sensitive organ or
group of organs. Thus it is only legitimate to use the word
'intensity' about feelings if we recognize that it refers to the
number of atoms involved. Diano sometimes even gives the
impression that he wants to ban the use of the word altogether,
but this is an unhelpful resolution of the semantic difficulties.
If we are to be forbidden to use words like 'intensity', we cannot
explain to a man what he means when he says 'My pain
increased' or 'A is in greater pain than B'. As we have seen,
we have to *interpret* these remarks in the sense that more atoms
have come to be involved in the pain of an organ, but there is
no reason why, when a greater number of sensitive parts of the
body feel pain, we should not be able to *say* that the person's
pain increased or even became more intense. Epicurus' theory
is designed to *explain* the physical experiences of our bodies
when we feel more pain (or more pleasure), and thus what we

[1] Eus., *PE* 14.21.3 (Us. 442). Mras' text (*GCS* 43²) reads μετρεῖσθαι γὰρ
αὐτὰ τῷ ποσῷ, εἰ καὶ οὐ τῷ ποιῷ. If this text did not refer to pleasure as well
as to pain, we might be tempted into supposing that, since pleasure is
associated with the order of atoms and pain with their disorder, then
pleasure could not be measured by degrees (but only by area), while pain
could. For, it might be argued, disorder *does* admit of degrees. But this
text shows that Epicurus thought that, while disorder itself admits of
degrees, the *degree* of disorderly motion of a particular atom does not
increase our feeling of pain. What matters is not how disorderly each atom
is, but how many atoms are disorderly.

mean when we say that pains or pleasures are more or less intense.

A passage of Diogenes of Oenoanda has been said to indicate that Epicurus had a more ordinary notion of the intensity of pleasures and pains.[1] Diogenes asserts that despite the widely recognized difficulties of evaluating our feelings, the pleasures and pains of the mind must be recognized as greater than the pleasures and pains of the body. Epicurus could not have held this view, it has been claimed, if he did not have some common-sense concept of intensity. Now it is certainly true that, when Diogenes of Oenoanda speaks of the greater pleasures and pains of the mind, he *could* be referring to a commonsense notion of intensity, but there is no reason to suppose that he was. Bodily feelings are localized and limited in time; mental feelings involve long-lasting memories and anticipations of comparatively brief bodily pleasures and pains, and thus, despite the thin distribution of soul atoms throughout the body, often involve a large number of atoms. Nor should we forget that soul and mind atoms, especially those of the unnamed variety, being smaller and finer, are more readily set in motion and can thus spread disturbances more easily throughout the personality. Anyone who feels great mental pleasure is on the way to becoming a sage, and thus can prevent whatever bodily pains he may have from assuming undue proportions in his mind. Anyone who is not a sage is liable to feel mental pain or worry, and people in that condition will not be able to control their reactions to purely physical events bringing purely physical pain. To take a concrete example: the stupid man who breaks his leg may, as we say, worry himself sick about it, thus demonstrating that the state of the mind can determine the state of the body, and that therefore mental pleasures and pains are in a sense both more severe in themselves and more serious in their effects. Through the soul-atoms scattered among all the sensitive areas of the body, they can induce a greater or less *amount* of pain throughout the whole person. Indeed in a sense mental pleasures and pains involve the whole person necessarily

[1] Steckel, *Epikurs Prinzip* 157–8; Diog. Oen., fr. 38, cols. 1–2 Chilton. Cf. Cic., *De Fin.* 1.55–6.

in a way that physical ones need not. Thus they necessarily (though indirectly) involve more atoms. So while it is right to recognize the importance of the passage of Diogenes of Oenoanda, we may conclude that it does not contradict our thesis. Even in Diogenes intensity of pleasure and pain need only equal the number of atoms involved in the pleasure and pain plus the duration of their movement. Each sense-bearing minimum feels either pleasure or pain, and in each individual there must be only a limited number of such minima. Hence, contrary to the view of Plato, there will be both maximum and minimum limits of both pleasure and pain.[1]

Condensing pleasure

According to *Basic Doctrine* 9, if every pleasure were 'condensed' (κατεπυκνοῦτο) and occurred throughout the whole organism or at least its most important parts, pleasures would never differ from one another.[2] Diano has assembled the scanty evidence from other sources about 'condensing',[3] and though scanty this fits together reasonably well. In the comic poet Damoxenus we read that Epicurus condensed pleasure in this way: he chewed carefully ('Επίκουρος οὕτω κατεπύκνου τὴν ἡδονήν, ἐμασᾶτ' ἐπιμελῶς).[4] The notion of condensing is further illumined by Alciphron who described the Epicurean Xenocrates as sitting on a bench embracing a dancing girl and looking at her lasciviously. According to Alciphron's Xenocrates this is the attainment of freedom from fleshly troubles and the

---

[1] Cf. *VS* 59; *BD* 18–21; *Pap. Herc.* 1251, col. 4 (Schmid). For the concept of limit in general see De Lacy, 'Limit and Variation', 104–13.

[2] There are serious textual difficulties about this Doctrine; Epicurus also added something about the time in which the 'condensed' pleasure should occur. A satisfactory explanation of this section of the evidence is not available and I have attempted to explain the text as far as possible without it. Diano's text (in *Epicuri Ethica*), Εἰ κατεπυκνοῦτο πᾶσα ἡδονὴ τ⟨όπ⟩ῳ καὶ χρόνῳ, is arbitrary. Others read τ⟨όν⟩ῳ, for which there is little justification. Perhaps τ⟨ῷ αὐτ⟩ῷ χρόνῳ is a possibility; it would certainly make sense for Epicurus to talk about amounts of pleasure *at the same time* being indistinguishable. For if some lasted longer they would be 'greater'.

[3] Diano, *SIFC* 12 (1935) 245 ff.   [4] Damoxenus, fr. 2 Kock.

condensed version of what is pleasing (τὸ τῆς σαρκὸς ἀόχλητον καὶ τὴν καταπύκνωσιν τοῦ ἡδομένου).[1] From these two passages a number of conclusions can be drawn.

First of all it is certain that 'condensing' implies squeezing out the maximum of pleasure, getting the highest possible amount of pleasure. From the examples provided by Alciphron and Damoxenus, we might form the impression that the Epicureans were excessively concerned to squeeze out every drop of *kinetic* pleasure, in these cases that of taste and sexual delight. But Alciphron makes the situation clear when he associates the condensing of pleasure with untroubledness of the flesh. For an Epicurean such untroubledness must mean a complete absence of pain. Hence the real condensing will be the attainment of a painless state of body and mind akin to and dependent on katastematic pleasure.

If we now return to *Basic Doctrine* 9 on 'condensing' pleasures, we can see what Epicurus means. He says that, if all pleasures are condensed, that is, maximized and spread over the whole organism, then pleasures will not differ from one another. This means that in terms of quality there is no difference between the katastematic pleasure of touch and the katastematic pleasure of taste or sight. *Qua* pleasure they are equally pleasurable, in so far as they all equally consist in an absence of pain. Hence it follows that, if they could all affect all parts of the body, they would be indistinguishable one from another. An extension of this doctrine in the moral sphere is provided by *Basic Doctrine* 8, where we read that no pleasure is bad *per se*. *Qua* pleasures all pleasures are equal. Kinetic pleasures are all variations on katastematic pleasures, and these katastematic pleasures are all equal *qua* pleasure. Hence the variations will all be equal in the moral and in any other sense, though we must always remember – and here Epicurus introduces his important note of caution – that when they are accompanied by pains they should be avoided.

[1] Alciphron, *Ep.* 3.55.8 ff. (Us. 442).

115

The selection of pleasures

In the letter to Menoeceus Epicurus says that, although we recognize that pleasure is the 'first good' and 'native' to us (σύμφυτον, συγγενικόν) – that is why it governs what we choose and what we reject – nevertheless we do not choose every available pleasure; indeed we pass over many pleasures because they cannot be enjoyed without concomitant unpleasantnesses.[1] Sometimes indeed we even choose particular hardships rather than more obvious pleasures, because we realize that by doing so our pleasure in the long run will be greater, that is, it will affect a greater number of our bodily constituents.[2] We will recognize that the particular pleasures which are associated or are likely to be associated with pains are most frequently the kinetic pleasures of the body. If such pleasures can be enjoyed without their accompanying pains, they may be chosen by the wise man, but often they cannot be.[3] Thus Epicurus will say to the young man troubled by sexual desires:[4] I understand that the movement of the flesh makes you too prone to sex. If you do not break the laws or good customs and do not upset any of your neighbours or waste your body or spend much-needed money, then gratify your inclinations as you wish. But, he adds, it is impossible for all these conditions to be fulfilled, and concludes that sexual relations never did anyone any good – that is, they are not necessary for the achievement of absence of pain – and a man is lucky if they do not do him any harm. The same attitude occurs elsewhere, as we shall see later, in connection with injustice.[5] Injustice, says Epicurus, is no bad thing in itself. If an Epicurean could be certain of avoiding detection, he would act illegally.[6] Unfortunately this

[1] D.L. 10.129 (Menoeceus).
[2] Aristocles, *ap.* Eusebius, *PE* 14.21.3 (Us. 442).
[3] Cf. *Basic Doctrine* 10, where Epicurus argues that he would not blame the pleasures of profligates if they could dispel fear and show us the limits of pleasure.   [4] *VS* 51; cf. Us. 62.
[5] *BD* 34. On the relative character of justice see now Müller, 'Sur le concept de Physis', 314–16, with especial reference to Polystratus, Περὶ ἀλόγου καταφρονήσεως, cols. 12 and 18 Wilke.
[6] Plut., *Adv. Col.* 1127D (Us. 134).

is not possible, though the fact that it is not possible should not disturb us.

What the wise man has to decide, therefore, is which pleasure can be safely gratified and indeed must be gratified if a degree of happiness is to be attained. Pleasures, as we have seen, are measured quantitatively, by the number of sentient constituents involved. Some are so slight that they escape notice altogether – Epicurus seems to have discussed this in some detail[1] – and obviously no one would go out of his way to secure them. There are many others, however, which present themselves to us as possibilities and we need to know how to evaluate them. Epicurus provides us with a criterion. We must also consider, he holds, what the consequences will be if we give rein to a desire for a particular pleasure. We must ask ourselves what we shall experience in each particular case both if we gratify a desire and if we do not.[2] Such questioning will lead us to a threefold classification of our desires. All desires, Epicurus finds, thus following a Platonic tradition, are either natural and necessary, natural and unnecessary, or unnatural and un-necessary.[3] Of necessary desires some are concerned with happiness, some with bodily untroubledness, others with life itself.[4] As the scholiast to *Basic Doctrine* 9 suggests, it is the fulfilment of natural and necessary desires which takes away pain, thus, of course, producing pleasure. We recall the cry of the flesh not to be hungry, not to be thirsty, not to be cold. It is natural for the flesh to cry in this way and dangerous for the soul to ignore it.[5]

Natural but unnecessary pleasures are those which, when tested, are found to be unnecessary in the sense that we are mistaken if we think our nature *demands* that they be fulfilled. Such fulfilment can only 'vary' pleasure, thus providing kinetic pleasure; it cannot take away pain. Sexual pleasure in particular would fall into this class. To think it is necessary is to be

---

[1] Cf. Cic., *De Fin.* 4.29 and see Us. 441 for Galen's work Περὶ τῆς κατ' Ἐπίκουρον ἀμαυροῦ ἡδονῆς.   [2] *VS* 71.
[3] *BD* 29 and its scholion; cf. Pap. Herc. 1251, col. 5–6 (Schmid) and Us. 456.
[4] D.L. 10.127 (Menoeceus).
[5] Us. 200. On the desirability of satisfying necessary desires see *VS* 21.

deluded by the intrusion of a vain opinion.[1] The same can be said about rich foods, the example chosen by the scholiast. Obviously food is necessary, but rich food only varies the pleasure.[2] It is important for the attainment of happiness to be able to reject such pleasures without discomfort. As Epicurus puts it in his characteristically rather violent manner: 'I am delighted with pleasure in the body when I live on bread and water, and I spit on luxurious pleasures (ταῖς ἐκ πολυτελείας ἡδοναῖς), not in themselves but because of the disagreeable things which accompany them.'[3] It is true that here Epicurus is probably extending his concept of luxurious pleasures beyond those which might be called natural (even though unnecessary), but essentially the point is the same. If we can do without a pleasure or leave a desire unsatisfied without suffering any ill effects, it is frequently best to do so. The Epicureans regularly held feasts on the twentieth day of the month,[4] feasts at which undoubtedly they indulged in a little unnecessary luxury, but normally such luxury should be avoided. If we are lucky, it provides not only katastematic, that is, essential pleasure, but also a greater amount of pleasure that is kinetic. If we eat cake, we get more kinetic pleasure than if we eat bread. If we are unlucky, however, luxury may be painful. Epicurus consistently advocated 'the simple life': not too much money, not too much

[1] On the intrusion of opinion see D.L. 10.132 (Menoeceus); *BD* 15, 30; *VS* 59; etc. For the idea that unnecessary desires of the mind which do not arise from bodily needs arise from opinion see Diano, *GCFI* (1940) 161. Diano interestingly compares Epicurus and the Stoics on the view that emotions follow judgments.

[2] For πολυτέλεια and its association with variation cf. *VS* 69, D.L. 10. 130 (Menoeceus) and Us. 181. Bailey (*Greek Atomists* 493), following the scholiast of *NE* 1118b8 (Us. 456), puts the desire for particular food into the class of unnecessary and unnatural desires. If this is right, the scholiast of *BD* 29 has made a mistake. There may have been some distinction, however, between different types of πολυτελῆ. Thus variations on natural needs (such as rich foods) are still natural and should be distinguished from totally unnatural needs such as those for 'status'. See Diano, *SIFC* 12 (1935) 258.

[3] Us. 181. Epicurus usually regards wealth as unsettling and dangerous; cf. *VS* 25.

[4] D.L. 10.18; Plut., *Non posse* 1089c; Cic., *De Fin.* 2.101; Pliny, *NH* 35.5.

good food. To be able to be satisfied with little is the freedom of self-sufficiency.[1]

Finally we come to the examples of pleasures which are neither necessary nor even natural, such as, to use the example given by the scholiast of *Basic Doctrine* 29, crowns and the setting up of statues in one's honour. All such vain pomp can only bring trouble. There is no possibility that indulgence in such pleasures will not involve serious risks of accompanying trouble and usually accompanying trouble in fact. The example of crowns and statues is doubtless chosen with reference to political life – and for the Epicurean such a life is too dangerous, too exposed, to be worth while. The class of unnecessary and unnatural pleasures is composed of 'outside luxuries', that is, luxuries quite irrelevant to basic personal survival. Luxurious food is at least food, and food is necessary, but crowns and statues are not basic. A papyrus adds several other things to our list of such inessentials: beauty, riches, marriage.[2]

It is therefore the aim of the wise man so to control his desires that he demands only katastematic pleasures of both mind and body. If he is able to secure a state in which he is free from pain and has a reasonable expectation that he will continue to enjoy such freedom, he is in a state of perfect happiness. The realization that because of man's mortality such happiness itself is limited in that sensation and hence all pleasure ends at death is not disturbing. Indeed so far from being disturbing it is a source of satisfaction. After death we can be completely confident that there is nothing to fear. Death, says *Basic Doctrine* 2, is nothing to us. For what has been dissolved has no sensation, and what has no sensation is nothing to us. Indeed the fear of death being removed, we can enjoy the fullness of pleasure, the highest happiness, in the instant. The man who is able to work the thing out properly and do the proper calculation of the amount of pleasure involved, will grasp that the same pleasure, that is, absence of pain, can be achieved in the instant as in an indefinitely long stretch of time.[3]

[1] *VS* 77; cf. *VS* 68, 69. But frugality too has a limit, *VS* 63.
[2] Pap. Herc. 1251, col. 15 (Schmid). On beauty cf. Lucr., 4.1190.
[3] *BD* 19.

PLEASURE

Nevertheless the mental pleasure of the instant is not complete without the reasonable expectation that at least no great evil will befall us in the future. We recall *Vatican Saying* 33 once more: the flesh cries out not to be hungry, not to be thirsty, not to be cold. Anyone who enjoys these things and expects that he will enjoy them would rival Zeus in happiness. In Cicero's version of the theme we hear that the happy man does not depend on what is to come for his happiness; but he is confident on that score.[1] Metrodorus talks about 'good expectation on the score of the continuation of the (katastematic) pleasure of the stomach'.[2] Finally we may turn to what is perhaps the best known of all Epicurus' descriptions of the happy life. As reported by Plutarch, it runs as follows:[3] the stable condition of the flesh and the confident expectation of its continuance contains the supreme and most certain joy for men who can work out the truth (τὸ γὰρ εὐσταθὲς σαρκὸς κατάστημα καὶ τὸ περὶ ταύτης πιστὸν ἔλπισμα τὴν ἀκροτάτην χαρὰν καὶ βεβαιοτάτην ἔχειν τοῖς ἐπιλογίζεσθαι δυναμένοις).[4] The word 'confident' (πιστόν) is important; if the Epicurean lacked a strong faith in the future, he could not be free from mental pains.

In many of the texts which refer to the expectation of pleasure to come, we also find emphasis on the importance of pleasures completed. In the *Tusculans* Cicero emphasizes the memory of pleasures previously experienced,[5] and Plutarch tells us that the Epicureans held that the memory of past goods is a very great factor contributing to a pleasant life.[6] Naturally such pleasures, like the pleasures deriving from a confident expectation of future goods, are pleasures of the mind; but they are, as we have seen, only the greater for that. Epicurus' own death-scene provides evidence of the importance of the role they can play, for with their aid the wise man can experience great happiness even at a time of great physical pain. Writing to Idomeneus,[7] Epicurus can say that he is happy. Although he is suffering greatly in his

---

[1] Cic., *De Fin.* 1.62. Cf. 1.57., *Tusc. Disp.* 3.33; 5.95, and other references given by Diano, *GCFI* (1942) 128–30 and *RAL* (1936) 851.
[2] Fr. 7 Körte (Plut., *Non posse* 1087D). [3] Plut., *Non posse* 1089D (Us. 68).
[4] Cf. also *VS* 39 and 34. [5] *Tusc. Disp.* 5.95.
[6] Plut., *Non posse* 1099D; cf. D.L. 10.122. [7] D.L. 10.22.

bladder and his stomach, he is able to set against these localized pains – localized, that is, in that they occur in a limited number of atoms in a specific part of the body – the memory of past philosophical conversations. Such memories make the soul rejoice and are thus, as Plutarch tells us the Epicureans held, a great factor contributing to the happiness of Epicurus himself.

The happiness which is a complete absence of pain from both body and mind is the happiness of the gods; men enjoy it in so far as they are able. They are able to progress far towards achieving their happiness, as we have seen, if they follow nature and the aid nature gives them, and do not let themselves be deluded by false judgments and opinions. Nature tells us that we are made in such a way that we do in fact pursue pleasure – katastematic pleasure – and eschew pain. There has been some discussion as to whether Epicurus means that we do in fact pursue pleasure or that we ought to pursue pleasure. For Epicurus the distinction would be almost meaningless. Apart from our nature, and what we naturally do, that is, what our first impulses are directed towards, we have no kind of moral obligation.[1] If the word 'ought' means anything precise for Epicurus in the proposition 'We ought to pursue pleasure' – and he does not seem to avoid 'ought'-forms of Greek words in this sort of context – it must mean 'is natural'. Thus 'we ought to pursue pleasure' would be exactly equivalent to 'we pursue pleasure naturally'.

As we have seen, it is katastematic pleasure with which the wise are primarily concerned. There has been an implicit, if not always explicit, disagreement as to the best way of translating the term 'katastematic'.[2] Some scholars have preferred 'static' or some equivalent of this; others have preferred 'constitutional'. In this chapter we have in general kept to the word 'katastematic', but it is to be hoped that the meaning we outlined for it has been maintained consistently. Although it is true that katastematic pleasures are static, in that they only involve the orderly motion of atoms, emphasis on their being static could be misleading. Indeed since katastematic pleasures may be very brief, it is necessary to recognize something more specifically

[1] Cf. Bailey, *Greek Atomists* 486.   [2] Merlan, *Studies* 4.

informative about them. It is helpful to relate 'static' (καταστηματικός) to 'state' (κατάστημα): the most important thing about katastematic pleasures is that they are, to adopt an Aristotelian definition, unimpeded pleasures of the natural state; unimpeded, that is, by the intrusion of anything painful. Since then katastematic pleasures are natural conditions of sentient beings, a word like 'constitutional' perhaps expresses the meaning of 'katastematic' in the least unsatisfactory way. Yet it must be emphasized that, although this word may be the most suitable we have, it is not an exact equivalent. Diogenes of Oenoanda distinguishes what is pleasant in 'states' (ἐν τοῖς καταστήμασι) from what is pleasant in actions (ἐν ταῖς πράξεσιν).[1] Katastematic pleasures exist in natural states of a 'healthy' organism as such; kinetic pleasures arise during certain activities of that organism.

The role of pleasure in ethics

It only remains to describe the impact of Epicurus' theory of pleasure as the 'end' on various traditional themes of Greek ethics: the importance of politics, the nature of justice, and the importance of the virtues in general. The relation of pleasure to friendship, a subject of great importance for the Epicureans, is best left for separate consideration.

Epicurus' attitude to justice, politics and wisdom should be already apparent. If the end is pleasure, and pleasure is to be understood in the first instance as absence of bodily pain and mental affliction, then politics is obviously condemned. 'Live unknown' is Epicurus' maxim – an exhortation to remain in private life which could still evoke a denunciatory treatise from Plutarch.[2] Epicurus will admit that the glory which is the aim of public life is pleasurable,[3] but the risks are great and the dangers unavoidable.[4] It is not wealth or importance or public office which makes a man happy; rather it is freedom from pain,

---

[1] Diog. Oen., fr. 28, col. 6 Chilton.
[2] For breaches of the rule against political action in Rome, above all in the case of Cassius, see Momigliano, *JRS* 31 (1941) 151–7.
[3] Plut., *Non posse* 1100A; cf. Us. 550.
[4] For further references to Λάθε βιώσας, Us. 551–60.

moderation in one's feelings and a capacity to distinguish what is natural.[1] What we need above all is safety, and in social life this means primarily safety from our fellow men;[2] retirement and a quiet life are the best means of achieving this. There are those who think that, if they become famous, they will achieve safety. Possibly they may succeed, but if they fail to attain safety, they have achieved nothing good whatever, for they have failed to secure what is natural.[3] Indeed elsewhere it seems that all public office is worthless almost by definition,[4] for any official is liable to inspire fear at some stage in his career. And yet Epicurus says that a man who inspires fear cannot be free of it himself.[5] Finally public life is competitive, and competitive behaviour is not necessary to obtain katastematic pleasure.[6]

So much then for politics, and the Platonic and Aristotelian conception of the necessity of public life goes by the board. Justice is the virtue above all to be associated with public life. We should therefore expect to find it reduced to comparative unimportance. In fact, like all the virtues, it is rigorously subordinated to pleasure. The aim of justice is to establish the maximum of security and untroubledness (ἀταραξία).[7] As far as the wise are concerned, says Epicurus, the laws exist, not that they may not be unjust, but that they may not suffer injustice.[8] As we have already observed, although Epicurus admits that the matter is problematical,[9] the wise man is prepared to act unjustly if there is no risk of detection; but he can never have certainty of that.[10] Hence he will act justly, for as *Basic Doctrine* 17 tells us, the just man is the most undisturbed, the unjust is full of great trouble.

What then do we mean when we talk about justice? Clearly we do not mean that the gods have a standard of justice or are concerned to punish those who transgress that standard, for the gods are not concerned with human affairs. Epicurus likes to

[1] Plut., *De Aud. Poet.* 37A.
[2] *BD* 14. For safety from our passions see *VS* 80.   [3] Cf. *BD* 7.
[4] Us. 554; cf. Plut., *Vita Pyrrhi* 20 (Us. 552); Lucr., 5.1127.   [5] Us. 537.
[6] *BD* 21.   [7] Clem. Alex., *Strom.* 6.2 (Us. 519).
[8] Us. 530. I prefer to translate χάριν τῶν σοφῶν as 'as far as the wise are concerned' rather than as 'for the sake of the wise'; cf. *VS* 31.
[9] Plut., *Adv. Col.* 1127D (cf. Us. 18).   [10] *VS* 7; cf. *VS* 70 and *BD* 34–5.

talk about that which is just and arises from nature,[1] that is, an idea of justice which we can arrive at by a consideration of how best to achieve our advantage, namely untroubledness. The naturalness of this concept is emphasized by the fact that Epicurus is willing to call it a general concept (πρόληψις),[2] that is, a concept based on sensation which has not been defiled by the intrusion of false opinion. What then is the context of this concept? It is that we properly use the word 'justice' to mean a pledge of mutual advantage between men by which they agree not to harm one another so that they may not be harmed themselves.[3] Thus justice is no kind of transcendent norm – the Platonic view is specifically rejected[4] – and we can only use the words 'just' and 'unjust' correctly where such contracts for mutual advantage have been made. Justice therefore is rigidly subordinate to the claims of personal security. If such security could be attained without it, it would have no meaning at all. Society is an empty concept; each man is concerned with himself.[5]

Justice, as we have said, is the principal political virtue, and Epicurus' treatment of it is a paradigm case of his treatment of virtue in general. 'I spit on the beautiful' (τὸ καλόν), he remarks – and 'the beautiful' has far more than an aesthetic sense, being more or less the equivalent of our term 'goodness' – 'I spit on the beautiful and those who pointlessly respect it when it produces no pleasure.'[6] And he tells Anaxarchus that he summons him to continuous pleasures, not to vain and empty virtues which are sure to involve us in disturbing expectations.[7] Thus although virtue is inseparable from pleasure and necessary if we are to be happy,[8] it is to be chosen not for its own sake but for the sake of pleasure. Beauty (τὸ καλόν) and the virtues and the like are to be honoured if they provide pleasure, but, if they do not, we must say goodbye to them.[9] And as Diogenes of Oenoanda put it, virtue is not an end but a means to an end.[10]

[1] *BD* 31. [2] *BD* 38. [3] *BD* 31, 32, 36.
[4] *BD* 33. [5] Lact., *Div. Inst.* 3.7.42 (Us. 523).
[6] Athen., 12, 547A; cf. generally Us. 511–12. [7] Plut., *Adv. Col.* 1117A.
[8] D.L. 10.132 (Menoeceus) and 138; *BD* 5; Pap. Herc. 1251, col. 14 (Schmid).
[9] Athen., 12, 546F (Us. 70).
[10] Diog. Oen., fr. 26, col. 3 Chilton. For moderation see Cic., *De Fin.* 1.47.

Since the virtues are thus wholly subordinated to pleasure as their standard (κανών),[1] and are in fact means to the obtaining of a natural and pleasurable state of life, we have further evidence that strictly speaking there is no concept of moral obligation or of moral evil in Epicureanism. Thus when we find it stated in Epicurean texts that the school did not regard all sins as equally serious,[2] we must not be misled into thinking that a sin or crime is anything other than an offence against the contract on which men have pinned their mutual hopes for security. This search for security provides the only kind of obligation a man may be said to have, and it is an obligation not of the moral law but of physiology. Bailey has restated the old view that Epicureanism is a system of uncompromising egoistic hedonism.[3] There is much truth in this, though we must reserve judgment on whether the egoism is complete until we have investigated the complex problem of friendship. But to say that Epicureanism is a hedonism can also be misleading. Strictly speaking, of course, it is true: the end is pleasure. But the highest pleasure is absence of pain, which, if continuous, is the katastematic pleasure of mind and body. Cicero several times draws our attention to the Peripatetic Hieronymus of Rhodes,[4] who to some extent provides a physical link between Epicurus and Aristotle. Hieronymus held that the end is freedom from pain, and Cicero, failing to grasp the more sophisticated position of Epicurus, complains that Epicurus himself ought to have talked exclusively in the same way as Hieronymus. But Epicurus has taken a further step. Freedom from pain *is* pleasure – and thus Epicurus becomes a hedonist, as Bailey points out. But it is an unusual kind of hedonism, and it could be as misleading to call him a hedonist *tout court* as it would be to say that he was a disciple of Hieronymus, because he believed that freedom from pain is the end. A variety of hedonism, a form of the theory that the end is pleasure, is an appropriate description of Epicurean ethics; but the distinguishing feature is that pleasure equals freedom from pain combined with safety,

---

[1] Cf. D.L. 10.129 (Menoeceus); Cic., *In Pis.* 68 etc.
[2] D.L. 10.120.
[3] Bailey, *Greek Atomists* 526.　　　　[4] *De Fin.* 2.8 and 16 etc.

whether from fear of the gods or of death or of any other mortal affliction, or from the purely 'fleshly' inconveniences of life. For if Epicurus is a typical hedonist, what are we to make of Aristippus, the man who believed only in his own variety of kinetic pleasure and had no confidence in the basically Aristotelian concept developed by Epicurus that the unimpeded activity of an organism is pleasant in so far as it is unimpeded?[1]

[1] For the Aristotelian background see Diano, *GCFI* (1940) 159.

7

THE PROBLEM OF FRIENDSHIP

It normally happens, as might be expected, that in accounts of Epicureanism a discussion of friendship forms part of the more general discussion of Epicurus' ethics and of the importance and role of pleasure in the Epicurean system. But there are a number of reasons for treating friendship as a case slightly apart. First there is the general point that for the ancients friendship was a most important subject and occupied a place in discussions of moral behaviour far more significant than would be allotted to it by a contemporary writer. Secondly within the school of Epicurus itself friendship had a great importance even by ancient standards. Thirdly the problem of reconciling the utilitarian and altruistic aspects of friendship led to divergences within the Epicurean school itself, as different individuals tried to interpret different maxims of Epicurus. It is therefore important to discuss in some detail whether Epicurus held a single consistent position on friendship and the relation of that position to his theories on the importance of pleasure, that is, of the absence of pain, in the ideal life.[1]

The background of Epicurus' theories of friendship, as of so much of his philosophy, is to be found in Aristotle. Besides the two books of the *Ethics* on friendship there are numerous other references elsewhere in the Aristotelian writings which indicate the context of Epicurus' ideas.[2] In much Greek philosophical thought both before and after Epicurus' time there was a strong tendency to conflate friendship with passion, φιλία with ἔρως. Above all this is true of much of the writing of Plato, and in particular of his dialogue *Lysis*. But for Epicurus, following here in the footsteps of Aristotle, the distinction must be kept clear. Although, as Philodemus tells us, passion is near to madness,[3] it

[1] The most recent general discussion, that of Diano, does not get to grips with the problems which Epicurean friendship poses (*Les Études Phil.* 22 (1967) 173–86).
[2] For this subject recently see Farrington, *The Faith of Epicurus* 28–31.
[3] Philod., *De Dis* 3, fr. 76, 8, p. 67 Diels; cf. Arrighetti, *PP* 10 (1955) 326–31. See above p. 10.

is not heaven-sent.[1] It is, in Epicurus' definition, an intense
desire for sexual relations accompanied by longing and distress.[2]
And sexual intercourse has never done anyone any good – that
is, it has never been necessary for the achievement of absence
of pain – and a man is lucky (or sensible?) if it does not do him
harm.[3] It is a constant source of frenzied desires (τὰς ἐπιθυμίας
τὰς οἰστρώδεις) which upset the security (σωτηρία) of one's
youth.[4] Fortunately, Epicurus somewhat optimistically
suggests, it can be easily quenched. If sight, association and
contact are removed, he asserts, the passion of love (τὸ ἐρωτικὸν
πάθος) will come to an end.[5] A more serious estimate of the
strength of passion is offered by Lucretius in the fourth book of
his poem, where we read a dramatic account of its effects and
how to moderate them by promiscuity or some other distraction.
But although Lucretius recognizes passion as a more troublesome foe to overcome, his attitude towards it echoes that of
Epicurus and, if our single relevant philosophical fragment is a
satisfactory guide, that of Philodemus also.[6] For Lucretius it is
desirable and simpler to avoid passion before being caught by
it, but even when caught it is possible to escape;[7] and escape is
essential if happiness is to be maintained.

Passion then brings pain as well as pleasure in its train;
specifically it threatens the safety, the quiet untroubled state
which is the aim of the wise man. Friendship, on the other hand,
improves our chances of living at peace and affords us the
necessary protection. It is therefore of great importance, and
anything which, by encouraging competition, prejudices our
chances of enjoying permanent and stable friendships, such as
political life, should be avoided. In the public life of the *polis*
we are not only risking the everyday dangers which will arise

---

[1] D.L. 10.118.
[2] Hermias, *In Phaedr.*, p. 76 Couvreur = Us. 483.
[3] *VS* 51; D.L. 10.118. Cf. Lucr., 4.1075 on how much more satisfactory it is
to have sexual relations if we are *sani* (non-passionate) than if we are
miseri (victims of passion). Cf. Kleve, 'Lucrèce, l'épicurisme et l'amour',
379.   [4] *VS* 80.   [5] *VS* 18.
[6] Kleve ('Lucrèce, l'épicurisme et l'amour', 381) draws attention to
Philodemus' poetry in this connection, with especial reference to the poem
to Philaenion (*AP* 5.121).   [7] Lucr., 4.1147–8.

from the hostility of our enemies, but even more seriously, we
face losing our friends.[1]

Passion destroys our security; friendship will help provide it.[2]
Indeed there is nothing which contributes more to the blessedness (μακαριότης) of our lives.[3] Friendship, asserts Epicurus,
dances round the world bidding all of us awake to an acknow-
ledged state of happiness.[4] And since friendship brings such
benefits to those who enjoy it, we seek it out for the sake of the
advantages it brings.[5] Yet it will only occur if one of the parties
takes the initiative and first bestows benefits on the other. These
benefits, if returned in kind, begin a friendship which will help
us to obtain that quietness of mind and body which is the
supreme pleasure.[6]

The problem which the Epicureans faced is clear. If friendships exist for the sake of advantage, and are employed in the
search for the highest pleasure, there may be a point at which
their claims will have to be set aside. In other words if my own
interests clash with those of my friend, do I simply set aside
the interests of my friend? And if friendships are undertaken
on this basis, how can they be genuine friendships at all, if each
party is aware that either he or his friend may betray the other
if it suits his own interest?

The dilemma is best set out by Cicero in the *De Finibus*.[7]
Torquatus, expounding the Epicurean position, begins with the
basic theme that of all the means to pleasure none is more fruitful than friendship. Epicurus' own life, Torquatus continues,
bore witness to his sincerity in the matter. But, he adds, some
Epicureans hold that we will not desire the pleasures of our
friends to the same extent as we desire our own. Torquatus
does not attribute this view to Epicurus himself and the context
makes it certain that it was not the master's position. Certain
critics of Epicurus, says Torquatus, hold that if we overvalue

---

[1] Cf. Philod., *Rhet.* 2, fr. 19, pp. 158–9 Sudhaus.   [2] *BD* 28.
[3] *BD* 27. Bollack's idea ('Les Maximes', 231–2) that τοῦ ὅλου βίου refers to
the 'full life' is attractive.   [4] *VS* 52.
[5] Cf. Cicero's opposition to this view in *De Amicitia* 27 and *De Fin.* 2.82.
[6] For the interpretation of διὰ τὰς χρείας at D.L. 10.120 and ἀπὸ τῆς
ὠφελείας in *VS* 23, cf. Bollack, 'Les Maximes', 222–6.
[7] *De Fin.* 1.65–70; cf. 2.82.

our friends' pleasures we destroy the very basis of friendship, namely utility. According to Torquatus this criticism is not well-taken.

According to Torquatus the orthodox Epicurean view is that pleasure cannot be separate from friendship, and by friendship he means genuine friendship. Hence a sham friendship in which either side is prepared to betray the other cannot be a genuine friendship and therefore cannot bring pleasure. In other words there is more hope of obtaining pleasure from the possession of friends than risk of pain from supporting other people's troubles and procuring them pleasure. We cannot obtain firm and lasting pleasure unless we love our friends to the same degree as we love ourselves. Hence the wise man will feel the same compassion for his friends' sorrows and joy for their pleasures as he does for his own. Above all friends are a source of confidence. If we possess them, we have high hopes of pleasures to come. The same point had been made by Epicurus himself. When examining the Epicurean theory of pleasure we noted the importance of the mental pleasure of hope or confidence. Hence we can recognize Torquatus echoing the words of Epicurus himself: it is not so much our friends' help but the chance to rely on that help (τῆς πίστεως τῆς περὶ τῆς χρείας) which helps us.[1] And Epicurus also shows us the reverse side of the coin. If we are injured by a friend, our whole life will be confused and upset because of the resulting distrust (ἀπιστία). Mental pleasures, as we know, are more important than pleasures of the body, and confidence for the future, which depends on the goodwill of our friends, is an essential part of the happy life.

Torquatus tells us in chapter 69 that the orthodox Epicurean position was attacked by the Academy. As a result of this controversy, he says, some members of the school, apparently of a later generation than Epicurus himself,[2] argued that, although friendship is originally formed for the sake of advantage, it later develops into a purely altruistic form so that we love our friends for their own sakes, even if no advantage (*utilitas*) derives to us from their friendship. Torquatus does not refute

[1] *VS* 34. For the translation see Bollack, 'Les Maximes', 228–9.
[2] See *De Fin.* 2.82.

this unorthodox position, though he clearly regards it as unorthodox. On the other hand he expresses himself favourably on a third position in the school, according to which wise men have made a compact to love their friends equally with themselves. This view, which could be consistent with what we spoke of as the orthodox Epicurean position, would make friendship something like justice. Both are to be contracts, the one not to harm and the other to help, albeit only to help a limited number of men who are one's friends.

We can see then the orthodox Epicurean view and the variant with altruistic overtones which was developed as a result of the criticism of the Sceptical Academy. Cicero tells us in the *De Finibus* (2.82) that he cannot find the heterodox view in the work of Epicurus himself, and we have argued that Epicurus did not hold it. But, before accepting this account, we must consider the puzzling statement that has come down as *Vatican Saying* 23. All friendship is desirable for itself (δι' ἑαυτὴν αἱρετή), but it starts from benefits bestowed. At first sight this statement seems to go beyond that of the orthodox Epicureans in the direction of altruism. How can Epicurus say that *all* friendship is desirable in itself, if it is only a means for the pursuit of pleasure? Surely he should have said that *no* friendship is desirable in itself but that *all* friendship is desirable for the sake of something else, that is, pleasure.[1] Indeed Epicurus' choice of the word 'desirable' (αἱρετή) is doubly striking, because, as we have seen, he argues elsewhere that, although all *pleasure* is good, it is not always to be chosen (αἱρετός). It would seem from this that the word 'desirable' (αἱρετός) has a special significance in Epicurean ethics: it refers to that which is both good in itself, namely pleasure, and good for the individual in the particular circumstances. But friendship is normally to be seen as good only for the achievement of pleasure, while in our text we find Epicurus saying that it is

[1] The word αἱρετή is a correction of Usener's which has been almost universally accepted. If, as Bollack wishes ('Les Maximes', 223–6) we retain the ἀρετή of the MS, the immediate problem changes, but it seems strange to speak of friendship as an ἀρετή, rather than a good (ἀγαθόν). And it is as odd to say that friendship is an ἀρετή (or a good) for its own sake as it is to say that it is αἱρετή for its own sake.

desirable for itself. It seems not unlikely that unorthodox Epicureans could have used this passage from the master to justify their more altruistic interpretations.

It is not clear where the solution of our problem lies, but perhaps some parallel Stoic theses may clarify Epicurus' intentions. After all Epicurus and Zeno were contemporaries, often thinking of the same problems and pondering over the same proposed solutions. Now in Stoic ethics we know that a certain class of things were called 'preferred' (προηγμένα). These preferred things were so named because they help in the formation of the ideal character; they are means to the end of the production of the wise man. Yet although their very name 'preferred' was designed to indicate that they are not good in themselves and therefore not to be chosen in and for themselves, the Stoics apparently were prepared to say that of things preferred some are preferred for their own sake and others for the sake of other things (ἐκ τῶν προηγμένων τὰ μὲν δι' αὐτὰ προῆκται, τὰ δὲ δι' ἕτερα).[1] This usage may provide a parallel for Epicurus. When Epicurus says that friendship is to be chosen for itself, perhaps he merely means not that it is ultimately valuable, for only pleasure is ultimately valuable, but that it leads directly and without intermediaries to the acquisition of pleasure. If he had said that it is valuable δι' ἕτερα, he would have meant that it is valuable because it produces other things which in their turn produce pleasure. But if this is the correct interpretation, we must admit that Epicurus' intention is not transparent. Bailey wrote, somewhat ambiguously, that 'it is probably safer to suppose that Epicurus did, as usual, found his advocacy of friendship on the purely utilitarian motive of personal advantage in protection and the pleasures of intercourse, but that on that foundation grew a true sense of the more unselfish enjoyment of friendship for its own sake'.[2] It is certain, if Cicero is to be believed, that such a sense developed, but there is no evidence that it developed in Epicurus himself. Indeed there is evidence to the contrary: one reason why Epicurus thought that friendship leads directly to pleasure was

[1] D.L. 7.107 (*SVF* iii 135).
[2] Bailey, *Greek Atomists* 520.

that it gives opportunities for benevolence. For Epicurus it is more pleasurable to confer benefits than to receive them.[1]

Since we are now clearer about the sense in which friendship is chosen for its own sake, we can consider its nature in more detail. Friendship leads directly to pleasure in the way that perhaps nothing else does. That is why Epicurus was able to say, as we saw, that of all the means to the production of a happy life friendship is the most important and the most fruitful. Since it is the most effective provider, we should not be surprised that the claims of friendship are considered as over-riding. The wise man sympathizes with his friend both in times of joy and in times of trouble. He is in pain if his friend is tortured as much as if he himself were the victim: such seems to be the sense of one of the more mutilated *Vatican Sayings*.[2] From Plutarch we hear that the wise man will endure great pains for his friends.[3] Finally Diogenes Laertius records it as Epicurus' opinion that there will be occasions when the wise man will die for his friends.[4] All this bears out the importance that Epicurus recognized must be attached to loyalty in friendship, if that friendship is to endure; and it confirms the strength of his conviction that it is possible to build loyalty up to the point of death for a friend on a utilitarian base. Diogenes indeed records that, in Epicurus' view, loyalty will be a principal characteristic of the wise man. According to Epicurus, he says, the wise man will face up to fortune and will not abandon a friend.[5]

Epicurus tells us that because of the self-sufficiency of the wise man he is better able to give than to accept from others.[6] Friendship is a relationship of mutual giving. Loyalty is one of its essential characteristics and we have noticed the terrible consequences that ensue if loyalty is betrayed. Hence, although friendship is the greater promoter of pleasure, yet since it is liable to compromise the self-sufficiency of the wise man and thus to involve doubts about his happiness in the future, it

[1] Plut., *Non posse* 1097A; *Philosophandum* 778C (Us. 544).
[2] *VS* 56.   [3] Plut., *Adv. Col.* 1111B.
[4] D.L. 10.121.   [5] D.L. 10.120.
[6] *VS* 44; cf. Plut., *Non posse* 1097A (Us. 544).

becomes essential that friendships be formed with the greatest care. Once a friendship is allowed to develop, Epicurus is prepared to let it flourish. But only a few should be allowed to develop; they are too demanding. Perhaps a comparison may be made with Epicurus' attitude to children. He warns the wise man off marriage,[1] chiefly, it seems, because of the inconveniences children cause, and he apparently advised that, even if born, they should not be reared.[2] Yet he seems to have felt obligations, and even affection, for the children of his friends.[3] Perhaps these obligations may be compared with those of friendship itself, for the wise man will be dependent on his friends in so far as he will trust them, sympathize with their misfortunes and take pleasure in their joys.

Bearing all this in mind, Epicurus takes care to make precise suggestions as to how friendships should be formed. Perhaps something of the least altruistic side of his position can be seen in *Vatican Saying* 39, where we read that the man who looks to his friends for constant satisfactions is not a friend at all. But we must remember that the parasite or sponger is a stock figure of ancient life and the Epicurean community would provide a choice target for parasites able enough to play the required philosophical games. But it is noticeable that, when Epicurus turns to the other side of the coin, and rejects the man who refuses to connect benefits with friendship at all, the emphasis again is on the fact that nothing good can be expected of such a man in the future. He destroys our hope of good things to come. The emphasis is not on the giving of the wise man but on his expecting. Epicurus' defence of this would, of course, be that in making friends we do look to our own pleasures. It is because we are assured of obtaining these that we fulfil, and pay in full, our part of the contract. We do not make the contract to give, even though we are better at giving than receiving, until we are assured that there is hope of good return. Again we notice the emphasis on hope. Epicurus does not talk about receiving; that,

[1] D.L. 10.119 and Us. 94; cf. Us. 525–6. For the correct text of Diogenes and parallel passages in later authors see Chilton, *Phronesis* 5 (1960) 71–3.
[2] Epict., *Disc.* 1.23.5.
[3] Cf. D.L. 10.19–21 and, if it is genuine, the letter to a child (113 Arr.).

he implies, would be mere bartering (καπηλεύει). Rather he thinks about our expectations for the future. Yet although friendship provides such advantages, we must not rush into it – the risks of betrayal are too great – nor must we accept into our friendship those who are too eager for it. They are as unsatisfactory as those who are too ready to avoid friendship altogether.[1]

Yet although the present enjoyment of benefits is at times played down by Epicurus for the sake of emphasis on the mental pleasure of expectation of future goods, future goods are still goods expected. And obviously if we expect goods in the future, we shall expect goods in the present also – for the future will in time become the present. In brief then there are two fairly closely related ways in which friendship shows itself the principal means of providing ourselves with a pleasant life. One way we have noticed already: it helps to provide us with safety. It protects us better than anything else from the envy and spite of our fellow men. If a man has no friends, his life is like that of a lion or a wolf. We must be careful with whom we eat and drink.[2] If we live without friends we are scarcely human, and the implication is clear: our life is the life of the jungle. Each man struggles for his own and safety is lost. We now see the dangers of politics and in general of the competitive life. Competition loses us friends, and loss of friends is loss of safety. Some men seek this safety in power and status, but they are misguided.[3] Retirement to the company of friends is the only way to achieve it.

Safety is in the first instance mere physical protection. But perhaps more important is the comfortable feeling of security that friends can bring us. As Cicero's Torquatus puts it, to be loved and to be the object of affection are pleasant because they make life safer *and* because they increase its fullness of pleasure.[4]

It is not merely safety, but a feeling of comfort that is a natural aim of man. And not only is it pleasant and therefore good to be loved oneself, but also the adoption of friendly or kindly feelings towards proper objects, such as wise men or the

[1] *VS* 28.   [2] Sen., *Ep.* 19.10.
[3] *BD* 7.   [4] Cic., *De Fin.* 1.53.

gods, is beneficial. Epicurus tells us that those who respect (σεβομένων) a wise man derive great benefits from their attitude.[1] Yet the wise man will not look for praise.[2] He, like the gods, is free from the need of it. Like those who worship the gods in the right way, those who behave in the right way towards the wise man will reap their due benefits.

It is a very good thing to have our friends around us;[3] hence Epicurus organized his 'school' as a society of friends. We enjoy their present company, we look forward to their friendship in the future and we look back to the joys of our past association with them. The memory of a dead friend is sweet, said Epicurus.[4] Lamentations are out of place, for they betray our ignorance of the nature of the world. We sympathize with our friends by concern for them, not by mourning, Epicurus tells us.[5] As if to emphasize the importance of the correct attitude towards friends who have died, Epicurus speaks of the matter in the last of his *Basic Doctrines*. Those who are safe from their neighbours will live together enjoying the most pleasant life. Their intimacy will be complete, but when one of them dies, they will not lament his death, for they will recognize that he does not need pity.[6] In a sense friendship provides the immortality for the group which death removes from each of its individual members. Friendship can be passed on for ever within the Epicurean community; perhaps this is at least a part of the reason why Epicurus can believe that, while wisdom and friendship are what generate a noble man, it is not wisdom alone which outlives each individual who possesses it. Friendship too is deathless, for the community of the wise lives on.[7] And even if the community of Epicurus were to die out, we should still have the gods to provide us with a paradigm of the life of friendship.

It has often been noticed that Epicurus' theoretical concern with friendship was matched by his practical behaviour to his friends. Ancient critics of Epicureanism tended to see a contrast

---

[1] *VS* 32.   [2] *VS* 64.   [3] *VS* 61.
[4] Plut., *Non posse* 1105D (= Us. 213).
[5] *VS* 66; see Diano *SIFC* 12 (1935) 66 for the meaning of this fragment.
[6] *BD* 40.
[7] *VS* 78. For the interpretation of this fragment see Bollack, 'Les Maximes', 233-4.

between the famous kindness and gentleness of Epicurus to his friends and the basic Epicurean doctrine that the life of happiness is the life of the maximum amount of pleasure. Plutarch complains that Epicurus says that he chooses friends for the sake of pleasure but is willing to endure very great pains on their behalf. The implication is that the two ideas are contradictory.[1] But Epicurus himself would reject this: we choose our friends with care for the sake of pleasure; but unless we are prepared to stand by them they will not be our friends, and the pleasure of and from friendship will be lost. It is in the light of this attitude that we must view various acts of Epicurus among his friends and disciples. He was opposed to a common store of goods on the grounds that this implied that the friends distrusted one another and would not behave towards one another in a friendly manner.[2] Only the wise man is able to thank those who benefit him adequately, Epicurus believes, and the gratitude of Epicurus to his friends and of his friends to himself is borne out by his correspondence. Ancient critics regularly accused the Epicureans of the grossest flattery and of excessive hyperbole in speaking of and to one another.[3] But the feeling of safety and consequent gratitude is probably genuine. And the attitude of intense gratitude to Epicurus long outlived his younger admirers like Colotes;[4] it can be found expressed in the strongest terms many centuries later in Lucretius' invocations to his master and in Diogenes of Oenoanda.[5]

It is easy to view Epicurean friendship as a kind of mutual admiration designed to make people feel cosy. There is some truth in this picture, since for Epicurus cosiness is worth having, provided it is based on a correct estimate of man's position in the world and is free from deluding sentimentality. But mutual admiration of this kind is not the whole of Epicurean friendship. The reality of the obligations of friendship must be emphasized; they sometimes bring pain and hardship to the wise man. The necessity of such obligations is in part that the

[1] Plut., *Adv. Col.* 1111B.   [2] D.L. 10.11.
[3] D.L. 10.118.   [4] Cf. Us. 141.
[5] Cf. the significance Lucretius attaches to his friendship with Memmius at 1.140–1.

joys of the mind are greater in the Epicurean sense than the joys of the body. But Epicurus is in the tradition of Aristotle in constantly remembering the claims of the self as well as the claims of the other in such a relationship. Just as Aristotle holds that a man who claims less for himself than he deserves is not a great-souled man, but is suffering from a lack of self-confidence and an excess of humility, so Epicurus insists on his rights as well as his duties as a well-spring of the pleasures of friendship for his friends. It is perhaps in this light that we should regard not only the seemingly excessive expressions of adulation bandied about by the members of the school, but also the insistence in Epicurus' will that the twentieth day of each month should be celebrated in perpetuity in honour of himself and his closest associate Metrodorus.[1] Similar festivities were to mark the anniversaries of his brothers and of his friend Polyaenus.

Epicurus has no interest in statues which may be erected in his honour,[2] but he wishes his friends to remember him. The difference between his attitudes to public and to private life is obvious here. Statues, like crowns, are the marks of vain popularity and its concomitant dangers. Friends, and private life where friendship is possible, provide security. The wise man, says Epicurus, will be respectful to monarchs if the occasion demands it,[3] and the occasion will demand it if such behaviour enables the philosopher to maintain himself quietly in the circle of his friends in private life. Among these friends he will expect his meed of honour, and he will receive it, but even here his relationships must be kept limited and unpretentious. He will give lectures, Epicurus says of the wise man, but not so as to win mass acclaim; he will give public readings, but not from choice. Those philosophers who acted otherwise – and there were many who did – are by implication condemned.

For the Epicureans, as we have seen, the chief aim of life is to secure tranquillity of mind and to avoid bodily suffering. Living the good life is compared to sailing a quiet and calm sea. When we form lasting friendships, we are in a haven from which the waves of politics and public life are excluded. The Epicurean theory of friendship deserves the attention of the student of

[1] D.L. 10.18.   [2] D.L. 10.121.   [3] D.L. 10.121.

antiquity not only because of Epicurus' philosophical attempt to base a theory of friendship on a doctrine of unswerving utilitarianism, but also because in his concept of friendship Epicurus shows himself at the opposite pole from the majority of the social thinkers of antiquity. Nothing is farther from Epicurus' concept of friendship than the Platonic ideal of a striving, motivated by passion, to reproduce in the temporal domain the ideal state which can be recognized by reason. Equally distant from Epicurus is Aristotle, when he holds that man is a creature who naturally needs social life and should therefore participate in the activities of the state. The Stoics inherited these and similar positions; Epicurus consciously rejects them, and offers us an alternative thesis about the good life for man. Most of his followers accepted this alternative thesis; a few, in the closing years of the Roman Republic, did not.[1]

[1] Cf. Momigliano, *JRS* 31 (1941) 151–7. According to Plutarch (*De Tranq. An.* 466A = Us. 555) even Epicurus admitted that those constitutionally unable to resist the attention of glory should enter public life as the lesser of two evils.

8

THE GODS AND RELIGION

The existence and structure of the gods

In his eulogistic address to Epicurus at the opening of book three of his poem, Lucretius declares that as soon as reason begins to proclaim the true nature of the universe, the terrors of the mind disperse and the marvellous nature of the gods is made manifest. They live in peace disturbed neither by wind, nor rain-clouds, nor snow, nor frost. Nature supplies all their needs and they are totally untroubled.[1] This is itself a poetical rendering of the first of the *Basic Doctrines* of Epicurus: that which is blessed and immortal neither has troubles itself nor provides troubles to anyone. It is constrained neither by anger nor by favour. For all such things exist only in what is weak.[2] These two texts provide us in embryo with most of what we can discover about the Epicurean gods – and first of all they tell us that such gods exist and that they are both blessed and immortal. We must enquire into the reasons why Epicurus is confident of these theses.

The gods exist, says Epicurus in the letter to Menoeceus, for our knowledge of them carries conviction.[3] We owe this knowledge to nature herself,[4] for in general men believe in gods and this belief is associated with a general concept (πρόληψις) deriving, like all general concepts, from direct experience.[5]

[1] Lucr., 3.14–24. [2] *BD* I (D.L. 10.139). [3] D.L. 10.123 (Menoeceus).
[4] Cic., *ND* 1.45. The idea that *natura* herself provides us with our general concept of the gods renders impossible the theory of Scott that the gods are identical with the images of the gods (*JP* 12 (1883) 212–47); it is even more destructive of the elaboration of Pfligersdorffer that these images are merely the projections of human ideals (*WS* 70 (1957) 250–1). Scott's theory of idol-gods may be closer to the view of Democritus, by whom Epicurus was certainly influenced in this matter, though Guthrie (*History of Greek Philosophy* 2.478–83) seems to think the contrary. For Democritus see also Bailey, *Greek Atomists* 175–7.
[5] D.L. 10.124 (Menoeceus); Cic., *ND* 1.43–4. The general concept of the gods must be distinguished from the false suppositions (D.L. 10.124) which lead us to suppose, for example, that the sun, moon and stars are divine (Lucr., 5.114; Plut., *Adv. Col.* 1123A).

Unlike many other general concepts, however, our concept of the gods does not depend on the evidence of our senses but on that of the mind, for the gods are 'seen' (θεωρητοί) by reason.[1] The most detailed account of our 'view' of them is provided by Cicero, in the first book of the *De Natura Deorum*,[2] and basing ourselves on a huge quantity of recent scholarship we are able to understand Cicero's elliptical but generally accurate presentation fairly well. Basically there are two stages in the process by which we acquire the essential knowledge of the gods, as we have already hinted. We first experience their existence; this is certain in some way since we 'see' them in the mind. Then we grasp their blessedness and immortality. These two facts provide us with a general concept of the gods, and, like all general concepts, it is indisputable.

According to Epicurus we can 'see' the gods both when we are asleep and when we are awake.[3] And our visions of them both when awake and when asleep can provide either true or false information. There is no reason to accept the view that dream-images are only likely to generate false opinion,[4] and indeed we derive evidence from them more frequently, since in the stillness of sleep the images of the gods, emitted as they are from compounds of small, fine atoms like those of the human soul,[5] can penetrate our minds more readily. This evidence tells us then that the gods exist, for we see them, and that they are anthropomorphic, for, as Cicero's Velleius puts it, they only appear to us in human shape.[6] For this latter view we not only have the direct evidence of the mind; the fact that the gods are anthropomorphic is also likely on *a priori* grounds. The human figure is the most beautiful figure we know, and it is therefore likely that the figure of the gods is similar, though probably

---

[1] Scholion to *BD* 1; cf. Aët., 1.7.34 (Us. 355).
[2] On Philodemus as Cicero's source for Velleius see Philippson, *SO* 19 (1939) 15–40; cf. Kleve, *Gnosis* 125. On Carneades as ultimate source for Cotta's critique see Philippson, *SO* 20 (1940) 21–44.
[3] Cic., *ND* 1.46.
[4] This suggestion has most recently been offered by Amerio, 'L'epicureismo e gli dei', 102–3 and Freymuth, *Zur Lehre* 28, note 5. *Contra* Kleve, *Gnosis* 36.
[5] Cf. Kleve, *Gnosis* 41 with the references given.
[6] Cic., *ND* 1.46; cf. scholion to *BD* 1; Us. 355–7.

larger, since for the ancients size was often a constituent feature of human beauty;[1] of all the creatures we know only men possess virtue, and they possess it because they have the power of reason. Since the gods also have the power of reason, Epicurus apparently argued, they must also have human form.[2] These arguments are weak, but they are only used to make the basic evidence provided by the seeing mind more credible to those foolish enough to distrust it!

We recall that in the first of the *Basic Doctrines* Epicurus tells us that anger and favour are not displayed by the gods. Such are the qualities only of beings that are weak; and Epicurus, as we shall see, laid considerable stress on the 'strength' of the gods. Hence when Cicero's Velleius continues his exposition of how the gods are seen not by the senses but by the mind, he tells us that in this way Epicurus was able to grasp their strength (*vis*) and their nature.[3] We must not understand this strength, however, to depend upon the 'solidity' of their bodies. On the contrary the bodies of the gods are fine; that is one reason why they cannot be grasped by the senses but only by the mind.[4]

There is another important way in which the bodies of the gods differ from human bodies. Epicurus teaches, says Velleius, not only that we grasp with the mind that their nature is without the normal solidity of bodies, but also that it is not *ad numerum*. This seems to mean that the bodies of the gods are being constantly renewed.[5]

[1] For the size of the images of the gods, though not of the gods themselves, see Aug., *Ep.* 118.28 and Sextus Empiricus, *Adv. Math.* 9.25; cf. Lucr., 5.1171. Again the origin may be Democritean; cf. Cic., *ND* 1.120.

[2] Cic., *ND* 1.48; cf. Philod., *De Sign.* 22, pp. 72–4 De Lacy.

[3] Cic., *ND* 1.49. Cf. Pease's commentary *ad loc.* for the use of *vis*.

[4] Cf. Lucr., 5.147–9, *tenuis enim natura deum longeque remota sensibus ab nostris* ... Cf. *perlucida*, *ND* 1.75; *perlucidos et perflabiles*, *De Div.* 2.40, with reference to the bodies of the gods.

[5] Bailey (*Greek Atomists* 445, note 2) is right to point out that the phrase *nec soliditate quadam nec ad numerum* in *ND* 1.49 is to be construed as an ablative of quality to be taken with *vim et naturam*, and that this is proved by the parallel passage at 1.105. For alternative (and incorrect) renderings see Pease, *ad loc.* For *ad numerum* and related problems see Appendix E.

Analogy and isonomia

We have discussed our knowledge of the gods in outline; it is necessary to consider it in more detail. As we have seen, in the first place this knowledge derives from the mind. We 'see' the gods both in dreams and in our waking hours and we see them in human form. But what is the process by which we understand the evidence that our minds provide? How do we understand the images which we see with our minds and relate them to the evidence of the senses? The answer is provided by Cicero, who says that the images are grasped (i.e. understood) *similitudine et transitione*;[1] but these words have proved difficult to interpret. The correct interpretation was proposed by Schwenke[2] and accepted by Philippson;[3] it has recently been expounded forcefully by Kleve.[4] It is that Cicero's Latin corresponds to the Greek phrase ἡ καθ' ὁμοιότητα μετάβασις, and that it refers to a process of understanding by analogy.[5] The objects of the mind (θεωρητά) are analogous to the objects of sense (φαινόμενα);[6] and we have evidence that the use of the word 'analogy' (μετάβασις) in this connection goes back to Epicurus himself. It is not a technical term only current among later generations of Epicureans.[7] Further information is provided by Sextus, who says that the Epicureans in general made use of analogy to explain our knowledge of the gods.[8] We form an idea that god is immortal and imperishable and complete in happiness by drawing an analogy from mankind (κατὰ τὴν ἀπὸ τῶν ἀνθρώπων μετάβασιν). This seems to be a similar argument to that which

---

[1] For this meaning of *perceptis* see most recently Kleve, *Gnosis* 93 ff. The Greek is probably καταλαμβάνω. In *ND* 1.109 we find *cerno* used. Both Greek and English also have seeing-words which can indicate an intellectual grasp.

[2] P. Schwenke, 'Zu Cicero De natura deorum (1.49f.)', *Neue Jahrbücher für Philologie und Pädagogik* 125 (1882) 623.

[3] Philippson, *Hermes* 51 (1916) 601 ff.

[4] Kleve, *Gnosis* 91–6.

[5] For the Greek phrase see *De Signis* col. 15, 6; 18, 15; 28, 35; 33, 23; 38, 27. Cf. Kleve, *Gnosis* 88.

[6] *De Signis* col. 37, 27–9.

[7] See Epicurus, Περὶ φύσεως 11 (24.[30.]2–3 Arr.) and D.L. 10.32.

[8] Sextus Emp., *Adv. Math.* 9.45. Cf. also Philod., *De Dis* 1, col. 2, 7–10, p. 10 Diels.

we have already noticed in the *De Natura Deorum*. There we found Velleius arguing that, since we are possessors of reason and of a particular shape, the gods, who also possess reason, must possess a similar shape. The point is made clearer by what follows, for Cicero says that it is the Epicurean view that the gods do not have a body but a quasi-body, not blood but quasi-blood. They are seen to be *like* us by analogy and thus have *similar* bodies and blood. As we have already observed, their bodies are much finer than ours; hence they cannot be identical but only similar in constitution and appearance.[1]

It is then by the aid of the mental operation of analogy that we understand the images of the gods which are constantly presented to our minds. These images succeed one another at such a rapid rate that we seem to get a single clear picture: *e multis una*, as Cicero puts it.[2] That at least being clear, we can proceed with our investigation of what these images depict. But we cannot go much further without reference to another general law of the cosmos, the law of *isonomia*. This too is mentioned by Cicero in the *De Natura Deorum* (1.50), first of all as a general principle that each thing in the universe must have its exact counterpart (*ut omnia omnibus paribus paria respondeant*) and then more specifically in the form of a theory that there must be no less a number of immortal than of mortal beings, and that the powers of destruction in the world must be counter-balanced by equal powers of conservation. Clearly these two theses are complementary, since even in their life in the *inter-mundia* the bodies of the gods are subject to the constant blows of moving atoms,[3] and are constantly being eroded by their throwing off of images. Unless these destructive pressures are

---

[1] Cf. Cic., *ND* 1.74–5 and Philod., *De Dis* 3, fr. 6, 5ff., p. 45 Diels, σῶμα κατ᾽ ἀναλογίαν. There is no need to re-examine here alternative inter-pretations of *similitudine et transitione*, since the views of Freymuth (*Zur Lehre* 23, 38), Bailey (*Greek Atomists* 447ff.), Pfligersdorffer (*WS* 70 (1957) 244ff.) and Diano (*GCFI* 30 (1949) 205ff.) have all been scrutinized and effectively criticized by Kleve (*Gnosis* 88–96). Freymuth and Bailey both regard *transitio* as a translation of ὑπέρβασις (cf. *ND* 1.109), and Bailey's interpretation is particularly unsatisfactory in that it depends on rendering *transitio* as 'succession'—which must be wrong.

[2] Cic., *ND* 1.109; cf. D.L. 10.50 (Herodotus); Lucr., 5.1176.

[3] Cic., *ND* 1.109.

balanced by some counterbalancing forces of replenishment, the gods could not be immortal. Hence when Cicero speaks of forces of conservation, he must refer to forces which lead to the conservation of bodies by the processes of actual replenishment.[1]

There is no doubt that the Epicureans recognized a very large, indeed a countless number of gods. Philodemus approves the piety of his sect in that they not only recognize all the gods of the Greeks but many others besides,[2] and this would seem to be logical if we accept that they postulated two kinds of gods, those of the popular cult who are fully individualized, like Zeus, and those others who are only specifically discernible like the Graces.[3] Indeed this theory helps to explain how there can be as many immortal as mortal beings. In any case *isonomia* is necessary, at least in the form that there must be powers of conservation equal in strength to the powers of destruction. If this were not so, as we have seen, the gods would not be immortal; yet we know by our general concept of them that they are immortal. If they were not, they could not be free from trouble nor enjoy perpetual security from pain both of mind and body.

If then there are gods, a principle of the *isonomia* of conservation and destruction must exist if they are to be immortal. As we have seen, Velleius also states that the principle of *isonomia* shows us that as many immortals as mortals must actually exist. In this form the principle is said to derive from the 'very great force of infinity'.[4] Lucretius argues in book two that there must be an equal distribution of animals of different species throughout the universe. If there are few elephants in Italy, there are many in India, so that the number is filled up (*numerumque repleri*).[5] This seems to depend, as Bailey saw, on the traditional argument (perhaps akin to that used by Democritus to support the random movement of atoms) that in the

---

[1] This interpretation disposes of the objection of Bailey that Velleius' 'doctrine of conservation' clashes with Lucretius' talk of creation in 2.569–76. But in the case of the gods conservation itself is a constant re-creation and replenishment of what is endangered.

[2] Philod., *De Piet.* 1, col. 17, 8–27, p. 84 Gomperz.

[3] See Appendix E.

[4] Bailey, *Greek Atomists* 462–4.   [5] Lucr., 2.535.

combinations of infinite numbers of atoms, there is nothing to produce any one combination in greater numbers than any other. Lucretius in fact proposes a theory quite close to that of Velleius that there must be as many immortals as mortals, for it is not difficult for any ancient thinker to hold that, if one kind of balance is maintained, then other balances are obviously present in the cosmos. If there is no reason why different species of animals should not have the same number of members, it was easy to argue that in general all different (and in particular all opposite) species should have equal numbers of members. Mortals and immortals are in a sense opposites; therefore there must be equal numbers of each.[1] As Bailey observes, as the doctrine of *isonomia* is expounded by Velleius, the existence of mortals, and therefore the predominance of the forces of destruction in this world, entails the existence of immortal beings and the predominance of the forces of conservation elsewhere.[2]

The life and activities of the gods

The Epicureans wish to emphasize above all that the gods do not concern themselves with human affairs. This theme, constantly echoed by Lucretius throughout the whole of his poem, perhaps indicates the mood of Epicureanism better than anything else. In fact it is probable that the reason for the apparently extraordinary hostility of Epicurus to his atomist predecessors is that they did not subordinate their physical enquiries, and the atomic theory itself, to the purpose of freeing mankind from fears of the gods and from the control of necessity, but senselessly and disastrously treated them as subjects of pure research;[3] which led in practice to absolute physical deter-

[1] Cf. Giussani, *Stud. Lucr.*, 251; Bailey, *Greek Atomists* 464.
[2] For the use of the doctrine of *isonomia* to explain the growth and decline of the cosmos see Solmsen, 'Epicurus on the Growth and Decline of the Cosmos'. For an appeal to *isonomia* to support the thesis that when dealing with ἄδηλα all possible causes are actual causes, though not necessarily in our world, see Lucr., 5.526–33.
[3] Cf. D.L. 10.13 on Leucippus. Bailey's note on this passage is amusing if sad (*Greek Atomists* 408): 'Epicurus' denial of his (Leucippus') existence was probably a playful form of his assertion of independence.' The

minism. Bringing the sympathy of a fellow ideologist to bear on this problem, Karl Marx was able to understand and explain the violence of Epicurus' attitude. On a matter as important as this, Leucippus and Democritus were in the role of objectivist deviationists.[1] As Epicurus put it: 'Vain is the word of a philosopher which does not heal any suffering of man.'[2]

As Lucretius and Plutarch, in his treatise on superstition, make clear, fear of the intervention of the gods was a factor in ancient life which could not easily be ignored, and many individuals appear to have lived their lives in constant dread.[3] It was of no avail for Cicero to deny this.[4] It was a fact of life for many, and Epicurus, as a healer of souls, regarded it as a matter of primary importance. In the Epicurean fourfold remedy for the ills of man, it is proclaimed first of all that god is not to be feared, then that death need not be a source of worry, then that it is easy to possess the good and to endure what is unpleasant.[5] But if the gods are not to be feared by anyone, there can be only one reason, namely that they are not concerned with human affairs, and, as we have seen, Epicurus emphasizes this in the first of his *Basic Doctrines*. The gods do not show anger or favour. From which it follows that they neither reward the good nor punish the evil. If the gods were troubled about how men behave, whether they are just or unjust, they would not enjoy undisturbed repose and happiness. Yet it is the nearly universal belief of mankind that they do enjoy such happiness, and the concept of god is meaningless if this belief is not upheld.

non-existence of Leucippus cannot, of course, be taken as fact (see Guthrie, *History of Greek Philosophy* 2.383). De Witt (*Epicurus* 67 and note 52) claims that D.L. 10.13 does not imply that Epicurus denied Leucippus' existence, but only that Epicurus denied that Leucippus was a philosopher. This mistranslation neglects the force of τινα (as Guthrie says, *op. cit.* 383, note 1). For attacks on Nausiphanes (the Democritean) see D.L. 10.8 and 73; Sext. Emp., *Adv. Math.* 1.3.

[1] Cf. Marx's dissertation, 'The Relation of Epicurus to Democritus', *Marx-Engels Gesamtausgabe*, Bd. 1 (Frankfurt 1927) and Farrington, *The Faith of Epicurus* 7–8.

[2] Porphyry, *Ad Marc.* 31 (Us. 221). Usener's attribution to Epicurus, accepted by Bailey, seems correct.

[3] On the problem of the fear of the gods see Festugière (tr. Chilton), *Epicurus* 51–6.   [4] Cic., *ND* 1.86.

[5] Philod., *Adv. Soph.* (P. Herc. 1005), col. 4, 10, p. 87 Sbordone.

Epicurus goes further than a denial that the gods concern themselves with the moral behaviour of mankind; it follows from his physics that the gods themselves are subordinate, just as mortal beings are subordinate, to the primary 'constituents' of the cosmos, namely atoms and the void. But apart from the fact that Epicurean physics precludes all possibility that the cosmos is made by the gods, this truth is apparent from observation of the world itself. If our world were the product of the gods, it would not have so much wrong with it. It would not be *tanta praedita culpa*.[1] In any case the view that the gods could form a concept of what worlds are like before there was a world is absurd. All concepts derive from the evidence of the senses and the mind, when the senses and the mind are directed to existent objects. Hence if nothing existed, no concept of a world could be found in the minds of the gods.[2] In brief, then, the world is not made by the gods, and human action is not judged by the gods. The gods, content with their perfect happiness, have no reason for concerning themselves with such things and good reasons not to do so – too much trouble is involved and this would be incompatible with their happiness. There is then, according to Epicurus, no such thing as divine providence, no teleological order in the world, since all apparent design is the result of the chance union of atoms,[3] and there is no divine retribution.[4] That there is no providence is the thesis which the ancients tended to find outrageous.[5] As originally proposed by Epicurus, it was probably aimed at the theological ideas not only of the general public, but also of the natural philosophers, who would, says Epicurus, make us slaves of necessity.[6] In particular Plato and Aristotle, by arguing for the divinity of the stars, had introduced new causes of terror, and both the letter to Pythocles and Lucretius' poem go to great lengths to make sure all divine activity is excluded from the operations of the heavenly bodies. What was originally designed by Epicurus as a

[1] Lucr., 5.199.
[2] Lucr., 5.181–6.
[3] Lucr., 4.823–57; D.L. 10.81.
[4] Lucr., 6.379–422.
[5] Cf. Us. 367–9 etc.
[6] D.L. 10.134. As Bailey points out (*Greek Atomists* 475), ἀπρονοησία is virtually a divine attribute for the Epicureans.

counterblast to the theologies of Plato and Aristotle could
equally be used by a later generation of Epicureans to demolish
the astral speculations of the Stoics and their associated doctrines of fate.[1] The gods then remain untroubled; they live in
the *intermundia*, the spaces between the individual cosmic
systems, and are at peace.[2]

Several times already we have referred to the fact that the
gods have the power of replenishment, that in their case the
powers of conservation are so effective that the erosion of their
bodies through the casting off of images and the possible
damage which might be done to their atomic structures by the
blows of passing atoms in the *intermundia* are counterbalanced by
an equal and opposite force which secures their immortality.
For if the gods were not immortal, they would not be free from
the bodily troubles of decay.[3] Even wise men can be free from
pain of the soul, but no man can hope to attain a permanent
state of freedom from bodily discomfort. The gods, however,
are superior in this respect. It remains to be seen how this
survival occurs. There are two schools of thought on this issue:[4]
those who argue that the survival of the bodies of the gods is
due to the working of external nature, and those who hold that
the gods know how to avoid destruction and act accordingly
as if by instinct. The former group of interpreters rely on such
texts as Lucretius 3.23, where we read that nature supplies the
gods with what they need; and it is obvious that, unless the gods
are 'renewed' by matter, they must ultimately perish. The
question is, how does 'nature' function in this case? Nature, we
recall, includes the processes of destruction as well as those of
conservation. How does it happen, then, that the gods 'receive
nothing evil' (κακοῦ παντὸς ἄδεκτος), as Philodemus seems to

[1] In Cic., *ND* 1.18 Velleius attacks Plato's Demiurge and the Stoic Providence in the same breath. On astral religion see Festugière, *Epicurus*
73–93.
[2] Cic., *ND* 1.18; *De Fin.* 2.75; *De Div.* 2.40; Lucr., 3.18–24; 5.154; Hipp.,
Phil. 22.3 (Us. 359); Philod., *De Dis* 3.8, 20ff., p. 26 Diels.
[3] That the gods are theoretically at risk from atoms in the *intermundia* seems
a certain deduction from D.L. 10.89 (Pythocles). Cf. Kleve, 'Die Unvergänglichkeit', 121; Cic., *ND* 1.114.
[4] Kleve, 'Die Unvergänglichkeit', 117–18.

put it?¹ Philodemus himself supplies the answer. It is because of the reason and excellence (ἀρετή) of the gods that they can secure their immortality.²

This text is not alone, but a passage of Origen best summarizes the Epicurean position.³ The gods of Epicurus, says Origen, are composites formed from atoms, and since in so far as their structure is concerned they are subject to dissolution, they arrange to shake off destruction-bearing atoms (πραγματεύονται τὰς φθοροποιοὺς ἀτόμους ἀποσείεσθαι). The best commentary on this is a passage of Lucretius, in which two means by which a body may be preserved and thus immortality secured are envisaged. The body will obviously be safer from death-dealing blows if nothing lethal comes near it. It will also be safe if the dangerous object 'recedes'. It is this latter process which Origen seems to be describing; the Epicurean gods are able to secure the withdrawal of harmful atoms. That by itself would not secure their immortality; they must also achieve the retention of the 'life-bearing' atoms which nature supplies. This must be an achievement of their 'reason' and 'excellence' if they are to survive. Now we may wonder how this 'reason' and 'excellence' is deployed. In other words what is the manner of the life-preserving activity of the gods? There is no specific answer to this in any Epicurean text, but Kleve seems to have found the solution. Like men, he argues, and presumably in the same way as men, the gods must have free will.⁴ That much seems to be verified by Philodemus,⁵ who says that if the gods wished for evil they would be doing evil now. Thus the origin of their action in warding off destruction is their own will and their own knowledge. Just as they concern themselves with eating, so they concern themselves with self-preservation (πραγματεύονται is the word Origen uses for their activity) and, since their bodies as well as their souls are perfect, they are bound to be successful.

¹ Philod., *De Dis* 3, fr. 7, 12ff., p. 45 Diels (Diels prints κατ[·] παντὸς ἀδεκ[τ . . .); cf. *De Dis* 1, col. 2, 14–15, p. 10 Diels.
² Philod., *De Dis* 3, fr. 82, 2ff., p. 13 Diels; fr. 44, 16ff., p. 57 Diels.
³ Origen, *Contra Celsum* 4.14; cf. Merlan, *Studies* 59, note 44. See also Philod., *De Dis* 3, fr. 80, p. 68 Diels (cf. Arrighetti, *PP* 10 (1955) 341–7).
⁴ Kleve, 'Die Unvergänglichkeit', 124–6.
⁵ Philod., *De Dis* 3, fr. 78, 4ff., p. 67f. Diels; cf. col. 7, 5ff., p. 24 Diels.

There is an objection to this thesis. Ancient opponents of Epicurus, such as Cotta in Cicero's *De Natura Deorum*, were in the habit of accusing Epicurus' gods of idleness.[1] But this sort of attack seems to derive from a misunderstanding (wilful or otherwise) of Epicurus' intentions. As we see in *Basic Doctrine* I, the gods are not inconvenienced in any way; they have no trouble (οὔτε. . .πράγματα ἔχει). That might easily be taken to mean that the gods have no business, that is, do nothing. Cotta seems to be thinking along these lines when he says that Epicurus' gods not only confer no benefits but do nothing at all. Epicurus, says Cotta, says that they have no *negotium*. The word *negotium*, however, means troublesome business, occupations which disturb leisure. But leisure (*otium*) is not idleness and Cotta has no reason to say that the gods do nothing (*non modo. . . exstare sed ne factum quidem omnino*). In fact, as we shall see, they do a number of things: at least they eat, drink and converse, according to Philodemus. So the objection disappears. The gods have the means to secure immortality; nature has provided them with everything necessary at no inconvenience to themselves. They make use of the powers they derive from nature and deploy their faculties on the material supplied by nature. They achieve their end without trouble or anxiety, for their knowledge of what is necessary is perfect and they have complete power to act. Now it might be argued that the gods do not need to use any unusual powers of self-preservation, since eating and drinking would make up for the atoms they lose. But this can hardly be right, for, although human beings may appear to retain their strength by eating and drinking, they do not in fact do so. Their skin wrinkles, their hair drops out and they eventually die as the forces of destruction come to predominate. But the gods are more successful; they *perpetually* replace the atoms lost *and* ward off dangerous atomic blows. Their action is as troublefree as eating, but not identical with it. It is simply *being* gods.

A further objection remains. After inspecting the details of divine life given by Philodemus, Bailey suggests that Philodemus worked out 'the anthropomorphic idea [of the gods] with a

---

[1] Cic., *ND* 1.102.

greater elaboration than his master would have approved. There is no evidence in the fragments of Epicurus himself or those of early generations of Epicureans to support the theological details which Philodemus recounts.'[1] It is impossible to prove Bailey wrong on this point, but there are indications at least that Philodemus is following the master fairly closely. When Sextus Empiricus considers the possibility that the gods have lungs and tongues and mouths, he speaks not of the myths of younger Epicureans but of the myths of Epicurus.[2] Furthermore the information we derive from Philodemus about the ability of the gods to achieve their own survival is certainly in accordance with *Basic Doctrine* 1. We recall that Epicurus says that to show anger or favour is the mark of weakness. All that is blessed and immortal thus possesses strength, and we can now see at least one area in which the strength of the gods is deployed. They are able to secure their own immortality while still remaining untroubled. We recall that Velleius points out that according to Epicurus we can grasp the *strength* and nature of the gods by reason.[3] If we did not grasp their strength, we could not understand their immortality and blessedness.

We know now that the gods will live for ever; we have not yet considered their origin. They are, as we know, atomic complexes. Did each atomic complex which is a god have an origin in time, or have all the gods existed from eternity? Clearly if the gods had an origin in time, more gods may be generated in the future, though since Epicurus holds that nothing can now occur which has not occurred at some time in the infinite past, these gods would presumably have to be indistinguishable from some of those already existing.[4] However, since we have argued earlier that the universe itself must exist eternally, and that the 'original' downward fall of atoms is only logically prior to the other causes of physical events, namely blows of atoms upon one another and swerves of atoms from their downward path, we are forced to the conclusion that, if the gods have an origin in time, there was once a time in which few, or perhaps no gods

[1] Bailey, *Greek Atomists* 469.
[2] Sextus Empiricus, *Adv. Math.* 9.178.
[3] Cic., *ND* 1.49.   [4] Cf. Us. 266.

existed. Such a conclusion flies in the face of the scraps of evidence which we have. According to Hippolytus it was the view of Epicurus that god is 'from eternity' (ἀίδιον).[1] Hippolytus' evidence may be dismissed as loosely expressed, though his words 'from eternity and imperishable' (ἀίδιον καὶ ἄφθαρτον) certainly seem to imply that the Epicurean gods have no beginning in time nor end in time. But there is a passage of Philodemus which settles the matter. The race of the gods 'has come into existence from eternity' (γεγονὸς δι' αἰῶνος), says Philodemus.[2] According to Merlan this suggests that Philodemus thinks that a god may both have come into existence and exist eternally, that is, have an eternal *dependent* existence.[3] That is a possible explanation. But it is not the only possibility. The phrase 'having come into existence from eternity' (γεγονὸς δι' αἰῶνος) serves another purpose admirably: the gods have existed eternally (δι' αἰῶνος), but their form, as we know, is constantly undergoing modification and restoration (*nec ad numerum*). Either way, the passage from Philodemus supports the evidence of Hippolytus that the gods have existed from eternity. We should emphasize again that if we accept that in Epicurean physics the downward movement of atoms is only logically prior to their swerve and their movements in other directions due to blows from one another, we can also accept that the existence of the gods from eternity is in no way contra-dictory to the physical principles of Epicurus.[4]

As we have already mentioned, Philodemus and probably Epicurus himself ascribed a number of specific activities to their gods. They eat and drink[5] and talk to one another.[6] Philodemus even supposes that their language is Greek or something very like it – the reason for this is probably that Greek was regarded as the only language that could admit of philosophical precision;[7] and from their conversations they derive unspeakable pleasure.

[1] Us. 359.
[2] If we accept Arrighetti's reconstruction of Philodemus, *De Dis* 3, fr. 79, p. 68 Diels (*PP* 10 (1955) 336).
[3] Merlan, *Studies* 59.   [4] Cf. Kleve, 'Die Urbewegung', 62.
[5] Philod., *De Dis* 3, fr. 77, p. 67 Diels; cf. Arrighetti, *PP* 10 (1955) 333.
[6] Philod., *De Dis* 3, col. 13, 36–9, p. 36 Diels.
[7] *Ibid.*, col. 14, 4–6, p. 37 Diels.

They do not become tired; therefore they do not need sleep, for sleep is akin to death.[1] Yet they have periods of rest.[2] They are friendly one to another, except apparently where their infinite numbers make such mutual acquaintance impossible.[3] As we might expect, the friendships of the gods involve us in some of the same questions as the friendships of men. In one passage Philodemus seems to suggest that, if the gods did not enjoy certain benefits from one another, their happiness would not be complete,[4] while elsewhere he observes that even though they favour one another (does this contradict Epicurus?) they are self-sufficient by themselves and are able to provide for their own most complete pleasure.[5] If these ideas are to be reconciled, the most probable explanation is that the favour the gods derive from one another is provided merely by their existence and not by positive acts of help. Just as satisfaction is to be gained by men from the contemplation of the gods, so the gods themselves derive pleasure from contemplation (and conversation) with one another. Thus their self-sufficiency and the completeness of their pleasures would be maintained even if each god were unique, but he can obtain a 'variation' of pleasure by conversation and the observation of his peers. It is essential to maintain that the happiness and pleasure of the gods is perfect. The best explanation of the puzzling passage in which Philodemus says that, if certain 'advantages' (χρεῖαι) were not obtained, then the happiness of the gods would not be complete (τέλειος), is that by 'complete' he refers to the enjoyment of certain additional kinetic pleasures which provide fresh variants on the katastematic pleasures which the gods constantly enjoy. We know, of course, that the absence of any particular kinetic pleasure cannot detract from the perfection of pleasure (that is, absence of pain) which the gods always possess.

Whatever difficulties the friendships of the gods may provide, there can be no doubt that the pleasures of the gods are *in fact* both katastematic and kinetic. In view of the repeated emphasis

[1] *Ibid.*, col. 12, 18, p. 34 Diels; cf. Lucr., 4.924.
[2] *Frag. Herc.*, pp. 167–73 Scott.
[3] Philod., *De Dis* 3, fr. 84, col. 1, 3–9, pp. 15–16 Diels.
[4] *Ibid.*, fr. 84, 2–4. [5] *Ibid.*, fr. 85, 5–7, p. 17 Diels.

by Epicurean writers on the calm quietness of the gods and the perfection of their pleasures, it seems superfluous to wonder whether the gods enjoy pleasures which can be classed as kata-stematic. But interpreters have professed themselves in doubt on the details, and in particular it has been urged that since we know both that the gods eat and that they derive (presumably) kinetic pleasure from conversations with one another, it is impossible to assume that *all* their pleasures are katastematic.[1] Indeed, it may be objected that, although they enjoy kata-stematic pleasures, it does not follow that *all* their pleasures are katastematic. Merlan, however, thinks this does follow from another passage of Philodemus where it is argued that, because the gods enjoy imperishability, they are free from the experience of any pleasures or pains from outside themselves.[2] What this means, according to Merlan, is that all their joys are within themselves. Hence they are all katastematic. Yet the problem of the kinetic pleasures of eating remains. The only solution, concludes Merlan, is that this is another example of the 'notorious' difficulties in Epicurean theology.

But it is not necessary to despair of a solution. If, as we have argued, all kinetic pleasures presuppose existing katastematic pleasures in the individual organs concerned, we must first assert that the gods enjoy complete katastematic pleasure, that is, they enjoy pleasure in every part of their being. That being so, what would their possible kinetic pleasure consist in? Obviously in 'variations' over greater or lesser areas of their bodies. Let us assume that the gods eat. If we interpret Philo-demus with Merlan, we should also assume they have no sense of taste – which is absurd – or that there is a contradiction. Probably, however, Philodemus only means by 'pleasures and pains from outside themselves' pleasures and pains which they cannot control and arrange, and which may actually increase the amount of pleasure enjoyed. The problem about kinetic pleasures, such as that of eating, is something like that about the pleasures of friendship. Without friendship the gods would still enjoy the greatest pleasure, but friendship brings them

[1] Merlan, *Studies* 17–18.
[2] Philod., *De Piet.* 2, col. 107, p. 125 Gomperz (Us. 99).

something new, that is, a variation on the pleasure they already possess. In terms of the amount of pleasure obtained the presence of friends brings no pleasure to those who are by themselves self-sufficient in regard to happiness. If we now try to generalize from this, we shall conclude that nothing outside the gods' control can increase or decrease their pleasure, which does indeed depend on their own constitutions. Pleasure cannot be brought up 'from outside' because it is already available in the highest amounts. But kinetic pleasures are not pleasures brought up from outside so as to increase the total pleasure in any particular organism; they are new ways of experiencing absence of pain.

Right religion

It seems that the same kinds of benefits which the gods bestow on one another are to a still larger degree available to men. As we know, the gods take no direct part in human affairs. Praying to them is of no avail if prayer is a mere request for help. In any case it is pointless for a man to pray for what he can provide for himself, namely happiness.[1] If gods heeded human prayers, ran the Epicurean argument, the human race would long since have become extinct, since men are constantly praying for disasters to fall on one another.[2] We can, in fact, neither achieve our wishes by begging from the gods, nor give them anything beneficial by our offerings.[3] Nevertheless prayer is to be recommended if properly used,[4] as is participation in the religious life of one's own country.[5] Such participation is a natural act.[6] Epicurus set his followers an example here: he

[1] VS 65.   [2] Us. 388.   [3] Lact., Div. Inst. 7.5.3.

[4] Cf. Hadzits, 'Significance of Worship'. D.L. 10.120 records that Epicurus said that the wise man will erect dedicatory statues. For an example of this practice being carried out—a herm of Phaedrus dedicated to the gods of Eleusis—see Raubitschek, Hesperia 15 (1949) 101–3.

[5] Cf. Philod., De Piet. 2, col. 108, 14, p. 126 Gomperz; col. 110, 25, p. 128 Gomperz; P. Oxy., 215, col. 2, 7 (SBB 1916, pp. 902–4). Cf. Schmid, 'Götter und Menschen', 144–7. Schmid ('Chi è l'autore?') has argued powerfully for Philodemus as the author of P. Oxy. 215, but the question of authorship is not very important for our purposes.

[6] Philod., De Piet. 2, col. 110, 5 ff., p. 128 Gomperz; De Musica 4.4.7–14 Kemke.

urged them to take part in sacrifices without worrying about false popular beliefs.[1] He himself participated with his fellow citizens in the festivities of the Anthesteria at Athens,[2] and was an initiate of the Eleusinian mysteries; he urged respect for oaths taken in the name of the gods.[3] From antiquity on many of Epicurus' opponents have regarded his behaviour as at best hopelessly inconsistent with his ideas and at worst a hypocritical safety precaution designed to protect Epicureans from the unpopularity and possible danger caused by their supposed irreligion.[4] There is a modicum of distorted truth in the latter suggestion, for Epicurus advised obedience to the laws and customs of one's own country as a means of living a life untroubled by political storms. But there are much more important reasons for the stand he took. First of all contemplation of the gods is a source of great pleasure. When our mind is concentrated on the images flowing from the gods, Velleius says, the greatest pleasures accrue as we understand their blessed and eternal natures.[5] This is more than that freedom from trouble which we achieve when we are liberated by correct beliefs about the gods from fears of reward and punishment. It is a delight of the mind, aroused by wonder at the excellence and happiness of immortal beings. Even Cotta, Cicero's opponent of Epicureanism, seems to admit that the Epicureans venerated the gods out of wonder at their nature, though he finds such wonder misplaced and senseless if the gods are such as the Epicureans hold them to be.[6]

Cotta's admission doubtless echoes the views of Philodemus, who says that the sage wonders at the nature and character of

[1] Philod., *De Piet.* 2, col. 108, 9, p. 126 Gomperz. Lucretius seems to be following Epicurus' example of honouring the ancestral gods but avoiding false belief in his invocation to Venus; cf. Kleve, 'Lukrez', esp. 91–3.

[2] Philod., *De Piet.* 2, col. 109, p. 127 Gomperz; cf. the recommendation to Polyaenus, *ibid.*, 2, col. 75, 25, p. 105 Gomperz.

[3] *Ibid.*, p. 104 Gomperz.

[4] Plut., *Non posse* 1102B; Philod., *De Piet.* 2, col. 78, p. 108 Gomperz; cf. Cic., *ND* 1.123 for the view of Posidonius on Epicurus as an overthrower of religion, and Plut., *Adv. Col.* 1125EF.

[5] Cic., *ND* 1.50. Cf. Atticus *ap.* Euseb., *PE* 15.5, where we learn that the ἀπόρροιαι of the gods are a source of great goods, and P. Herc. 168, col. 1, 9, with Philippson, *SO* 19 (1939) 38.   [6] Cic., *ND* 1.117.

the gods and tries to draw near it as if he desires to touch it and be with it. Such a man, says Philodemus, should call wise men the friends of the gods and gods the friends of the wise.[1] Elsewhere Philodemus tells us that those who retain in their memory the forms of the best and most blessed beings, namely the gods, are among those to be admitted to the regular banquets of an Epicurean community.[2] And we know that such attitudes are not a growth of later Epicureanism, where it might at least be arguable that they are a reaction to Stoic beliefs. We can find them in a well known passage of Epicurus himself which Philodemus quotes: 'Every wise man has pure and holy opinions about the divine and has understood that this nature is great and holy. But particularly at festivals does he come to a grasp of it because he constantly has its name on his lips and, through a more vivid experience, grasps the immortality of the gods.'[3] Finally we may appeal to a further letter, perhaps also by Epicurus himself.[4] It is argued that mere partaking in sacrifices is not a firm basis for piety. What we need to secure this firm basis (τὸ βέβαιον εὐσεβείας) is in the first instance a proper understanding of the best thing we can conceive, namely the gods. Such an understanding is itself blessed. We should stand amazed at it and reverence the divine experience.[5] Contem-

---

[1] Philod., *De Dis* 3, col. 1, 14, p. 16 Diels.

[2] Cf. Philod., *De Epicuro*, fr. 8, col. 1, p. 70 Vogliano.

[3] Philod., *De Piet.* 2, col. 76, p. 106 Gomperz (Philippson, *Hermes* 56 (1921) 373).

[4] As claimed by Diels in his edition of P. Oxy. 215 (*SBB* 1916, pp. 886–909). Cf. Festugière, *Epicurus* 64–5. But Schmid's arguments for Philodemus as author are strong (see above p. 156, n. 5).

[5] For the interpretation of this very difficult text I have followed Schmid ('Götter und Menschen', 137–8), as do Merlan (tentatively) in *Studies* 29 and Pfligersdorffer (*WS* 70 (1957) 251; *AAHG* 11 (1958) 148). The older view of Diels (supported, for example, by Festugière) is reaffirmed by Barigazzi in 'Uomini e dei'. It seems that in the context of the papyrus the recognition of an object for τὸ διειληφέναι καλῶς gives a clearer sense. If we do not allow an object and translate as 'clear perception', the question 'Clear perception of what?' is not easy to answer convincingly. If Epicurus wished to say 'true understanding', a phrase like ὀρθὴ γνῶσις would have been a better way of saying it. The text is as follows: μακαριώτατον μέν τι νόμιζε τὸ διειληφέναι καλῶς, ὃ τὸ πανάριστον ἐν τοῖς οὖσι διανοηθῆναι δυνάμεθα. It should perhaps be added that I do not accept Schmid's

plation of the gods is a source of pleasure, and should be valued as such. The vivid experience by which at festivals we can 'grasp' the immortality of the gods, the sense of pleasure which accompanies such awareness – all this adds up to a doctrine of the kinship of the wise with the gods. As has often been recognized,[1] it is an Epicurean version of the Platonic ideal of the attainment of likeness to the gods – and this attainment and its accompanying happiness is achieved by a right recognition of the gods' natures. The idea that the wise man strives to touch and be with the true nature evokes a clear echo of the *Symposium*. As we have known since the work of Bignone, Epicurus sets himself up as the rival and supplanter of Plato and Aristotle; hence it should afford no surprise that in the last sentence of an Epicurean letter on true and false varieties of piety, the climax is a slighting reference to Plato.[2] The wise man is indeed the rival of the gods for happiness,[3] for the pleasures of the soul are superior to those of the body,[4] and the wise man can enjoy the pleasures of the soul. It is true that the gods are immortal, but the perfection of happiness does not depend on its continuation over infinite time.[5] Likeness to the gods is a joyful reality for the wise man and an ambition to be achieved by the novice.[6] We recall how Lucretius hails Epicurus as a god himself.[7]

This is the context in which we should view passages stating the benefits accruing to mankind from the gods. There are many such passages, but one of the most interesting is a mutilated text in Philodemus, in which Epicurus seems to be

interpretation of θεωρία in a later section of this same papyrus. The text is τιμῶν αὐτὴν τὴν θεωρίαν σαυτοῦ ταῖς συγγενέσι κατὰ σάρκα ἡδοναῖς. Schmid takes θεωρία to mean 'contemplation of the gods'. Diels' 'philosophic theory' seems preferable, particularly in view of the phrase 'doctrine most worthy of belief' above.

[1] Particularly clearly by Schmid, 'Götter und Menschen', 127–40.
[2] P. Oxy. 215.
[3] VS 33.
[4] Diog. Oen., fr. 38 Chilton.
[5] BD 19, 20.
[6] D.L. 10.135 (Menoeceus); cf. the letter to his mother in Diog. Oen., fr. 52, col. 4 Chilton.
[7] Lucr., 5.8; cf. Plut., *Adv. Col.* 1117B for Colotes' attitude to Epicurus.

taking part in a conversation with the god Asclepius.[1] Some of the gods, Asclepius assures Epicurus, are well disposed toward him. We should not read too much into this. It is merely a vivid rendering of a number of Epicurean themes which should now be familiar. It tells us that some of the gods are friends of the wise man, Epicurus. That only *some* of them are his friends accords with a passage we observed earlier, where we noticed that, since there are so many gods, they cannot all be one another's friends. Presumably the same idea is now applied to men. More striking, perhaps, is the notion of the goodwill (εὐμένεια) of these gods which Epicurus is said to enjoy. But this should not be interpreted as active benevolence.[2] It is not that the gods exert themselves in any way to help the wise man; that would be in complete contradiction with the basic principles of Epicurean theology. Rather they smile upon him, as it were; they are well-disposed towards him. Thus the text is to be interpreted in the light of more general statements of the benefits which men gain from the gods. We have seen already how benefits, indeed the greatest pleasures, accrue to the man who concentrates his mind on the images flowing perpetually from the bodies of the gods and recognizes their nature. Only the good man is capable of recognizing such gods as they really are and thus of benefiting from them. It is only in this restricted sense that the gods actually show goodwill to mankind. The gods appreciate the wise man and the wise man derives pleasure from contemplating the gods. This contemplation, as we have seen, reflects the wise man's achievement of likeness to the objects of his contemplation.

There are other passages in Epicurean writings in which the thesis that the benevolence of the gods is passive is fully

---

[1] Cf. Jensen, *Ein neuer Brief* 15 (Philod., Περὶ κακιῶν 1, col. 1, 11 ff.). Philippson (*Phil. Woch.* 54 (1934) 154–60) argues that it cannot be proved that Epicurus is the speaker. I am not convinced by this, but even if it is true, it does not affect our cautious treatment of the passage. That Epicurus recognized individual gods (Zeus, Poseidon, Demeter, etc.) is clear from Plut., *Adv. Col.* 1119C–1120A.

[2] Jensen's text is by no means certain, but his restoration of εὐμ]ενεία[ς μετ]ασχὼν has a good deal of plausibility. Philodemus speaks of Zeus the Saviour (*De Morte* 3.33). This again does not refer to action on the part of a god.

supported. According to Philodemus Epicurus spoke in the thirteenth book of his treatise *On Nature* of the gods' being akin to some men and alien to others (περὶ τῆς οἰκειότητος... πρός τινας...καὶ τῆς ἀλλοτριότητος).[1] But here a new notion is introduced, that of the alienness of the gods to some, presumably to the bad (who are here at least equated with the foolish). That too seems to have been the doctrine of Epicurus himself in a famous passage of the letter to Menoeceus.[2] The impious man, says Epicurus, is not the man who rejects the gods of the many, but the man who attaches the beliefs of the many to the gods. For the statements of the many about gods are not (founded on) general concepts (προλήψεις) but false suppositions. As a result of this fact (ἔνθεν) the greatest injuries are brought down upon bad men because of the gods, and benefits are brought down (upon the good). What Epicurus is arguing is that it is *because* there are both true and false opinions current about the gods that the gods can cause both good and harm. If one has true opinions about the gods, this is a source, as we have seen, of very great pleasure. But if one's opinions about the gods are false, then we know the evils that can ensue: terror of the divine vengeance, superstitition, dread of death. Epicurus can say that these evils arise 'from the gods' (ἐκ θεῶν), since they could not occur if we did not know that the gods existed. That is why we have rendered ἐκ θεῶν somewhat loosely as 'because of the gods'. The gods are the cause of evils in the sense that without their existence these evils would not exist either. And Epicurus has already observed that not only the wise but also 'the many' recognize their existence through clear knowledge (ἐναργής...ἡ γνῶσις). In conclusion therefore we can see how this section of the letter to Menoeceus

---

[1] Philod., *De Piet.* 2, col. 106, p. 124 Gomperz.

[2] D.L. 10.123–4 (Menoeceus). I accept the text as printed in Long's Oxford edition of Diogenes. Schmid's recent emendations ('Götter und Menschen', 120) are unnecessary since the meaning is quite satisfactory with much less rewriting of the text. Usener's βλάβαι τε for the βλάβαι αἴτιαι of the MSS has great persuasiveness and makes excellent sense. It is much to be preferred to Stark's recent proposal βλάβαι αἰτιαταί (*Hermes* 93 (1965) 420–2). Gassendi's addition of τοῖς ἀγαθοῖς after ὠφέλειαι certainly gives the sense intended, though it is just possible that it was understood rather than written.

supports the passage from Philodemus in its suggestion that the gods are not only akin to the good but that they are 'alien' to the bad. This 'alienness' is to be understood in the sense that the bad misread the gods' natures and are thus 'alienated' from them. Hence comes the evil of fear.

If this interpretation is correct, we can understand the next sentence of the letter to Menoeceus clearly enough. The text reads as follows: 'For those always accustomed to their own virtues accept those like themselves, and regard all that is not like themselves as alien.' The problem is: Who are those 'accustomed to their own virtues' (ταῖς γὰρ ἰδίαις οἰκειούμενοι ἀρεταῖς)? Is Epicurus talking about the gods,[1] or does he mean the good and wise?[2] Or is the phrase indefinite, referring to people in general? We should notice that the word 'for' (γάρ) tells us that the sentence is designed as an explanation of its predecessor. And according to its predecessor goods or ills arise for mankind because of the gods for the particular reason that good men have right and beneficial beliefs and bad men have wrong and damaging beliefs. In other words we should expect this sentence to make a statement about how the opinions of both good and bad men arise. And if, with Bailey, we translate ταῖς γὰρ ἰδίαις οἰκειούμενοι ἀρεταῖς as 'for *men* being accustomed to their own virtues', we get precisely this sense. What Epicurus is saying is that men judge the character of the gods according to their own virtues or lack of them. Good men recognize that the gods are as they are, happy and unconcerned with mankind; bad men imagine that the gods are violent like themselves and for ever threatening punishments, being angered at human activities and human failings. As Lucretius puts it,[3] 'Unless you spew all these errors from your mind and put far from you thoughts unworthy of the gods and alien to their peace, their holy powers, besmirched by you, will often do you harm'.

[1] Jensen, *Ein neuer Brief* 79; Schmid, 'Götter und Menschen', 120.
[2] Barigazzi, *Hermes* 81 (1953) 145–58.
[3] Lucr., 6.68–71; cf. Philod., *De Dis* 1, col. 16, 19, p. 28 Diels (ταραχήν) and *De Piet.*, p. 100, 9 Gomperz, a passage wrongly interpreted by Diano (*Ep. Eth.* 100f.). See also Schmid, 'Götter und Menschen', 103, note 28, and 104, and for further references Kleve, *Gnosis* 118, note 4.

When we read the poem of Lucretius, we can easily be misled into supposing that Epicurean thought about the gods is almost entirely negative. It is true, as we have seen, that there are sections of his work in which Lucretius speaks about the blessed life of the gods in the *intermundia*, but more frequently we are learning of the evils and tragedies which false beliefs can produce and from which the enlightened philosophy of Epicurus can release us. Perhaps this is because, as has often been held, the poem is incomplete, and a last book, if it had been written, would have corrected the false impression. Be that as it may, our other evidence about Epicureanism, in particular that of Cicero, Philodemus and Epicurus himself, gives a more complete picture. For an Epicurean it is an important fact that there are gods, and piety, on which treatises were written by Epicurus himself[1] and by Philodemus, is an important virtue. It is also an important fact that the gods enjoy perpetual happiness and provide a model of perpetual happiness for mankind. For the good man true beliefs about the gods are as valuable as false beliefs are harmful to the bad and foolish. The point needs to be emphasized. Philodemus' writings, as we have them, contain a great deal of evidence about the gods; it might be imagined that this evidence has exaggerated the importance of the gods for Epicurus himself. We have attempted to argue in this chapter that, although the gods are not to be feared, and although prophecy is a fruitless exercise,[2] yet correct beliefs and even properly motivated practices of religion both aid our enjoyment of present pleasures and help to strengthen our hopes that such happiness will continue.

[1] D.L. 10.28.
[2] D.L. 10.135; cf. Diano *SIFC* 12 (1935) 237–9. Cf. Cic., *ND* 2.162.

9

POSTSCRIPT

A book of this sort could not usefully end with a chapter called 'Conclusion'. It has been our aim not to argue a thesis but to describe the essential characteristics of the philosophy of Epicurus. Nor have we attempted, except in minor instances, the perhaps valuable task of comparing Epicureanism with other post-Aristotelian philosophies. The only appropriate way to sum up our account would be to re-emphasize the reasons why Epicurus engaged in philosophical speculation and to state the place of his thought in its historical context. The first objective is not difficult to achieve. For Epicurus philosophy must be a pragmatic activity. Philosophical enquiry is important since it enables us to secure to a high degree that absence of pain which is humanity's primary need.

As for Epicurus' place in the history of Greek thought, that too is reasonably clear. In company with most of his contemporaries he rejects any form of philosophical idealism. In physics Epicurus reasserts the pre-Socratic tradition – but always subordinating natural philosophy to ethics – and he refines earlier atomism to meet the objections of Plato and Aristotle. In politics, ethics and religion he asserts the values of private life and rejects the claims of the city; in doing so he rejects by implication, though without full awareness of the revolutionary nature of his views, the basic fibre of Hellenism. In many important respects Epicurus condemns ancient society and refuses to accept its assumptions.

APPENDIX A

GENERAL CONCEPTS AND INNATE IDEAS

It might seem that the account we have given of general concepts (pp. 26–30) is complete. Basing ourselves on Diogenes Laertius, and finding confirmation in passages of Epicurus himself, we have argued that general concepts arise as the result of sensations. We have also mentioned that the Stoics took over the term 'general concept' from the Epicureans and we have argued, following Sandbach, that they used it in a similar sense. But the main point of Sandbach's article was to demonstrate that when the early Stoics used the term 'general concept' they were not thinking of any kind of innate idea.[1] If Sandbach is right then in maintaining that the Stoic and Epicurean uses of the term are basically similar—and certainly there is no statement to the contrary in any ancient author—it would follow that Epicurean general concepts are not innate ideas either. That is also the natural conclusion of our discussion in Chapter 2.

Basing himself largely on the account of general concepts given by Cicero, however, De Witt takes exactly the opposite view. For him the word of Diogenes is not to be trusted because it conflicts with Cicero's expert knowledge.[2] De Witt adduces a number of arguments about the way he thinks general concepts are formed and claims that since Diogenes' Epicurus makes mistakes in this area, he cannot be the historical Epicurus. Nor, argues De Witt, could it possibly be the case that Epicurus placed general concepts of such things as horses and oxen in the same logical category as the concept of justice.[3] It is clear, however, that despite the philosophical weaknesses of Epicurus' position, we cannot maintain that he did not hold it simply because it is wrong. In some other areas, as De Witt himself admits, Epicurean positions seem ludicrous.[4]

Of little more validity is De Witt's claim that the etymology of the Greek word πρόληψις (general concept), in particular the prefix πρό (before), suggests that general concepts precede sense-experience, that is, that they are innate ideas. But the 'preceding' aspect of a general concept can be accounted for without any such drastic solution. Our general concept of the gods is our basic knowledge of them: it is that they are immortal and blessed. It is not, for example, our knowledge that they eat and drink. Our general

---

[1] Sandbach, ''Εννοια and Πρόληψις'; cf. also Rist, *Stoic Philosophy* 134.
[2] De Witt, 'The Gods of Epicurus' and *Epicurus* 142–50.
[3] De Witt, *Epicurus* 144.
[4] *Ibid.* 141 for what De Witt calls Epicurus' ridiculous judgment about the size of the sun.

concepts then could be our prior knowledge, in the sense of our basic knowledge, not our innate ideas of things.

In fact De Witt's case rests entirely on a text of Cicero. If his interpretation of this text were correct, at least it could be argued that Cicero thought that Epicurus believed in innate ideas. We would then have to consider whether Cicero's beliefs are reliable. On the other hand, if Cicero's text does not imply innate ideas, De Witt's case disappears. The relevant passages of the *De Natura Deorum* are as follows:[1] *intellegi necesse est esse deos, quoniam insitas eorum vel potius innatas cognitiones habemus...Quae enim nobis natura informationem ipsorum deorum dedit, eadem insculpsit in mentibus ut eos aeternos et beatos haberemus.*[2] There are two main problems. What are these *insitae vel potius innatae cognitiones?* In what sense is nature said to engrave beliefs about the eternity and happiness of the gods on our minds? According to De Witt the word *innatus* implies that we have innate ideas of the gods. The matter is not, however, so easily settled. Cicero himself seems to suggest that our primary knowledge of the gods derives from images which appear to us when we are awake or in dreams.[3] But if we have innate ideas, why should we need such images? In fact De Witt's whole case rests on his assumption that *innatus* must *mean* 'inborn' or 'innate', and this assumption is by no means self-evidently true. Sandbach has recently pointed out that the combination of *insitus* and *innatus* is a Ciceronian cliché.[4] If so, it need not be taken too literally. If a thing is deeply engrained, it might be said to be inborn, though strictly speaking it would not be. And we might ask ourselves what Greek original Cicero is translating. Kleve wants to associate *innatus* with the Greek συγγενικός and refer it not to innate ideas but to the built-in structure of every soul capable of forming general concepts.[5] There are other possibilities too. The Greek might have been ἔμφυτος, which, as Sandbach pointed out in connection with the general concepts of the Stoics, can mean not only inborn but ingrown or implanted.[6] This is a matter on which certainty is impossible, but Sandbach's suggestion that we are dealing with a Ciceronian cliché referring to the notion of 'deep-rootedness' offers the most likely solution. If that is right, Cicero is not foolishly talking about innate ideas at one moment and concepts deriving from dreams and other images the next. As for the notion of *nature* engraving such general concepts on the mind, there is nothing in that to suggest that they are innate. Rather the text is more naturally interpreted to mean that when there is a mind, that is, after birth, general concepts are engraved on it through the functioning of

[1] Cic., *ND* 1.44–5.
[2] Cf. *notionem impressit, ND* 1.43.　　　　[3] *ND* 1.46.
[4] Review of Kleve, *Gnosis* in *CR* n.s. 14 (1964) 272.
[5] Kleve, *Gnosis* 34. For a full discussion and rebuttal of De Witt see Kleve, *Gnosis* 23–34.
[6] Sandbach, '῎Εννοια and Πρόληψις', 48.

the senses, as the account of Diogenes Laertius would have us believe. In sum there is no reason to deny that the accounts of a general concept given by Cicero and by Diogenes Laertius are complementary.

APPENDIX B

THE WEIGHT OF THE DEMOCRITEAN ATOM

In the atomism of Leucippus and Democritus the question of the weight of atoms is linked with that of their motion. There is a good deal of evidence to suggest that for Democritus the original motion of the atoms is confused. They wander at random through the universe, collide at random, entangle and separate from one another at random and occasionally link up in such a way as to produce a vortex-like movement which leads to the formation of worlds.[1] If this is the case, then Democritus would have had no use for a theory of the 'natural' motion downwards of atoms due to weight, and, as Guthrie points out, when Simplicius says that according to Democritus atoms were 'naturally motionless', this must mean that they have no 'natural' motion in the Aristotelian sense. Simplicius knew his sources too well to say that the atoms naturally have no motion at all. Guthrie also draws our attention to a passage of Cicero, in which it is said to be an error limited to the Epicurean version of atomism to suppose that the atoms are carried perpendicularly downwards because of their weight.[2] But although Democritus apparently did not think that atoms have a natural movement perpendicularly downwards because of their weight, it does not follow that he denied weight to them altogether. Indeed a minority of commentators has long argued the plausible position that, since according to Aristotle Democritus *did* claim that atoms have weight, we should accept this testimony.[3] Democritus would certainly have rejected the notion that there is such a thing as 'up' and 'down' in an infinite universe, while still giving weight to his atoms.

There is good evidence in Aristotle that Democritus distinguished the atoms from one another by weight. The weight of Democritus' atoms varies with their size, says Aristotle in the *De Generatione*,[4] and Theophrastus speaks

---

[1] For a recent survey of the evidence see Guthrie, *History* 2.400–2.
[2] Cic., *De Fin.* 1.17.
[3] Brieger, *Die Urbewegung*; Liepmann, *Mechanik*.
[4] *De Gen. et Corr.* 326a9. Inevitably attempts have been made to emend this passage away.

in a similar vein in the *De Sensu*.[1] Guthrie tries to evade the implications of these passages by adducing another from Simplicius which refers to the fact that atoms in a vortex, not atoms floating freely in the void, have weight. But it does not follow that because atoms in a vortex have weight, atoms freely floating in the void do not.[2] As we have seen, Simplicius knows that for Democritus atoms have no 'natural' movement downwards; they move at random. Hence when in his commentary on the *Physics* he says that they move through the air because of their weight, he uses a word which, as Guthrie points out, cannot refer to *downward* movement.[3] But that does not mean that Simplicius is confused. Quite the contrary is probably the case. Simplicius knows that the Democritean atom has weight *and* that it does not move 'downwards' because of its weight. He may be misreading Democritus in suggesting that it moves *because* of its weight at all, but there is no reason to deny that he believes (correctly) that weight is one of its properties. Bailey was right to observe that Democritus thinks of weight as a secondary property, that is, a derivative of size, and that he has no notion of absolute weight, and describes atoms as 'heavier' or 'lighter' than one another. Yet granting all that, we still have to admit that the Democritean atom has weight.[4] Even though there is no standard by which weight can be understood – except by the comparison of one atom with another – the atoms are still 'relatively' heavy. Epicurus might have called them 'incomprehensibly heavy'.[5] Indeed Democritus may have hoped to indicate this relativity of weight when he spoke, if Simplicius records him accurately, of things *seeming* light and heavy.[6]

---

[1] *De Sensu* 61.
[2] Guthrie, *op. cit.* 403; cf. Simp., *In De Caelo*, p. 569, 5 Heiberg.
[3] Simp., *In Phys.*, p. 1318, 35 ff. Diels. The textual questions about the corrupt περιπαλαίσεσθαι do not seriously affect the argument. Democritus may have called his original random motion παλμός (Aët., 1.23.3 = DK 68A47).
[4] *Greek Atomists* 131.
[5] Bailey admits that weight in an absolute sense pre-dates Epicurean atomism. He attributes its introduction to Nausiphanes (*op. cit.* 129). This may be true if the phrase 'absolute weight' is used to describe a weight which induces a natural movement 'perpendicularly' downwards.
[6] *In De Caelo*, p. 569, 5 Heiberg.

APPENDIX C

THE GROWTH AND DECLINE OF
THE COSMOS

The processes of the growth and decline of the cosmos are described in some detail towards the end of the second book of Lucretius' poem. Solmsen, however, has drawn a false contrast between Epicureanism and the atomism of Democritus.[1] He draws attention to the theory of Democritus, as reported by Hippolytus, that the cosmos (world) is in a state of acme until it is no longer able to accept anything additional from outside. But that seems to be also the position of Epicurus in the letter to Pythocles (89), for he says that the period of maximum development of the cosmos will last as long as the cosmos is capable of receiving new materials, presumably to make up for its constant losses. Epicurus' phrase προσδοχὴν...ποιεῖσθαι seems, despite Solmsen, to be the equivalent of Democritus' ἔξωθέν τι προσλαμβάνειν. In other words for both Democritus and Epicurus the process of receiving new material, the 'watering' of the foundations, eventually comes to an end. At this stage the world begins to go into decline. There is no evidence in Epicurus that, when the decline has begun, the intake of new material *merely* fails to compensate for the loss of old. Rather Epicurus seems to hold to the view of Democritus that after the acme intake ceases altogether. And although such texts as Lucretius 2.1118–19 (*ut fit ubi nilo iam plus est quod datur intra / vitalis venas quam quod fluit atque recedit*) might give some credibility to Solmsen's idea that there exists an Epicurean view different from that of Democritus, Lucretius does not in fact say that the world goes on taking more atoms after passing its most developed point. Thus although we must note Solmsen's emphasis on the way Epicurus (by his word 'watering') and Lucretius (by his parallel between the growth of the earth by reception of atoms and the growth of man by the reception of food) both seem to be talking of the growth of the world as though it were like a living being,[2] we should not press the parallel too far. It seems to be only in the period of growth that the parallel holds. Lucretius tends to give a false impression – though strictly speaking he accepts Epicurus' position – because his poetic rendering of the comparison between man and the world overshadows his philosophical intentions. Indeed he says in the case of *living things* that after the attainment of their acme input no longer balances output; that is what deceived Solmsen. But he does not apply the account of the decline of living things to the decline of the cosmos. In the decline of the cosmos no atoms

[1] Solmsen, 'Epicurus on the Growth and Decline of the Cosmos'.
[2] Cf. Aëtius, 2.4.10.

169

APPENDIX C

are taken in. Rather they batter against and help undermine the foundations
of the world.

Perhaps Solmsen would emphasize the fact that the mood of Lucretius'
account is different from that of Epicurus. At least that is true of the passage
in which the poet suggests that we ourselves are living in a declining period
of the present cosmos.[1] He repeats this view elsewhere in the poem, but it is
not found in the writings of Epicurus himself. Above all there is no trace in
Epicurus of the mood of Lucretius when he voices his prayer that the last day
may not come in his own lifetime.[2]

APPENDIX D

THE RELATION BETWEEN
KINETIC AND KATASTEMATIC
PLEASURE

There are a number of objections to the theory that kinetic pleasures supervene on katastematic pleasures, some of which must be taken seriously.
One of the less serious is the argument that if the theory were correct and, for
example, the pleasure of eating and drinking is of the palate alone, then the
palate should be able to enjoy this pleasure whether we are hungry or not.
We all know, however, that it is possible to eat and enjoy eating when we do
not need to eat, and if we overeat to excess the pleasure may continue *in the
palate* while we feel pain elsewhere. Even when it ceases in the palate, this
would be because the atoms of the palate are disturbed by events in the
rest of the body. Conversely, if we eat when we are hungry, more and more
parts of the whole organism are gradually restored to their natural state, to
the enjoyment of katastematic pleasure, on which, of course, kinetic pleasure
may supervene.

Following Bignone, however, Merlan finds difficulties in a passage of the
De Finibus.[3] Cicero's text is as follows: *restincta sitis stabilitatem voluptatis habet,
illa autem voluptas ipsius restinctionis in motu est.* Clearly a distinction between
katastematic and kinetic pleasure is intended. Clearly *restincta sitis* refers to
the katastematic pleasure of the stomach. According to Diano, *voluptas
restinctionis* would have to be the kinetic pleasure not of the stomach *and* of the
palate, which, according to Merlan, would be 'what common sense would

[1] Lucr., 2. 1150–74.
[2] Lucr., 5. 104–9; cf. Green, 'The Dying World of Lucretius'.
[3] Cic., *De Fin.* 2.9; see Diano, *RAL* (1936) 842ff.; Merlan, *Studies* 12.

170

take these words to mean', but of the palate alone – and this Merlan finds a difficult leap to make. But the difficulty is exaggerated and Diano's interpretation is right, as the *De Finibus* itself indicates. After the distinction between katastematic and kinetic pleasure has been made and the example of the quenching of thirst given, Cicero says that he cannot understand what the Epicurean Torquatus means when he says that kinetic pleasures 'vary' our former pleasant sensations (*quae faciat varietatem voluptatum*) but that 'that pleasure' (*illam . . . voluptatem*) is not increased. Thus the nature of a kinetic pleasure is specifically said to be a variation upon an already existing pleasure; and that already existing pleasure must be a katastematic pleasure. The passage is paralleled by another from the *Tusculans*,[1] in connection with which Merlan himself says that 'all examples of kinetic ἡδονή given by Cicero consist in ποικίλλειν, i.e. presuppose katastematic ἡδονή'.[2]

A second argument offered by Merlan is much more interesting. He wonders how Diano applies his theory to the pleasures of the mind. If philosophical discussions can remove our fears of the gods or of death, must we assume that we experience no kinetic pleasure of the mind during these discourses? 'Or that it is another part of the mind which is afraid of death and another which enjoys the philosophical discourse?' Further, as Merlan points out, one of the *Vatican Sayings* tells us that the process of learning coincides in time with our enjoyment (ἀπόλαυσις).[3] From this Merlan argues that, since learning must provide a kinetic pleasure, if we assume Diano's theory that all kinetic pleasure presupposes the katastematic pleasure of the part of the organism in which it takes place, we have also to assume that no learning takes place unless the mind is 'pacified'. And how is the mind to be pacified without instructions, asks Merlan? And how can instruction take place without κίνησις of the mind?

The questions are not as difficult as Merlan supposes, and the conclusion which he draws does not follow. He asks how the mind is to be pacified without instruction. The answer is that unless something in the mind, and in Epicurean terms that means some atoms of the mind, is already pacified, then no learning of any kind can take place. We know that in some sense the enjoyment of katastematic pleasure is our natural state. If we are so mentally disturbed that none of our mind atoms is moving regularly, Epicurus would think that we are incapable of learning; we have become totally unnatural. Thus when we learn, we have a pacified section of the mind, and on Diano's theory that section will experience the kinetic pleasures involved in learning. In the course of this learning, naturally enough, the pacified area will increase and we shall be able to enjoy a wider and wider

---

[1] Cic., *Tusc. Disp.* 3.46–7.
[2] Merlan, *Studies* 11.
[3] *VS* 27.

range of mental pleasures. Thus although Merlan's objection looks strong, and there are no direct references in ancient texts which can be deployed against it, there is no reason why kinetic pleasures of the mind should not be understood in the same way as kinetic pleasures of the body, both depending on previously existing katastematic pleasures in the part of the organism directly involved. Indeed, if Diano's theory were wrong, Epicurus would have to think that in the case of mental pleasures the same organ (the mind) experiences pleasure and pain at the same time. That would involve him in a contradiction of which he could hardly have been unaware.

APPENDIX E

VARIETIES OF EPICUREAN GODS

In the *De Natura Deorum* (1.49) Cicero says that the Epicurean gods are not seen *ad numerum*.[1] It has been recognized that these words are a translation of the Greek κατ᾽ ἀριθμόν and refer in some way to individual identity. The individual identity of the gods is somehow unlike that of the solid bodies which we recognize with the senses. It is tempting to connect the phrase *ad numerum* in Cicero with a part of the scholion to Epicurus' first *Basic Doctrine*, for after pointing out that the gods are recognized by reason, the scholiast continues with the words οὓς μὲν κατ᾽ ἀριθμὸν ὑφεστῶτας, οὓς δὲ κατὰ ὁμοείδειαν; and these words again refer to the gods. The interpretation of Cicero's *ad numerum* must await clarification of the scholion.

Merlan has argued that the scholion tells us that Epicurus recognized two kinds of gods, those who are fully individualized, like Zeus, and thus discernible from one another, and those which only differ specifically, like the Graces.[2] Of the latter class each species would contain many gods who cannot be distinguished from one another. The existence of such a class of specifically discernible but individually non-discernible gods has an *a priori* likelihood, since there is no reason why, among the combinations of atoms which form the bodies of the gods, there should not be many gods composed of exactly similar atoms arranged in exactly similar ways. And there is no doubt that, unless the scholion is emended, Epicurus is shown to have posited these two kinds of divinities. Many attempts have been made to avoid this conclusion, and they should be briefly mentioned. Some scholars have tried to emend the text;[3] others have argued that οὓς μὲν...οὓς δέ

[1] Cf. Pease, *ad loc.* for references.
[2] Merlan, *Studies* 38–97; see also 'Zwei Fragen'.
[3] E.g. G. F. Schoemann, third edition, 1865. See appendix to 1.37 (p. 105).

means 'in one way. . . in another way',[1] and thus that only one class of divinities is in question. These attempts would appear more plausible if they had supporting evidence, and less plausible if Merlan could produce other passages supporting the thesis that there are two kinds of divinities in Epicurus. We should consider his claim to have done this.

Merlan offers us a passage from Philodemus' *De Dis*.[2] Diels prints the text as follows: διὰ δὴ τὰ προειρημένα κ(αὶ) καλῶς ἔχει τιμᾶν, καὶ σέβεσθαι καὶ ταῦτα, [κ]αὶ μᾶλλον ἢ τὰ κατασκευαζόμενα πρ(ὸς) ἡμῶν εἴδη, καὶ τοὺς νέους θεούς, ἐ[πεὶ] τὰ μὲν ἀεὶ συνάπτεται τοῖς [γε] σεβασμοῦ τοῦ παντὸς ἀξίοις, τὰ δ' οὐχ ὁμοίως.

According to Merlan there are two kinds of 'worshipables' mentioned in this passage;[3] others have disagreed and claim that there are three.[4] Merlan's objection to three is strong,[5] but for our present purposes what matters is how many kinds of worshipables the Epicureans themselves recognized and what were their grounds for distinguishing them. And although Merlan thinks that the sense of the passage is obvious, Philodemus provides no indisputable evidence that he is talking about the kind of distinction Merlan needs. It is certain that καὶ ταῦτα refers to one class of worshipables, and very probable that another group is implied. But we cannot deny that it is not certain that these two groups are the groups mentioned in the scholion. The *De Dis*, though not harmful to Merlan's case, cannot be used to support it without reservations.

Merlan thinks that some of Epicurus' gods are indiscernible and some are not. Other scholars, notably Diano[6] and Krokiewicz,[7] have gone further. According to Diano all Epicurus' gods are indiscernible. As Merlan has pointed out,[8] this is false: Cicero and Philodemus both indicate, one

---

[1] Cf. Philippson, 'Zur epikureischen Götterlehre', 580, and many others, most recently Kleve, *Gnosis* 61.

[2] *De Dis* 3, col. 10, 2 ff., p. 29 Diels. Merlan in general follows the interpretation of Diels. However the reading πρὸς ἡμῶν εἴδη καὶ τοὺς νέους θεούς may not be the best. Freymuth (*Zur Lehre* 17), perhaps rightly, prefers ἕδη καὶ ναούς, which is much nearer the papyrus.

[3] Merlan, *Studies* 38–44.

[4] E.g. Philippson, 'Die Götterlehre', 171–5; Freymuth, *Zur Lehre* and 'Methodisches', 234–44.

[5] In particular the view of Philippson and Freymuth that the *intermundia* are deserving of worship seems strange and unsupported. Since Merlan's book an unduly pessimistic article of Moreschini's has appeared (*PP* 16 (1961) 342–72). Moreschini follows Philippson's view of the scholion (pp. 348 ff.).

[6] Diano, *Epicuri Ethica* 118 ff.

[7] Krokiewicz, 'De dis Epicuri', 100.

[8] Merlan, *Studies* 51. Gigante's attempt (*Rend. della Accad.* n.s. 28 (1953) 119–32) to show that Philodemus thought all gods indiscernible depends

explicitly, the other indirectly, that Epicurus recognized both male and female divinities.[1] Krokiewicz' thesis is stronger: he argues that the gods only differ in sex. All male divinities are indiscernible and all female divinities are indiscernible. There is no evidence in favour of this view, except perhaps the passage from Cicero's De Natura Deorum (1.49) where it is said that the nature of the gods is such that they have no soliditas and in some way cannot be grasped ad numerum. But if this passage is accepted as evidence that none of the gods can be recognized as individuals, we must go back and explain away the scholion which says that some gods are numerically distinguishable, others only distinguishable by species. Indeed Krokiewicz says that there are only two species of gods, male and female.

There is no need to interpret Cicero in this way. Cicero explains what he means in a later passage of the De Natura Deorum in which it is suggested that just as the form (species) of god has no soliditas, so 'it does not remain the same ad numerum' (1.105). It is not difficult to interpret this passage in such a way as not to contradict the scholion, though we have to admit that Cicero's ad numerum (=κατ' ἀριθμόν) is not in fact used in the same sense as the κατ' ἀριθμόν of the scholiast. All bodies throw off images constantly, and this throwing off of images represents a gradual erosion of the object itself. In the case of things mortal nothing can be done about this erosion. In the case of the gods means are at hand by which the erosion is counterbalanced by a constant replenishment of physical substance. If the bodies of the gods are constantly replenished by atoms exactly similar to those which are thrown off, they do not remain 'exactly the same', but 'very similar'. This phenomenon is what is referred to by Cicero's phrase ad numerum (though not by the scholiast), and may also be the subject of a strange passage in Aëtius in which it is said that one of four kinds of immortal things recognized by Epicurus is the class of 'similars' (ὁμοιότητες).[2] As Cicero says (De Natura Deorum 1.105), neque deficiunt umquam ex infinitis corporibus similium accessio; and again (1.49), cum infinita simillumarum imaginum species ex innumerabilibus individuis (scil. atoms) existat et ad deos adfluat.[3]

on a wild restoration of De Morte 4.3; contra Merlan, Studies 62–6. I have not discussed Metrodorus, fr. 12 Körte, because, as Merlan has shown (Studies 60–2), no restoration so far offered is convincing and the text cannot therefore be used to support argument.

[1] Cic., ND 1.95; Philod., De Dis 3, col. 5, p. 22, 26–7 Diels (πάντε[ς τ]ε κ(αὶ) πᾶ[σ]αι).

[2] Aët., 1.7.34. Cf. the scholion to BD 1 (ἐκ τῆς συνεχοῦς ἐπιρρύσεως τῶν ὁμοίων εἰδώλων ἐπὶ τὸ αὐτὸ ἀποτετελεσμένων).

[3] species, given by the MSS, must be the right reading, as is confirmed by its appearance in 1.105. The point at issue is that the 'appearance' of the gods is constantly changing in so far (and only in so far) as it receives a 'face-lift' by the arrival of existentially different (though perhaps almost identical) atoms. For the alternative reading series and its supporters see

Finally we should look at another passage of Philodemus.[1] Philodemus says that atomic complexes (here called ἑνότητες)[2] can be maintained not only from 'numerically' identical atoms, but also from atoms that are specifically but not 'numerically' identical. Both types of complex can retain a recognizable identity. The context of the passage makes it clear that Philodemus is discussing the gods, and his argument is that they enjoy permanent happiness even though they are perpetually renewed by the addition of *only specifically* identical atoms.[3] This seems to suggest that, although they do not remain 'exactly the same' (*nec ad numerum?*), they still retain their individual identity.

We may conclude that the argument for kinds of gods is not affected by the *ad numerum* passage of Cicero. But, although it depends on the scholion alone, it is probably correct. When Cicero says that the gods cannot be grasped *ad numerum* he refers to the fact that Zeus' body is constantly renewed by fresh atoms and thus does not remain 'the same'. When the scholiast says that only one class of gods exists κατ' ἀριθμόν, he means that Zeus is distinguishable from Apollo, but that the Graces are indistinguishable.

Pease, *ad loc.* Too much has been made of the word *imagines* in Cicero. If *imagines* are thrown off by the bodies of the gods, it is precisely *imagines* which need restoring.

[1] *De Pietate* 2, col. 80, p. 110, 4ff. (Us. 40 and corrigenda p. lxxvii). Cf. Bailey, *Greek Atomists* 453 (for comments on the unnecessary textual variants of Scott and Philippson) and Merlan, *Studies* 53.

[2] Philippson, 'Zur epikureischen Götterlehre', 589ff., originally held this view of ἑνότης, but later wrongly decided the reference was to atoms (*Hermes* 53 (1918) 376); the latter position is also that of Bailey (*Greek Atomists* 454) and Freymuth, 'Methodisches', 237ff. Merlan (*Studies* 54–5) argues for a return to the rendering 'atomic complexes'. Philod., *De Dis* 3, col. 11, 6, p. 31 Diels (τὰς ἐξ αὐτῶν ἑνότητας = gods), seems to support Merlan's interpretation.

[3] It is unnecessary to follow De Witt (*Epicurus* 264–6) who seems to think that this passage suggests that there are two kinds of gods, one which changes and the other which does not.

GLOSSARY OF TECHNICAL TERMS

ἄδηλον – inaccessible to the senses, remote and obscure

αἴσθησις – sensation

ἀκαταπληξία – undisturbedness

ἀταραξία – untroubledness

διάνοια – mind

εἴδωλον – image

ἐπαίσθημα – act supervening on sensation, act of comprehension

ἐνάργεια – self-evident truth

ἐπιμαρτύρησις – confirmation, supporting evidence

ἐπίνοια – thought

ἔρως – passion

λογισμός – calculation, reasoning process

μετάβασις – analogy

οὐκ ἀντιμαρτύρησις – absence of contrary evidence

πρόδηλον – accessible to the senses

πρόληψις – general concept

φανταστικὴ ἐπιβολὴ τῆς διανοίας – image-making contact of the mind

φαντασία – presentation

BIBLIOGRAPHY

Details are given of all books and articles mentioned in the text as well as a selection of other works on Epicureanism.

Alfieri, V. E., *Atomos Idea* (Florence 1953).
'L'atomo come principio intelligibile', *Epicurea in memoriam Hectoris Bignone* (Genoa 1959) 61–8.
Amerio, R. 'L'epicureismo e gli dei', *Filosofia* 4 (1953) 97–137.
'L'epicureismo e il bene', *Filosofia* 4 (1953) 227–54.
Arrighetti, G. 'Filodemo de dis III Fr. 74–82, Pap. Herc. 157', *PP* 10 (1955) 322–56.
'Sul problema dei tipi divini nell'epicureismo', *PP* 10 (1955) 404–15.
'Filodemo de dis III, col. x–xi', *Studi classici e orientali* 7 (1958) 83–99.
'La structure de la lettre d'Épicure à Pythoclès', *ACGB* (Paris 1969) 236–52.
Bailey, C. *Epicurus. The Extant Remains* (Oxford 1926).
The Greek Atomists and Epicurus (Oxford 1928).
Barigazzi, A. 'La μονή della terra nei frammenti ercolanesi del lib. xi del περὶ φύσεως di Epicuro', *SIFC* 24 (1950) 3–19.
'Epicurea', *Hermes* 81 (1953) 145–62.
'Uomini e dei in Epicuro', *Acme* 8 (1955) 37–55.
'Cinetica degli εἴδωλα nel περὶ φύσεως di Epicuro', *PP* 13 (1958) 249–76.
'Il concetto del tempo nella fisica atomica', *Epicurea in memoriam Hectoris Bignone* (Genoa 1959) 29–59.
'Épicure et le scepticisme', *ACGB* (Paris 1969) 286–93.
Bignone, E. *Epicuro* (Bari 1930).
'L'ΑΕΙΦΥΕΣ nella teologia epicurea (a proposito del Pap. ercol. 1055)', *RFIC* 61 (1933) 433–44.
L'Aristotele perduto e la formazione filosofica di Epicuro (Florence 1936).
Björck, G. 'Βλάβη, Αἰτία', *Glotta* 24 (1936) 251–4.
Bloch, O. R. 'État présent des recherches sur l'épicurisme grec', *ACGB* (Paris 1969) 93–138.
Bollack, J. 'Les Maximes de l'Amitié', *ACGB* (Paris 1969) 221–36.
Boyancé, P. *Lucrèce et l'épicurisme* (Paris 1963).
Brescia, C. 'La *philia* in Epicuro', *GIF* 8 (1955) 314–32.
Brieger, A. *Die Urbewegung der Atome bei Leukippos und Demokritos* (Halle 1884).
'Die Urbewegung der demokriteischen Atome', *Philologus* 63 (1904) 584–96.
Brink, C. O. 'Callimachus and Aristotle', *CQ* 40 (1946) 11–26.
Chilton, C. W. 'Did Epicurus approve of marriage? A study of Diogenes Laertius x, 119', *Phronesis* 5 (1960) 71–4.

Cole, T. *Democritus and the Sources of Greek Anthropology*, American Philological Association Monographs, no. 25 (1967).

Crönert, W. *Kolotes und Menedemos* (Leipzig 1906).

'Die Epikureer in Syria', *Jahreshefte d. Österr. Archaeol. Inst.* 10 (1907) 145-53.

De Falco, V. *L'Epicureo Demetrio Lacone*, Biblioteca di Filologia Classica 2 (Naples 1923).

De Lacy, E. 'Meaning and Methodology in Hellenistic Philosophy', *PR* 47 (1938) 390-409.

De Lacy, P. and E. 'Ancient Rhetoric and Empirical Method', *Sophia* 6 (1938) 523-30.

Philodemus: On Methods of Inference. A Study in Ancient Empiricism, American Philological Association Monographs, no. 10 (1941).

De Lacy, P. 'The Epicurean analysis of language', *AJP* 60 (1939) 85-92.

'Lucretius and the History of Epicureanism', *TAPA* 79 (1948) 12-23.

'Epicurean Epilogismos', *AJP* 79 (1958) 179-83.

'Colotes' First Criticism of Democritus', *Isonomia* (ed. Mau and Schmid) (Berlin 1964) 67-77.

'Limit and Variation in the Epicurean Philosophy', *Phoenix* 23 (1969) 104-13.

De Witt, N. W. 'Notes on the History of Epicureanism', *TAPA* 63 (1932) 166-76.

'Epicurean Contubernium', *TAPA* 67 (1936) 55-63.

'Organization and Procedure in Epicurean Groups', *CP* 31 (1936) 205-11.

'The Epicurean Doctrine of Gratitude', *AJP* 58 (1937) 320-8.

'Epicurus: περὶ φαντασίας', *TAPA* 70 (1939) 414-27.

'The gods of Epicurus and the Canon', *Tr. Roy. Soc. of Canada* 36 (1942) 33-49.

'Epicurus: all sensations are true', *TAPA* 74 (1943) 19-32.

Epicurus and his Philosophy (Minneapolis 1954).

Diano, C. 'Note epicuree', *SIFC* 12 (1935) 61-86, 237-89.

'Questioni epicuree', *RAL* 12 (1936) 819-95.

'La psicologia d'Epicuro e la teoria delle passioni', *GCFI* 20 (1939) 105-45; 21 (1940) 151-65; 22 (1941) 5-34; 23 (1942) 5-49, 121-50.

'Note epicuree', *ASNP* 12 (1943) 111-27.

'Dissentio–Διαισθάνομαι e il Problema della Memoria', *RAL* 4 (1943) 265-70.

Epicuri Ethica (Florence 1946).

'Questioni epicuree', *GCFI* 30 (1949) 205-24.

'Épicure: la philosophie du plaisir et la société des amis', *Les Études Philosophiques* 22 (1967) 173-84.

Diels, H. 'Philodemos über die Götter, Erstes Buch', *Abh. d. Kön. Preuss. Akad. der W., phil.-hist. Kl.* 7, 1915; 'Drittes Buch', 8.4 (text) and 5 (commentary), 1916.

'Ein epikureisches Fragment über Götterverehrung, Oxy. Pap. 2.215', *Sitz. Kön. Preuss. Akad. d. W.* (1916) 885–909.

Drabkin, I. E. 'Notes on Epicurean kinetics', *TAPA* 69 (1938) 364–74.

Düring, I. *Aristoteles* (Heidelberg 1966).

Easterling, H. J. 'Quinta Natura', *Mus. Helv.* 21 (1964) 73–85.

Escoubas, E. 'Ascétisme stoïcien et ascétisme épicurien', *Les Études Philosophiques* 22 (1967) 163–72.

Farrington, B. 'Karl Marx – Scholar and Revolutionary', *Mod. Quart.* 7 (1951–2) 83–94.

'La amistad epicúrea', *Notas e Estudios de Filosofía* 3 (1952) 105–13.

The Faith of Epicurus (London 1967).

Festugière, A. J. (trans. C. W. Chilton). *Epicurus and his Gods* (Oxford 1955).

'Recenti Contributi sulla γνῶσις θεῶν in Epicuro', *Athenaeum* 42 (1964) 214–22.

Freymuth, G. *Zur Lehre von den Götterbildern in der epikureischen Philosophie* (Berlin 1953).

'Eine Anwendung von Epikurs Isonomiegesetz (Cic. *de Nat. deor.* 1.50)', *Philol.* 98 (1954) 101–15.

'Methodisches zur epikureischen Götterlehre', *Philol.* 99 (1955) 234–44.

'Zu Philodem περὶ θεῶν Buch III Kol. 8 und 9', *Philol.* 102 (1958) 148–53.

Fritz, K. von. 'Nausiphanes', *RE* 16, cols. 2021–7.

Furley, D. 'Lucretius and the Stoics', *BICS* 13 (1966) 13–33.

Two Studies in the Greek Atomists (Princeton 1967).

'Knowledge of Atoms and Void in Epicureanism', in *Essays in Ancient Greek Philosophy*, ed. J. P. Anton and G. L. Kustas (Albany 1971) 607–19.

Gigante, M. 'Filodemo De Morte iv. 3', *Soc. naz. di scienze, lettere ed arti, Napoli, Rend. della Accad. di Arch., Lett., e Belle Arti*, n.s. 28 (1953) 119–32.

'Filodemo, De Morte iv 37–39 (Pap. Herc. 1050)', *PP* 10 (1955) 357–89.

'Philodemi De Morte iv col. iv–ix (Pap. Herc. 1050)', *PP* 13 (1958) 51–76.

'Philodème: Sur la liberté de parole', *ACGB* (Paris 1969) 196–217.

Giussani, C. T. *Lucreti Cari De rerum natura libri sex, vol. I (Studi lucreziani)–IV* (Turin 1896–8).

Green, W. M. 'The Dying World of Lucretius', *AJP* 63 (1942) 51–60.

Grilli, A. 'Su alcuni frammenti di Filodemo', *PP* 12 (1957) 23–45.

Grimal, P. 'L'Épicurisme romain', *ACGB* (Paris 1969) 139–68.

Guthrie, W. K. C. *History of Greek Philosophy* 2 (Cambridge 1965).

Guyau, M. *La morale d'Épicure*[5] (Paris 1910).

BIBLIOGRAPHY

Hadzits, G. D. 'The Significance of Worship and Prayer among the Epicureans', *TAPA* 39 (1908) 73–88.

Huby, P. 'The Epicureans, Animals and Freewill', *Apeiron* 3 (1969) 17–19.

Jensen, C. *Ein neuer Brief Epikurs* (Berlin 1933).

Kleve, K. 'Die "Urbewegung" der epikureischen Atome und die Ewigkeit der Götter', *SO* 35 (1959) 55–62.

'Die Unvergänglichkeit der Götter im Epikureismus', *SO* 36 (1960) 116–26.

'Cicerone e la teologia epicurea', *Atti del II Congresso Internaz. di Studi Ciceroniani* 2 (Rome 1961) 471–7.

'Wie kann man an das Nicht-Existierenden denken? Ein Problem der epikureischen Psychologie', *SO* 37 (1961) 45–57.

'Zur epikureischen Terminologie, 1. Λόγος und διάνοια; 2. *Res occultae, animo videre, manu tractare* (Cic., *nat. deor.* 1.49)', *SO* 38 (1962) 25–31.

Gnosis Theon (*SO* supp. 19) (Oslo 1963).

'Lukrez und Venus (*De rer. nat.* 1.1–49)', *SO* 41 (1966) 86–94.

'Lucrèce, l'épicurisme et l'amour', *ACGB* (Paris 1969) 376–83.

Krokiewicz, A. 'De dis Epicuri', *Eos* 32 (1929) 91–120.

'Nauka Epikura', *Bull. Int. de l'Acad. Polon.* (Krakow 1929) 39–54.

Liepmann, H. C. *Mechanik der Leukippisch-Demokriteischen Atome* (Leipzig 1886).

Luschnat, O. 'Die atomische Eidola-Poroi-Theorie in Philodems Schrift De Morte', *Prolegomena* 2 (1953) 21–41.

Marx, K. *The Relation of Epicurus and Democritus*, Marx-Engels Gesamtausgabe, Bd. 1 (Frankfurt 1927).

Mau, J. *Zum Problem des Infinitesimalen bei den antiken Atomisten* (Berlin 1954).

'Raum und Bewegung, zu Epikurs Brief an Herodot 60', *Hermes* 82 (1954) 13–24.

'Über die Zuweisung zweier Epikur-Fragmente', *Philol.* 99 (1955) 93–111.

Merbach, F. *De Epicuri Canonica* (diss. Leipzig 1909).

Merlan, P. 'Zwei Fragmente der epikureischen Theologie', *Hermes* 68 (1933) 196–217.

'Lucretius: Primitivist or Progressist?', *JHI* 11 (1950) 364–8.

Studies in Epicurus and Aristotle (Wiesbaden 1960).

'L'univers discontinu d'Épicure', *ACGB* (Paris 1969) 258–63.

Mewaldt, J. *Epikur, Philosoph der Freude* (Stuttgart 1949).

Mins, H. F. 'Marx's Doctoral Dissertation', *Science and Society* 12 (1948) 157–69.

Momigliano, A. 'Su alcuni dati della vita di Epicuro', *RFIC* 63 (1935) 302–16.

Moreau, J. 'Épicure et le physique des Dieux', *REA* 70 (1968) 286–94.

Moreschini, C. 'Due Fonti sulla Teologia epicurea', *PP* 16 (1961) 342–72.

Moutsopoulos, E. 'Le "clinamen", source d'erreur?' *ACGB* (Paris 1969) 175–81.

Müller, R. 'Sur le concept de Physis dans la philosophie épicurienne du droit', *ACGB* (Paris 1969) 305–18.

Mugler, R. 'L'invisibilité des atomes', *REG* 76 (1963) 397–403.

Pease, A. S. M. *Tulli Ciceronis De natura deorum liber primus* (Cambridge, Mass., 1955).

Pfligersdorffer, G. 'Cicero über Epikurs Lehre vom Wesen der Götter (*nat. deor.* 1.49)', *WS* 70 (1957) 235–53.

Review of Freymuth, *Zur Lehre*, *AAHG* 11 (1958) cols. 147–54.

Philippson, R. 'Polystratus' Schrift περὶ Ἀλόγου Καταφρονήσεως', *Neue Jahrb. f. d. Klass. Alt.* 12 (1909) 487–509.

'Philodemus' Buch über den Zorn', *Rh. Mus.* 71 (1916) 425–60.

'Philodemus', *RE* 19, cols. 2444–82.

'Zur epikureischen Götterlehre', *Hermes* 51 (1916) 568–608.

'Nachträgliches zur epikureischen Götterlehre', *Hermes* 53 (1918) 358–95.

'Zu Philodems Schrift über die Frömmigkeit', *Hermes* 55 (1920) 225–78, 364–72; 56 (1921) 355–410.

Review of Jensen, *Ein neuer Brief*, *Phil. Woch.* 54 (1934) 154–60.

'Die Götterlehre der Epikureer', *Rh. Mus.* 83 (1934) 171–5.

'Die Quelle der epikureischen Götterlehre in Ciceros erstem Buche De natura deorum', *SO* 19 (1939) 15–40.

'Die Akademische Kritik der epikureischen Theologie im ersten Buche der Tuskulanen [he means De natura deorum] Ciceros', *SO* 20 (1940) 21–44.

Raubitschek, A. E. 'Phaidros and his Roman Pupils', *Hesperia* 15 (1949) 96–103.

Rist, J. M. *Stoic Philosophy* (Cambridge 1969).

Sandbach, F. H. '"Εννοια and Πρόληψις in the Stoic theory of knowledge', *CQ* 24 (1930) 44–51.

Schmid, W. *Epikurs Kritik der platonischen Elementenlehre*, Klass.-Phil. Stud. 9 (Leipzig 1936).

Ethica epicurea: pap. herc. 1251 (Leipzig 1939).

'Zur Geschichte der herkulanensischen Studien', *PP* 10 (1955) 478–500.

'Götter und Menschen in der Theologie Epikurs', *Rh. Mus.* n.F. 94 (1951) 97–156.

'Epikur', *RAC* 5, cols. 681–819 (Stuttgart 1962).

'Chi è l'autore del. Pap. Oxy. 215?', *Misc. di Studi Alessandrini in memoria di A. Rostagni* (Turin 1963) 40–4.

Schottländer, R. 'Kynisiert Epikur?', *Hermes* 82 (1954) 444–50.

'Epikureisches bei Seneca? Ein Ringen um den Sinn von Freude und Freundschaft', *Philol.* 99 (1955) 133–48.

Schwenke, P. 'Zu Cicero De Natura Deorum (1.49f.)', *Neue Jahrbücher für Philologie und Pädagogik* 125 (1882) 613–33.

BIBLIOGRAPHY

Scott, W. 'The physical constitution of the Epicurean gods', *JP* 12 (1883) 212–47.

Smith, M. F. 'Fragments of Diogenes of Oenoanda Discovered and Rediscovered', *AJA* 74 (1970) 51–62.

Smith, M. F. 'New Fragments of Diogenes of Oenoanda', *AJA* 75 (1971) 357–89.

Solmsen, F. 'Epicurus and Cosmological Heresies', *AJP* 72 (1951) 1–23.

'Epicurus on the Growth and Decline of the Cosmos', *AJP* 74 (1953) 34–51.

'Αἴσθησις in Aristotelian and Epicurean thought', *Med. der Kon. Ned. Akad. van Wetenschappen, Afd. Letterkunde* 24 (1961) 239–62 (1–24).

Stark, R. 'Epicurea', *Hermes* 93 (1965) 420–8.

Steckel, H. *Epikurs Prinzip der Einheit von Schmerzlosigkeit und Lust* (Diss. Göttingen 1960).

'Epikur', *RE* Supp. 11, cols. 579–652.

Steinmetz, F. A. *Die Freundschaftslehre des Panaitios* (Wiesbaden 1967).

Stocks, J. L. 'Epicurean Induction', *Mind* 24 (1925) 185–203.

Tuilier, A. 'La notion de φιλία dans ses rapports avec certains fondements sociaux de l'épicurisme', *ACGB* (Paris 1969) 318–29.

Usener, H. *Epicurea* (Leipzig).

Vlastos, G. 'Minimal Parts in Epicurean Atomism', *Isis* 52 (1965) 121–47.

Vogliano, A. *Epicuri et Epicureorum scripta in Herculanensibus papyris servata* (Berlin 1928).

'Autour du jardin d'Épicure', *E. Pap.* 4 (1938) 1–13.

Westman, R. *Plutarch gegen Kolotes. Seine Schrift 'Adversus Coloten' als philosophiegeschichtliche Quelle* (Acta Phil. Fenn. 7, Helsingfors 1955).

INDEX

Academy 2, 8, 130, 131
Alexander the Great 3
Amerio, R. 141
anima 76, 78, 79, 80, 81, 99
animus 76, 78, 79, 80, 81, 86, 90
Antigonus Monophthalmus 6, 9
Aristoxenus 74
Aristippus 103, 126
Aristotle ix, 2, 3, 14, 47, 53, 54, 56, 74, 78, 95, 101, 102, 103, 105, 125, 127, 138, 148, 159, 164, 167
Arrighetti, G. x, 24, 35, 42, 96, 127, 150, 153
atoms: size 44, 45, 61, 148, 150; number 45, 67; weight 49, 50, 51, 61, 92, 167, 168; blows 46, 49, 50, 51, 92, 167, 168; movement 46, 49, 59, 85, 167; 'parts' 52, 53, 54, 55; shape 45, 46, 61, 67; swerve 42, 48, 49, 50, 51, 52, 91, 92, 93, 94, 97, 152, 153

Bailey, C. x, 22, 23, 25, 34, 35, 42, 44, 52, 55, 56, 60, 64, 65, 67, 73, 76, 83, 85, 89, 98, 118, 121, 125, 132, 140, 142, 144, 145, 146, 148, 151, 152, 162, 168, 175
Barigazzi, A. 4, 46, 47, 66, 158, 162
Batis 7
Bignone, E. ix, 9, 11, 44, 159, 170
Bollack, J. 129, 130, 131, 136
Brieger, A. 167
Brink, C. O. 3

canonic 14–40, 69, 100
Carneades 141
Cassius 122
chance 51, 52, 98
Chilton, C. W. 134
Cicero ix, 14, 51, 16, 17, 36, 92, 93, 102, 105, 106, 111, 120, 129, 130, 131, 135, 141, 142, 143, 144, 145, 146, 147, 151, 152, 157, 163, 166, 167, 170, 171, 172, 174, 175
Cole, T. 70
Colotes 8, 137, 159
colour 63, 65
compounds 58–66

condensing pleasures 114, 115
contact of the mind 18, 32–7
criterion of truth 14–17, 37, 100
Cyrenaics 103

De Lacy, P. and E. 4, 18, 39
De Lacy, P. 35, 90, 114
De Witt, N. W. x, 2, 5, 6, 8, 10, 11, 19, 30, 147, 165, 166, 175
death 119, 120, 136, 154, 161, 171
Demetrius Laco ix
Demetrius Poliorcetes 9
Democritus 1, 4, 5, 6, 10, 41, 44, 45, 46, 51, 52, 53, 54, 59, 63, 68, 80, 81, 87, 93, 140, 142, 145, 147, 167, 168, 169
Demosthenes 3
development of doctrine 8
Diano, C. ix, x, 27, 35, 88, 90, 96, 103, 104, 106, 107, 108, 109, 110, 111, 112, 114, 118, 120, 126, 127, 136, 144, 162, 163, 170, 171, 172, 173
Dicaearchus 74
Diels, H. 158
Diogenes of Oenoanda ix, 31, 47, 52, 72, 73, 93, 113, 114, 122, 124, 137
dream-images 33, 141
Düring, I. 17, 30

Easterling, H. J. 78
Epictetus 27, 98
error 23, 24, 88, 91, 161
Eudoxus 7, 9
evidence 38–40

Farrington, B. x, 127, 147
feelings 18, 30–31
Festugière, A.-J. 147, 149
flattery 11, 137
free will 4, 90–9, 150
Freymuth, G. 141, 144, 173, 175
friendship 127–39, 154, 155, 160
Furley, D. 18, 25, 29, 33, 34, 45, 46, 47, 49, 53, 60, 77, 78, 81, 91, 92, 93, 94

Gassendi, P. ix, 18
general concepts 26–30, 88, 124, 140, 161, 165–7

INDEX

Gigante, M. 10, 173
Giussani, C. ix, 18, 34, 78, 146
gods 26, 31, 41, 74, 85, 123, 140–63, 165; activities of, 146–56; two kinds of, 145, 172–5
Green, W. M. 170
Guthrie, W. K. C. 45, 53, 63, 140, 147, 167, 168
Guyau, M. 52

Hadzits, G. D. 156
Hedeia 7, 10, 11
Hermarchus 7, 8, 10, 12
Herodotus 8
Hesiod 1
Hieronymus of Rhodes 125
Huby, P. 97
human acts 91–99
Hypereides 3

ideology ix, 5, 147
Idomeneus 7, 12, 120
images 18, 19, 21, 24, 32, 83, 84, 85, 95, 160, 175
intermundia 144, 149
isonomia 144–6

Jensen, L. 160, 162
judgment, true and false 37–40
justice 122, 123, 124

katastematic pleasure 102, 103, 104, 105, 106, 107, 108, 109, 110, 111, 115, 121, 122, 154, 155, 170, 171, 172
kinetic pleasure 102, 103, 104, 105, 106, 107, 108, 109, 110, 111, 115, 126, 154, 155, 170, 171, 172
Kleve, K. x, 24, 31, 37, 50, 83, 128, 141, 143, 144, 149, 150, 153, 157, 166
Krokiewicz, A. 50, 173, 174

language development 72, 73
Leonteus 7
Leontion 9, 11
Leucippus 5, 6, 41, 68, 146, 147, 167
Liepmann, H. C. 50, 167
Long, H. S. 38, 161
Lucretius ix, x, 28, 36, 41, 43, 45, 46, 53, 54, 55, 56, 57, 59, 60, 61, 62, 64, 65, 69, 70, 72, 74, 75, 76, 77, 79, 80, 81, 82, 83, 87, 90, 91, 93, 94, 97, 98,

Lucretius *cont*
109, 110, 128, 145, 146, 147, 148, 149, 157, 159, 162, 163, 169, 170
Lysimachus 7

marriage 132
Marx, K. 147
Mau, J. 47, 53
memory 86, 89, 96, 113, 159
Merbach, F. 28
Merlan, P. x, 46, 50, 71, 101, 103, 109, 121, 150, 153, 155, 158, 170, 171, 172, 173, 174, 175
Metrodorus ix, 7, 8, 10, 11, 12, 13, 104, 105, 120, 138
Mewaldt, J. 101
mind 32–36, 37, 83, 88–89, 171, 172
Mithres 7
Momigliano, A. 6, 7, 122, 139
moral obligation 121, 175
Moreschini, C. 173
motion 39, 43, 46, 90
Moutsopoulos, E. 8

natural impulses 103, 105, 106, 135
Nausiphanes 4, 5, 6, 8, 93, 147, 168
necessity 68, 93, 98
Neocles 1
non-existent objects 23, 24, 33, 34, 84, 88

origin of civilization 70–3
other worlds 67

pain 30, 78, 82, 100–26, 137, 155
Pamphilus 1
Parmenides 41
Pease, A. S. 142, 175
Pfligersdorffer, G. 140, 144, 158
Philippson, R. 141, 143, 157, 158, 160, 173, 175
Philodemus ix, x, 9, 18, 27, 30, 33, 39, 40, 107, 127, 128, 141, 145, 149, 151, 152, 153, 154, 155, 156, 158, 160, 161, 163, 173, 175
Plato ix, 1, 2, 14, 47, 51, 52, 73, 74, 86, 101, 105, 107, 114, 127, 148, 149, 159, 164
pleasure 30, 78, 82, 100–26, 131, 133, 137, 157, 159, 170–2
Plutarch ix, 8, 14, 46, 56, 63, 64, 78, 102, 104, 122, 133, 137, 147

INDEX

Polemeus 6
politics, dangers of 3, 128, 129, 135, 138
Polyaenus ix, 7, 10, 11, 12, 138
Posidonius 157
position of earth 47, 48, 69
Praxiphanes 3
providence 147, 148
Pyrrho 4
Pythocles ix, 2, 8, 12

qualities 55, 61–6

Raubitschek, A. E. 156
religion 71, 156–163
rhetoric 8
Rist, J. M. 51, 91, 98, 165

Sandbach, F. H. 27, 165, 166
Schmid, W. 1, 156, 158, 159, 161, 162
Schoemann, G. F. 172
Schwenke, P. 143
Scott, W. 140, 175
'seeds' 42, 59
Seneca 98
sensation 17–25, 55, 80–8, 89
sex, sexual morality 10, 11, 100, 101,
    115, 116, 127, 128
shape of earth 47
Simplicius 57, 58, 167, 168
smell 63, 64, 87
Smith, M. F. 47, 52
Solmsen, F. 32, 77, 82, 146, 169, 170

soul 63, 64, 74–99, 100
Speusippus 9
Stark, R. 161
Steckel, H. 113
Stoics 27, 28, 51, 79, 99, 106, 118, 132,
    149, 158, 165
swerve, see 'atoms'

taste 63, 64, 87, 100
Themista 7, 10, 11, 12
Theophrastus 2, 3, 10, 63, 167
time 47, 59, 66
Timocrates 8
touch 83
Tuilier, A. 11

Usener, H. ix, 2, 22, 42, 132, 161

'variation' of pleasure 106–8, 115, 156
vibration 59
virtue 124, 125, 162, 163
vision 22, 23, 24, 84–7
Vlastos, G. 32, 53, 54
Vogliano, A. 6, 12
void 35, 39, 40, 42, 43, 56–8, 61, 67,
    89, 148, 168

will 90–9

Xenocrates 2

Zeller, E. 3